THE CANAL

THE CANAL

ASPECTS OF UNITED STATES PANAMANIAN RELATIONS

Sheldon B. Liss

UNIVERSITY OF NOTRE DAME PRESS
Notre Dame • London

Library of Congress Catalog Card Number: 67-22147
Manufactured in the United States of America

FOR GLADYS,
whom I promise not to involve,
but always will

Orden no es una presión que desde fuera se ejerce
sobre la sociedad, sino un equilibrio que
se suscita en su interior.

Order is not a pressure which is imposed on society
from without, but an equilibrium which
is set up from within.

José Ortega y Gasset

Table of Contents

Acknowledgements

This book had its genesis while I was involved with a project dealing with the United States-Mexican conflict over the Chamizal region.[1] From the time that I began to contemplate the ultimate effect of United States concessions to Mexico upon other hemispheric disputes, and in particular the one involving Panama, I have received able guidance from numerous sources.

Space precludes individual recognition of the many institutions and their reference specialists, in both the United States and Panama, who suffered with my impossible requests and rendered valuable services.

Analysis of the material presented herein would have been impossible without the insights offered by scores of individ-

1. See the author's *A Century of Disagreement: The Chamizal Conflict 1864–1964* (Washington: University Press of Washington, D. C., 1965). Changes in the course of the Rio Grande caused the Chamizal, formerly appended to the Mexican side of the river, to shift and attach itself to the United States' shoreline. In 1911 the problem was submitted to International Arbitration, but the Arbitral Tribunal's decision was rejected by the United States. During the Kennedy Administration the United States offered to settle the conflict on the basis of the 1911 award, and a considerable portion of the territory in dispute was returned to Mexico.

uals in Panama including the man in the street, communists, nationalists, professors, politicians, diplomats and government functionaries.

I am indebted to Panama's *Ministerio de Relaciones Exteriores* and the Department of State of the United States, and the late Dr. E. Taylor Parks in particular, for cooperation offered an individual who has a proclivity for involvement in restricted areas. A special note must be made of the Panamanian "Young Turks"[2] who, with refreshing candor and disregard for personal safety, assisted my comprehension of the situation on the Isthmus, as did their counterparts in the various United States agencies in Panama.

To Miss Maryanne Lomberger goes a thank-you for her painstaking work in checking footnotes and references which saved countless hours of labor. Special mention goes to Dr. Michael J. Francis, Mr. Dominic D. Lorenzo and Miss Theresa Lapenta, who read the manuscript and made numerous valuable suggestions.

My greatest debt of gratitude, as always, extends to my family, who persevered at home during my tenure in Panama and who patiently withstood my irritability while this work progressed. To Steven and Jacqueline, who frequently wondered what could be so interesting to their father that he rejected their offers to engage in play, goes the hope that someday they will understand.

S.B.L.

2. These well educated and unselfish men, most of whom hold positions of respect, are striving to eliminate bureaucratic corruption and weaken the hold of the oligarchy which impedes progress in their nation.

CHAPTER
ONE

Panorama

United States-Panamanian relations have been turbulent from their inception and Americans and Panamanians have not always been conscious of all the issues involved in dealings between their nations. The presence of United States institutions and citizens in Panama has led to frequent agitation in favor of freedom from Yankee intervention since 1903, when Panama, with the assistance of the United States, broke away from Colombia.

Sporadic outbreaks of terrorism have increased since the bloody anti-United States upheaval of January, 1964. Immediately upon entering Panama one is aware of symbols of violence rather than tranquility. Khaki uniformed members of Panama's *Guardia Nacional* (National Guard) are everywhere. Their military bearing, coupled with the fact that they travel in pairs and are often armed with shotguns, is cause for immediate apprehension.

The campus of the University of Panama is sprinkled with signs condemning both the United States and the oligarchy which rules the nation. Politics, both international and national, dominate conversation, and tempers flare easily. Pressure for social and political reform has been mounting in

Panama, and government officials are prepared for the lid to blow off momentarily.

Panama, the third largest of the six republics on the Central American Isthmus, encompasses some 29,000 square miles and for centuries has been one of the crossroads of the world. She has the smallest population in Latin America, and her greatest economic assets are the Panama Canal[1] and the Canal Zone which surrounds it.

It is a nation which is preoccupied with the Canal and whose people, for the most part, live alongside the Canal or in the port cities of Panama and Colón. The Panamanians are a conglomerate people, over eighty-five per cent of whom are of Negro, Indian or *Mestizo* (mixed) origins. This racial diffusion causes many problems and exacerbates relations with the United States.

By Latin American standards, health and educational levels in Panama are high. This is attributable to United States influence which is evident everywhere as women scurry about the streets in slacks and shorts and shops display signs written in both English and Spanish. Interestingly, this is one Latin American nation where the term *gringo,* as applied to Americans, is often an endearing figure of speech, rather than a derogatory term as in most Latin American nations. Panama, a name derived from an ancient Indian term meaning "many fish," has for its national colors red, white and blue; dollars are the common denomination of exchange; and slot machines in the government operated casinos indicate "payoffs" in English rather than Spanish. Even the cost of living in Panama approximates that of the United States and is exceedingly high by Latin American standards.

With the construction of a passage between the two major

1. In mid-1964 the estimated population was 1,200,000 and by 1970 should reach 1,410,000.

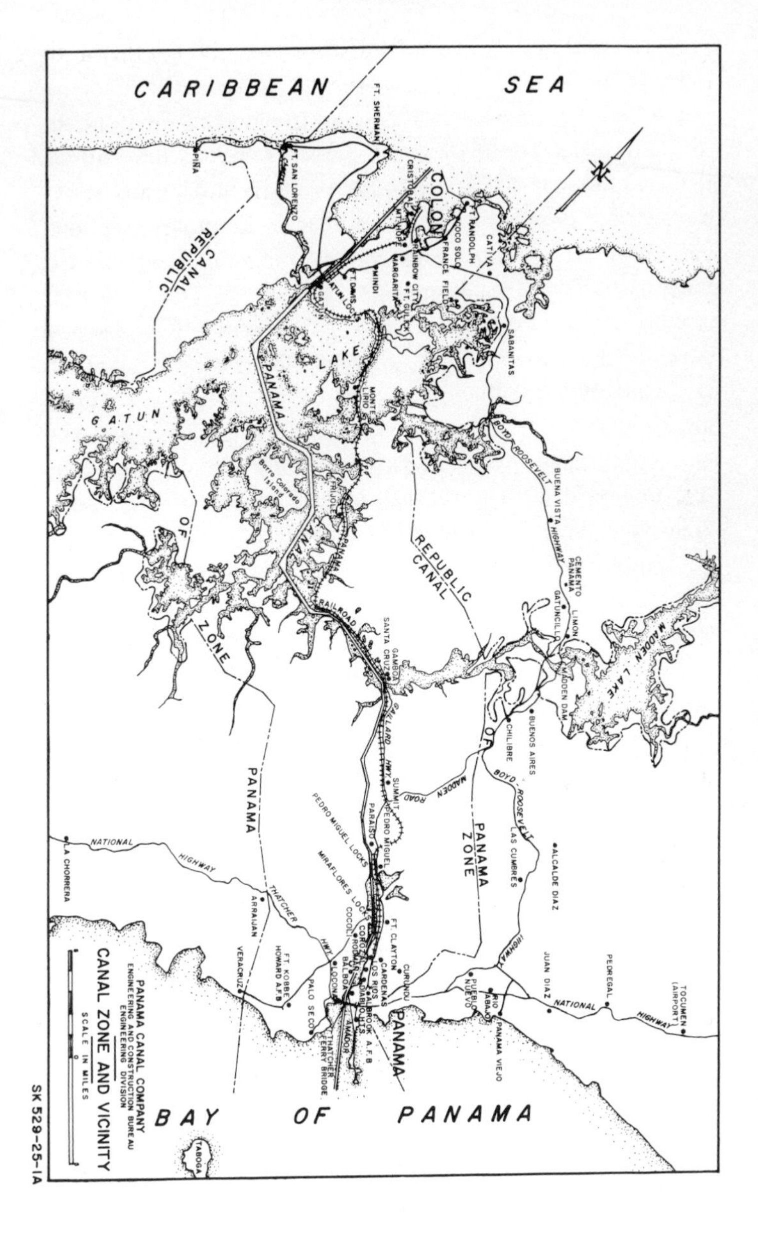
CARIBBEAN SEA
BAY OF PANAMA
GATUN LAKE
MADDEN LAKE
PANAMA CANAL
COLON
PANAMA
REPUBLIC OF PANAMA
CANAL ZONE
PANAMA CANAL COMPANY
ENGINEERING AND CONSTRUCTION BUREAU
ENGINEERING DIVISION
CANAL ZONE AND VICINITY
SCALE IN MILES
SK 529-25-1A

hemispheric land masses in the Americas the problems of Panama began and have yet to be resolved. The Panama Canal has often been a political and psychological barometer of United States relations with Latin America, and current readings indicate a need for improvement. The United States has never viewed the Panama Canal as a natural resource, but rather as a hemispheric necessity. On the other hand, Panama has traditionally adhered to the view that the Canal is indeed a natural resource and should be exploited for her benefit. She contends that this unique resource has been exploited by the United States to the exclusion of her own interests.

A multitude of problems exists in Panama and, at one time or another, all evils have been laid at the feet of the United States. Relations between the United States and Panama have not existed under the best of circumstances and the tensions and frustrations which have evolved are complex. The problems between both countries are not going to be easily resolved, and both the United States and Panama will never be fully satisfied. But it is important that the desire to reach a better accord be shared by both nations. During this century millions have been spent on physical modernization in Panama. Now expenditures must be made in the realms of social betterment and human understanding.

The relations of the United States with Panama have naturally been influenced by their diverse interests in the Isthmus. From the outset of United States interest in what was formerly a province of Colombia, Panama has been somewhat of a hairshirt. On numerous occasions this tiny Latin American nation has challenged the United States, and the ability of the United States to handle these challenges reflects its image to Latin Americans, be it strong, weak, or vacillating. The United States attitude toward the other nations of the Americas has often been reflected in Panama, and Latin Americans have searched for indications of new United States tacks in inter-American diplomacy.

United States policy with regard to Panama has been anachronistic, its actions usually following events after they occurred. Whenever the United States reacted or failed to react to situations in Panama, there have been international repercussions. The eyes of the hemisphere focus upon United States policy in Panama and because of extended tenure upon Panamanian soil the Colossus of the North is often accused of imperialism.

One wonders how the treaty granted in perpetuity under which the United States controls the Panama Canal and the Canal Zone is to be construed in light of contemporary world, hemispheric and Panamanian problems. Certainly United States assurances of "titular sovereignty" over the area in dispute are insufficient to negate the presence of ten thousand American troops on Panamanian territory. Is it any wonder Panama claims that American occupation is inimical to the concept of national sovereignty and the credos of the Inter-American System, when over thirty thousand privileged citizens of the United States live in what is tantamount to an American enclave in Panama? One can easily see why mid-twentieth century United States relations with Panama remind the world of United States policies during the era of the Spanish American War.

While the United States emphasizes the need for planning Panama's future, the Panamanians are primarily concerned with the present. Panama tends to theorize when pragmatisim should be the order of the day. While those in the United States chart progress leading to a better way of life in Panama, the Panamanians are pondering whether or not the United States infringes upon their sovereignty and violates their cherished doctrines of non-intervention and self-determination. Conceding that these questions are meaningful, it is doubtful that they should dominate a nation to the detriment of the well-being of its populace.

The impasse caused by separate United States and Panamanian goals is not the only factor which hinders progress in Panama today. The agencies of the United States government which are involved in Panamanian affairs often pursue different objectives. The Pentagon and the Department of State frequently differ as to military versus diplomatic goals in Panama; and when these quandaries are compounded by factors such as United States economic interest in the nation, hemispheric feelings and world opinion, the obvious result is chaos. If the United States has not been able to agree upon its own objectives, can the less politically sophisticated Panamanians be expected to interpret United States policy and simultaneously plan their own future?

Periodically the United States has been able to satisfy Panama's nationalistic desires by making concessions such as permitting the Panamanian flag to fly in the Canal Zone. But this type of acquiescence satiates the Panamanian appetite only temporarily, and further demands are always forthcoming. The Panamanians have never been reluctant to publicly express their dissatisfaction with United States policies and American cultural arrogance.

Although many of the accusations of the Panamanians are exaggerated, one must bear in mind that affluent nations are often scapegoats. The people of Panama, both indigenous and of Iberian descent, want recognition, not for their willingness to accept United States aid but for themselves and their original contributions to "American culture."

Panamanians are now demanding the re-establishment of their sovereignty over territory occupied by the Panama

Canal and the Canal Zone.[2] As the Panamanian journalist Leopoldo Aragon cogently stated, the titles of two volumes accurately depict the attitudes of his countrymen about relations with the United States. The first book refers to the treaty governing the Canal and environs and is entitled: *Authentic History of the Scandalous Negotiations of the Panama Canal Treaty;* and the second: *Panama-United States Relations. A Situation that must be changed for the welfare of Panama and the honor of the United States. True History born of the Panama Canal Treaty, born from fraud, perfidy, inequity, dishonor, coercion, chicanery, menace, disloyalty and injustice.*[3]

The Panamanian Constitution of 1946 defines the nation as a centralized democratic republic. The right of revolution is basic to Panamanian politics and has loomed large in the country's history. Panama, like Mexico, professes an institutionalized type of constitutionalism, but Panama's middle and lower class elements have yet to be entirely integrated into the electoral process. Since World War II the Panamanian government has been unstable as six presidents have been deposed by violent revolution and one eliminated by assassination.

Politics in this tropical land is a colorful game of intrigue. A viable political party system is nonexistent, and the nation is controlled by some forty to fifty families. This entrenched oligarchy resembles the *Fronda* which has traditionally stagnated Chilean politics. Names such as Arias and Boyd have been household words in Panama for decades and promise to be for years to come.

2. By "re-establish" the Panamanians refer to the fact that their Republic was formed two weeks prior to the Canal Zone, which was then carved out of Panamanian territory.

3. Leopoldo Aragon, "Has the Panama Canal a Future?" *The New Republic* (July 30, 1962), pp. 16–17.

The oligarchy relies upon *personalismo* (personalism) and the *caudillo* (military chief) for power. The oligarchy also utilizes United States occupation of Panama's territory as an outlet through which is directed popular dissatisfaction. Conveniently the blame for any inequities perpetrated by the rulers is shifted to the United States via the Canal and the Zone. The oligarchy is deceitful; to the people of Panama it expresses Yankeephobia while simultaneously courting the favor of the United States. Certainly Panama will never have good government until the oligarchy is overthrown. Thus by syllogistic logic one might conclude that relations with the United States will never be harmonious until the oligarchy is removed. On the other hand, Panama has a conservative regime with some modicum of politcial democracy and this leaves her further advanced than many of her sister Latin American republics. Panamanians, politicians, intellectuals and proletarians alike, are never satisfied and constantly grope for more. Even the vast bureaucracy seems, at times, to advance only its own economic and political ends.

In light of the hemispheric menace emanating from Havana, Moscow, and Peking, it is obvious that United States relations with Panama must be adversely affected. Panama is not a primary target of communism in the Americas, but nevertheless a threat is imminent. One wonders whether or not the United States has mastered the technique of coping with hemispheric eruptions which have appeared with greater frequency since the ascendency to power of Fidel Castro. When severe rioting took place in Panama in January, 1964, the Panama Committee for the Defense of the Cuban Revolution immediately took credit for the violence directed against the United States. What does this portend for the future? How significant are the pro-Castro placards which line the walls of public edifices in Panama? Is the communist movement potentially strong in Panama? Will the agents of Havana, Moscow and Peking be successful in their attempts to capitalize upon the poor state of United States relations with Panama to the extent of fomenting a revolution? Will recurrent political upheavals play into the hands of some embryonic Castro who may lead Panama down the road to communism? Could the United States realistically entertain thoughts of leaving Panama and possibly create a vacuum to be filled by some strongman or those connected with international communism? Does Panama desire the departure of United States citizens and installations from her shores, or is the communist threat precisely what is necessary to extract further concessions from the powerful neighbor to the North?

CHAPTER
TWO

Historical Backgrounds

When the first European, Rodrigo de Bastidas, reached Panama in 1501, he could hardly envision the magnitude of the Isthmus' future. As more Spanish caravels arrived, the search for gold was intensified. A shortened route from the Atlantic Ocean to the Pacific Ocean was not found by Magellan, who conceived of going around Cape Horn or passing through the straits that were to bear his name. When sea routes were found to be too long the Spaniards turned to overland crossings, and when Vasco Núñez de Balboa first crossed the Isthmus of Panama in 1513, he initiated a ceaseless march of traffic. Panamanians are still proud of the curious Balboa who discovered the Pacific, surveyed the Panama route across the Central American Isthmus and found that there existed a difference in the levels of the respective oceans.[1]

The *Conquistador* Hernán Cortés was certain that no natural waterway existed between the Atlantic and the Pacific, and he expressed a desire to construct a sea passageway through Panama, Darien, Nicaragua, or Tehuantepec. The dreams of the foresighted Cortés went for naught as it was

1. It was not until 1524 that Charles V of Spain ordered the first official survey of a proposed canal route across the Isthmus of Panama.

almost three centuries before serious consideration was again given to the construction of an interoceanic waterway.

The Congress of Central America in 1823 was instrumental in arousing United States interest in a trans-Isthmian waterway. Secretary of State Henry Clay was stimulated by Señor Cañas, the Congress's diplomatic representative in Washington, and contemplated construction of a canal. In June of 1825 the Congress of Central America offered concessions for the construction of a canal, and as a result the *Central American and United States Atlantic and Pacific Canal Company* was capitalized. However, the five million dollars which was ultimately subscribed was insufficient to undertake such an ambitious project.

1826

When the first hemispheric conference, under the aegis of Simón Bolívar, was called for Panama in 1826, it was surmised that a canal might be a major topic of discussion. However, when delegates from the United States, which received a belated invitation, failed to make an appearance at the conference, pan-Americanism was off to an inauspicious start, and progress toward canal construction was thwarted. Bolívar formally proposed the canal project, but aside from the conclusion of a contract between a New York builder, Aaron H. Palmer, and the Republic of Central America, the idea was a failure.[2]

1839

Some years later, President Martin Van Buren dispatched John L. Stephens to the Panama area to survey the possibilities of canal construction. In 1839, Stephens' reports estimated the cost of such a project as approximately twenty-five million dollars, and Washington rejected it on the grounds that it was too risky and temporarily deferred plans for an inter-oceanic canal.

2. The $5,000,000 proposed for the project proved too costly.

In 1845, Louis Napoleon of France explored the idea of obtaining concessions for a canal in Nicaragua, but the collapse of the French monarchy channelled his attention in other directions. The following year the American Chargé signed a treaty with the Republic of New Granada,[3] guaranteeing the right of transit across the Isthmus of Panama. This pact guaranteed New Granada that perfect neutrality would prevail on the Isthmus. In actuality the treaty granted the United States control over the territory with the proviso that all nations were to have access to the route. The United States was now the protector of the Isthmus, but Colombia still claimed sovereignty over the area.

With the beginning of railroad construction across the Isthmus the United States invoked her rights as protector and between 1846 and 1903 often deployed troops in the area. But United States' influence on the Isthmus did not deter foreign powers from endeavoring to make inroads in the area. In 1848, the King of Holland obtained a contract to build a canal in Nicaragua, only to have his plans postponed by a revolution in the Netherlands. His plans were rapidly overshadowed by the California Gold Rush during which the movement to find a faster means of crossing the Isthmus gained impetus. People found that it was easier to cross the jungles of Panama than the American West, yet neither route was entirely satisfactory. The Gold Rush spurred the economy of Panama which led ultimately to the completion of a trans-Isthmian railway, which again whetted the appetites of those who desired a waterway from the Atlantic to the Pacific.

During the middle of the nineteenth century Great Britain

3. In 1830 the area now designated Colombia reverted to its viceregal name, New Granada. In 1858 it became the Granadine Confederation, in 1861 the United States of Colombia, and finally in 1886 the Republic of Colombia.

was contending with the United States for spheres of influence in the Caribbean. Despite the prohibitions of the Monroe Doctrine, the British had designs on the Central American Isthmus. The conflict between Great Britain and the United States was partially resolved by the Clayton-Bulwer Treaty of 1850, under whose terms both nations promised never to maintain exclusive control over the proposed new route across the Isthmus and pledged themselves to neutrality and to the support of the construction of a canal.[4]

The period following the conclusion of the Clayton-Bulwer Treaty was one of enthusiasm for the construction of the Panama railroad. Between 1850 and 1855, approximately nine thousand laborers died in Panama's swamps in an effort to link the Atlantic with the Pacific by rail. The dream was fulfilled by 1855 when the Isthmus was bisected successfully by a railroad, which is still in operation.

Once again attention was focused upon an interoceanic canal. The Cass-Yrisarri Treaty was signed between the United States and Nicaragua on November 6, 1857. Under its terms both nations were to share equal rights over any interoceanic route to be constructed. Unfortunately, this treaty was never ratified by the Congress of Nicaragua which feared further concessions to the United States. The attitude of the Nicaraguans gradually changed and a decade later the Dickinson-Ayon Treaty granted the United States the right to construct a canal in return for guaranteeing Nicaragua's neutrality.

Secretary of State William Seward negotiated a treaty with Colombia in 1868 for exclusive United States rights to construct a canal across her territory. The treaty was not ratified

4. These covenants were applicable to both the proposed routes across Panama and Tehuantepec.

in either Colombia or the United States and in 1870 President Grant appointed an Interoceanic Canal Commission to survey the situation. After six years of erratic work the Commission reported unanimously in favor of a route across Nicaragua.

Meanwhile the center of attention shifted from the United States to Europe. The International Engineering Congress held in Paris in 1879 paved the way for European construction of a canal in Panama. The United States attempted to invoke the Monroe Doctrine and unsuccessfully warned the Europeans not to extend their interests to the Central American Isthmus. So infuriated was President Rutherford P. Hayes by the intentions of the French that in a message to Congress, in March of 1880, he stressed that the United States was committed to the idea of a canal under her own control and under no circumstances could consent to surrender this control to a European power.

Some might have been dissuaded by the convincing argument of President Hayes, but not the French. Ferdinand de Lesseps, the builder of the Suez Canal, was attracted by the possibility of a similar achievement in America. The Universal Oceanic Canal Company, of which he was president, purchased from Colombia for ten million dollars a concession to construct a canal. The *Compagnie Universelle du Canal Interocéanique de Panama* (Universal Interoceanic Canal Company of Panama) was capitalized and the French firm began to formulate plans for canal construction. The United States asserted that this constituted a violation of the Monroe Doctrine, but de Lesseps and company disregarded the American objections and in 1880 announced that they were about to embark upon a one hundred sixty-eight million dollar canal project.

The task before the de Lesseps combine was formidable and the area to be cleared for the canal virtually impassable.

In the 1880's the port city of Colón had been described as " . . . a foul hole, by comparison, the ghettoes of White Russia, the slums of Toulon, Naples, and old Stamboul . . . deserve prizes for cleanliness. There are neither sewers nor street cleaners . . . toilets are quite unknown, all the rubbish is thrown into the swamps or onto rubbish heaps. Toads splash in the liquid muck . . . rats infest the solid filth . . . snakes hunt both toads and rats; clouds of mosquitoes swarm into the homes."[5] Under such adverse conditions, the Universal Interoceanic Canal Company of Panama commenced work in 1881 upon a project that was to last for eight years and cost almost four hundred million dollars. With the work one-third completed the project failed.

The United States still favored construction of a canal in Nicaragua, and the Spanish American War of 1898 re-emphasized the need for a route that would speed traffic from California and Oregon to the Caribbean. During the War when it took the battleship *Oregon* sixty-nine days to complete the trip from the Philippines around Cape Horn to Cuba, Congress was convinced of the necessity of a shortened route and instructed President Theodore Roosevelt to build the much discussed canal.

The British were no longer included in the United States plans for a canal across the Isthmus, and the process of abrogating the Clayton-Bulwer Treaty was initiated. On February 5, 1900, Secretary of State John Hay and Lord Pauncefote, the British Ambassador to the United States, signed a treaty which provided that the United States could operate an Isthmian canal alone, as long as the territory was neutralized. The British failed to ratify the treaty, and Hay and Pauncefote had to renegotiate. By November 18, 1901, they con-

5. Author anonymous.

cluded a second pact which abrogated the Clayton-Bulwer Treaty and provided that the United States could control, manage, defend and fortify a canal, but it was to be neutralized in much the same manner as had been the one in Suez. European opposition to, or competition with, United States canal interest was waning.

In 1902 the United States purchased rights for a new Panama canal company to succeed the defunct French firm. The Panamanians now feared that the United States might still proceed with plans for a canal over the alternate route in Nicaragua, which would subsequently cause severe losses to Panama. This fear, coupled with American "Manifest Destiny," in what Samuel Flagg Bemis has called an "epoch of protective imperialism,"[6] would ultimately lead to revolution in Panama.

In 1903 a French group led by Philippe Bunau-Varilla was interested in recouping losses sustained in the collapse of the French Canal Company. Capitalizing on anti-Colombian sentiment in the Province of Panama, Bunau-Varilla offered his services to the Panamanians who were seriously considering rebellion. Panama was desirous of seceding from Colombia and thereby becoming the sole recipient of any benefits to be derived from the construction of a canal across its territory. The Panamanians dispatched Dr. Manuel Amador to the United States to seek support for their cause. Immediately, Mr. Bunau-Varilla offered to assist the Panamanians in eliciting support from the United States and, with more audacity than commitment, Bunau-Varilla promised Dr. Amador that United States funds and support would be forthcoming within two days after revolution broke out in Panama.

6. See Samuel F. Bemis, *The Latin American Policy of the United States* (New York: Harcourt Brace & World, Inc., 1943), p. 140.

In return for this assistance, the avaricious Bunau-Varilla requested that he receive the potentially lucrative position as Panama's representative in Washington.

Since the Hay-Herran Treaty of January 22, 1903, had authorized the transfer of property rights from the French Canal Company to the United States and given the United States the right to construct a canal and control it for a hundred years, the Americans were desirous of gaining a foothold in Panama. The fact that Philippe Bunau-Varilla fomented the revolution in Panama is undeniable, and President Theodore Roosevelt and the United States have never been completely exonerated from complicity. In fact Mr. Bunau-Varilla boasted to President Marroquin of Colombia that if the Hay-Herran Treaty were not ratified, then either the Nicaraguan route would be chosen, or Panama would rebel under the protection of the United States.[7]

When the United States vessel *Nashville* sailed for Colón on October 31, 1903, a revolution simultaneously erupted in Panama. The role of the United States in the actual rebellion was minimal, but the Americans assured the success of the revolution by prohibiting Colombian troops from landing to put down the insurgents.[8] Significantly, insofar as future United States-Panamanian relations were concerned, at the time of the revolution there were no overt signs of Panamanian hostility to United States assistance. Certainly the interests of the people of Panama and the United States were compatible.

On November 6, 1903, the United States formally entered into diplomatic relations with the Republic of Panama, and from that date forward the two nations have continuously

7. See *Foreign Relations of the United States,* 1903, p. 193.

8. This action was taken on the pretext of protecting United States property.

been involved in one type of conflict or another. By the Hay-Bunau-Varilla Treaty, signed in Washington on November 18, 1903, the United States guaranteed the independence of the newly formed Republic of Panama. In return for ten million dollars in gold and the annual payment of $250,000, the United States received the use and occupation of a zone ten miles wide across the Isthmus of Panama from Colón to Panama City and the use of adjacent territory necessary to the construction and operation of a canal.

Whatever had been the role of the United States in the revolution in Panama, she now had vested interests in the nation. When President Roosevelt averred: "I took the Canal Zone and let Congress debate, and while the debate goes on the Canal Zone does too,"[9] he created cause for deep concern. Never again would the United States be able to extricate herself from the affairs of Panama. President Roosevelt being contemptuous of Latin American politics had resorted to "Big Stick" tactics to achieve his goals. In reference to the situation in Panama he asserted: "You don't have to foment a revolution, all you have to do is take your foot off and one will occur."[10] From the days of Theodore Roosevelt this type of tactlessness has endured and has not endeared the United States to the Panamanians.

The United States was now a party to something which it did not fully comprehend. Secretary of State John Hay, who negotiated the treaty with Panama, knew nothing of the needs or interests of the Panamanians, and many of his successors in office would be equally ignorant. Although Secretary Hay

9. Mercer D. Tate, "The Panama Canal and Political Partnership," *The Journal of Politics* (February, 1963), p. 119. The statement was made on December 29, 1903.

10. See Edwin Lieuwen, *Arms and Politics in Latin America* (New York. Frederick A. Praeger, Inc., 1961), p. 261.

might be absolved of blame in the Panama matter, one could question whether or not his failure to come to grips with the situation is excusable.

The United States took advantage of the chaos and instability in Panama in 1903 to extract advantages which still exist. There can be no doubt that the treaty between the United States and the newly emerged Republic of Panama favored the Americans. Article II of the pact gave the United States control and use of lands and waters in perpetuity, placing Panama at a disadvantage.[11] The 1903 Treaty started relations between the United States and Panama off on the wrong foot. The 1903 agreement was backed by the Hay-Pauncefote Treaty, between the United States and Great Britain, and pledged that the canal was to be open and free to vessels of commerce and war from all nations. It has been meaningless because the agreement has been unilaterally interpreted over the years, and Panama has in this sense been a protectorate of the United States.

Anti-Americanism arose in Panama almost immediately after the revolution in 1903, as Washington continuously applied the treaty with little regard for the views of the Panamanians and this led to a steady stream of criticism. According to William C. McCain, the first official controversy after the establishment of the Republic of Panama was one dealing with sovereignty over ports of entry, tariffs, customs houses and a postal service.[12] This initial conflict was subsequently settled by Secretary of War William Howard Taft, who journeyed to Panama in June of 1904 in an effort to propitiate the Panamanians. Problems between the two nations mounted

11. Contracts in perpetuity are generally not recognized in international law.

12. See William McCain, *The United States and The Republic of Panama* (Durham: Duke University Press, 1937), p. 23.

rapidly, as Panama became a haven for United States investment. As early as 1903 the famous United Fruit Company owned extensive interests in the railroad and banana industries in Panama.

Theoretically Panama was not an exclusive creation of the United States, as it was also desired by the Panamanians. But freedom from Colombia brought other encumbrances to what Philander C. Knox termed a "vest pocket Republic."[13] And to a degree he was correct in assuming that Panama would now be held on a fob and manipulated by the United States. The real injured party in the 1903 conflict was Colombia. Washington refused to arbitrate the matter, but by 1922 the United States indemnified Bogotá by payment of twenty-five million dollars.

Secretary of War William Howard Taft, to whom fell the task of supervising the building of the Panama Canal, knew no more about Panamanian affairs than did Secretary of State John Hay. Furthermore, Taft lacked interest in the nation and regarded it as one of the "dirty republics" of Latin America.[14] Such a lack of United States compassion and understanding could hardly augur well for the future.

The United States was confronted with problems from the outset in Panama. The new Republic had a constitution, but was going to encounter difficulty in implementing it and would frequently call upon the United States for help. Colombia still posed a threat to Panama and was a potential nuisance to the United States. However, the Colombian situation was eventually ameliorated by the Root-Cortés-Arosemena Trea-

13. See Lawrence O. Ealy, *The Republic of Panama In World Affairs* 1903–1950 (Philadelphia: University of Pennsylvania Press, 1951), p. 20.

14. "W. H. Taft to Horace D. Taft," July 3, 1904, as found in the *Taft Papers*.

ties between Panama, Colombia, and the United States.[15] But Panama's internal problems were not so easily solved. Less than a year after the establishment of the nation it was necessary for the United States to intervene a *coup d'état*. After this abortive revolution the United States brought pressure to bear against the military in Panama. As a result, in 1904 the army was abolished, providing another source of anti-Yankee feeling as the United States was given a strong pretext for intervention in the nation on the grounds that it was necessary to the maintenance of order. The Monroe Doctrine had been amended by the Roosevelt Corollary of 1904, which justified United States intervention. Panama felt that unilateral intervention in her affairs on the part of the United States could come at any time, and it did.

During her early years Panama relied upon the United States to maintain internal stability in the nation. For example, on the eve of Panama's election in December of 1905, President Amador requested that the United States act as official observer on the grounds that if the Americans did not do so Panama might have to rebuild her military.[16] Thus the United States was thrust into Panamanian politics and forced to take a greater role in the nation than she desired. The presence of American troops on Panamanian soil was from the outset construed as occupation, or at least intervention. United States military personnel were never cordially wel-

15. Three treaties were concluded, one between Colombia and the United States, one between Panama and the United States, and one between Panama and Colombia. By their terms Colombia was given the right to transport ships through the Canal duty free, while her agricultural and manufactured products were to be afforded the same treatment as were United States products. Also Panama was to indemnify Colombia, and boundaries between the two nations were drawn.

16. McCain, p. 65.

comed, and throughout the early years the nations were often at odds with one another over beatings administered to American sailors by Panamanian police.

American bankers began to ingratiate themselves in Panamanian life as early as 1906 when they launched joint ventures with local groups. It was the same year that Secretary of War William Howard Taft first recognized Panama's "titular sovereignty" in the Canal Zone, and the United States flag was first flown in the Zone after a visiting United States Senator complained of its absence.[17] Gradually the flag of Panama disappeared from view as American influence began to overshadow local interests. Panamanians complained bitterly as the United States established its own postal service, customs-house and commissaries in the Canal Zone. The drain on the economy of Panama was not severe and more than compensated for by the influx of new American capital into the nation, but a source of lingering dissension was established.

As the years passed it became virtually impossible for the United States to remain out of Panamanian affairs. Panama relied upon the United States in times of crisis and yet resented the presence of the Yankees. When a boundary dispute broke out with Costa Rica in 1907, the good offices of the United States were solicited by Panama in order to resolve the problem.[18] In May of the following year, Panama's Foreign Secretary Arias requested United States supervision of elections in order to prevent frauds.

As the United States became involved in the affairs of Panama, she too began to make demands. From May 19, 1904, when the United States officially took control of the Canal Zone, the Americans sought and literally expropriated land under the provisions of the 1903 Treaty, which stipu-

17. Tate, p. 127.
18. *For. Rel. of U.S.* (1901), p. 773.

lated that the United States was entitled to additional territory required for military installations. Panama began to feel that the entire Isthmus might eventually be deemed of strategic value and occupied. As demands for land increased,[19] a serious bone of contention developed.

Despite the accomplishments of men like Dr. William C. Gorgas, who exterminated the malaria-carrying mosquitoes in Panama during the canal building era, Panamanians became more hostile to the United States. After the successful completion of the Panama Canal, Panamanians would have preferred the departure of the Americans.

THE PANAMA CANAL AND CANAL ZONE

On January 7, 1914, the first vessel, the self-propelled crane boat the *Alex La Valley,* passed through the Panama Canal.[20] With the opening of the interoceanic waterway, United States penetration into the Caribbean and Central America increased enormously. New York banks began to spring up throughout Panama and the Caribbean, and the United States became closely identified with financial exploitation in the region.

The newly constructed Canal became the focal point of Panamanian life. It was regarded as Panama's primary natural resource, even though a good portion of it was attributable to man's engineering techniques. Certainly most of the progress that has occurred in Panama is a result, either directly or indirectly, of the Canal. Theoretically, Panama has become a great shipping power because of the advantages to

19. The United States made fourteen requests for additional territory between 1908 and 1930.

20. It was not until August 15, 1914, that the *S. S. Ancon* made the first official ocean-to-ocean transit.

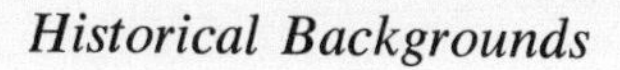

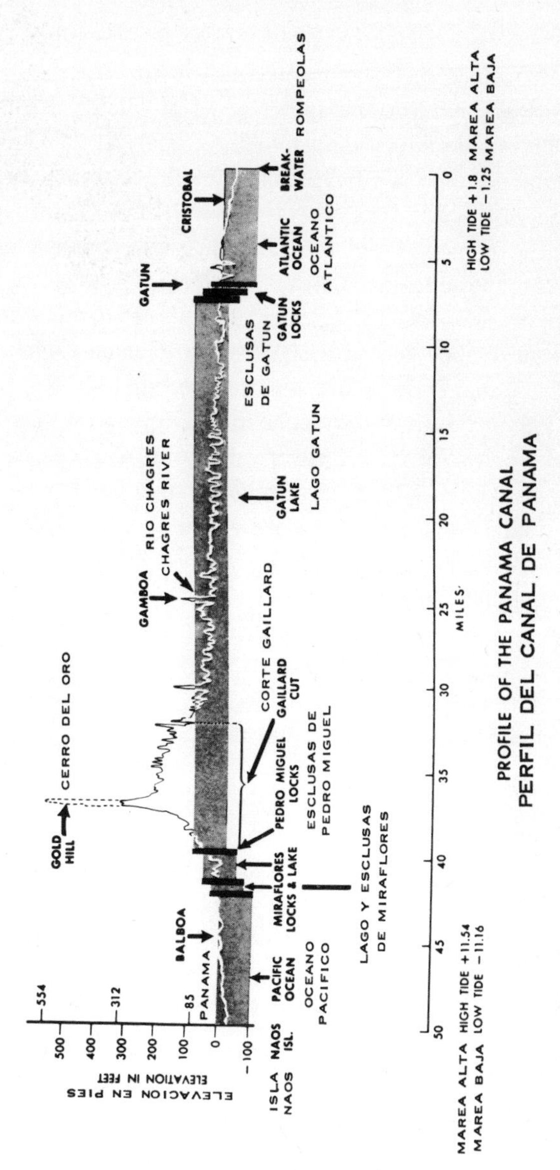

PROFILE OF THE PANAMA CANAL
PERFIL DEL CANAL DE PANAMA

nations which utilize Panamanian maritime facilities.

When the Canal first opened an average of five ships a day passed through it; some day it would provide transit for over ten thousand vessels annually. The Canal cut 7,873 miles of travel from the sea voyage from New York to San Francisco and 8,868 miles from the trip from New Orleans to San Francisco, and placed the United States nearer to desired mineral resources in Bolivia and Chile. By avoiding sailing around "The Horn" ships could save more than ten times the amount of their tolls if they used the Panama Canal.

The Canal Zone, a strip which spread some ten miles across the Isthmus, was placed under the jurisdiction of the Department of the Army and governed by an officer of the Engineer Corps, and the construction of the Canal was carried out under military supervision. The United States Army employed about four or five hundred Panamanians in the original labor force, and thousands of laborers were imported from the West Indies. Racial problems originated with the importation of Jamaican Negro labor to work on the Canal and are still a thorn in the side of the United States.

Ownership of the Canal and the Canal Zone was placed in the hands of a single stockholder of the Panama Canal Company, the Secretary of the Army, who approves the appointment of the Canal Zone Governor and holds him answerable for both the Zone's civil government and the operation of the Canal. The authority of the Governor has been shared with a board of nine to thirteen directors who have jointly made policy for the Canal and the Zone, subject to acceptance by the Secretary of the Army.

Travelers in the Canal Zone derive the impression that they are in the midst of a gigantic military installation, and by the same token the Panamanians have felt that an important segment of their territory is occupied by the forces of the

United States. This notion cannot be dispelled even when visiting the residential areas within the zone which resemble American enclaves.

The Canal itself is a source of wonder even in this age of missiles and spacecraft. Ships enter the Canal from Balboa on the Pacific side or from the Atlantic entrance at Cristobal which is some twenty-seven miles farther west. A vessel entering the Canal from the Atlantic Ocean goes from Cristobal Harbor to Gatun Locks (a distance of seven miles), is initially raised by a series of locks to Gatun Lake (eighty-five feet above sea level), passes thirty-one miles of lake through Gaillard Cut to Pedro Miguel Locks where it is lowered (thirty-one feet) to Miraflores Lake. A mile to the south the vessel is then lowered through Miraflores Locks (fifty-four feet) to the Balboa Harbor which is at sea level, and then proceeds into the Pacific Ocean.

The Panama Canal system contains six locks each way, each being a thousand feet long and one hundred-ten feet wide. The draft limitation is thirty-seven feet and numerous passenger, freight, and naval vessels now find it impossible to pass safely through the Canal.[21] The locks have always been militarily vulnerable and Panamanians have feared that a sunken ship might obstruct traffic in the Canal. The Panama Canal operates on the machinery originally installed, and it now takes about eight hours for a vessel to pass through its water, if unobstructed. Canal passage, which is limited to daylight hours for the sake of safety, is frequently slowed by traffic congestion or single lane traffic necessitated by repairs or maintenance.

When first constructed the Panama Canal was of strategic

21. To accommodate the vessels now in existence, it is desirable that a canal be sea level, and at least 1,000 feet wide and 250 feet deep.

importance to the United States Navy which in the early decades of the twentieth century did not maintain both Atlantic and Pacific fleets. Now the primary use of the Canal is merchant marine travel between the two coasts of the United States and between the eastern coast of the United States and the western coast of South America and Asia.

The Canal Zone occupies a small area in comparison to the total territory of Panama. Many are lured to the Zone from rural areas in the hope of securing employment, which creates a vast pool of unskilled workers. However, there is and has been a lack of trained manpower needed to run the Canal, which necessitates the importation of United States workers. Panamanians ignore the fact that they are incapable of handling the operation of the Canal themselves and treat the United States role in their country as a classic example of nineteenth century imperialism. They feel that the United States has placed not only the Canal area but the whole nation under its hegemony.

Panamanians are correct when they allege that the Canal is monopolized by the United States. But that is not to say that Panama has been entirely excluded. Legally the status of the Canal is neutral and the Republic of Panama has the right to transport vessels, and troops, with no payment required. Although the Zone has been granted to the United States in perpetuity, funds spent in the area and enuring to the Republic of Panama are considerable. In comparison to other Latin American nations, the economic interests of the United States in the Canal are not inconsiderable.

The United States currently pays Panama $1,930,000 annually, considerably more than the sum agreed upon in 1903, and spends between forty to fifty-five million dollars a year in the Republic of Panama on supplies and tourism, as a result of the Canal.[22] Certainly the $5,158 average toll received per Canal transit does not leave an enormous profit for the Panama Canal Company or the United States.[23] The Canal Corporation itself is considered a non-profit organization, and the fact that excess funds are channelled into repairs and improvements has never been fully understood by the man in the street in Panama. Panamanians have no legitimate argument when they assert that the United States keeps duplicate sets of books and is enriching herself at their expense.

THE ERA OF INTERVENTION

Article 136 of the original Constitution of the Republic of Panama permitted United States intervention, and for the first three decades of its history the Republic was a de facto protectorate of the United States. Acting in accordance with the Treaty of 1903, the Constitution of Panama and the Roosevelt Corollary to the Monroe Doctrine, the United States sought to secure stability and order in Panama. As the United States intervened on behalf of the newly created nation it made inroads into every facet of Panamanian life.

During the first decades of the twentieth century even the mere threat of United States intervention proved helpful to Panama. At various times the Americans were compelled to take over public health problems in Panama in order not to jeopardize the operation of the Canal and the Canal Zone. It is a lasting tribute to the United States that Panama is one of the least disease ridden nations in Latin America.

22. "Servicio Información De Los Estados Unidos," *Boletín de Prensa y Radio Panamá,* República de Panamá, Comunicado No. 330 (20 de abril de 1965), p. 378.

23. Tolls are levied on a net tonnage basis and amount to about 90 cents a ton for laden ships and 72 cents for unladen vessels.

A prime illustration of the futility of attempting to assist Panama was the election of 1912, which Washington agreed to oversee and wound up implicated in fraud charges.[24] Entanglements of this nature ultimately cast a shadow upon the United States. On July 4 of the same year anti-Yankee riots broke out in Cocoa Grove and resulted in the death of one American and injuries to nineteen others.[25] Washington requested an explanation and proper action by the government of Panama, but it was not immediately forthcoming. The intentions of the United States had become suspect in Panama, and dealings with the northern neighbor had to be handled discreetly as not to arouse adverse public opinion. By 1916 the incident was finally settled when Panama agreed to pay minor damages to the United States.[26] The length of time necessary to settle this altercation was indicative of the growing disdain for the United States presence in the Republic of Panama.

By 1913, the Panamanian government, sensing the need for stability in the nation, agreed to permit the United States to intervene in her affairs. By the addition of an amendment, similar to the more famoús Platt Amendment in Cuba's Constitution, Panama provided for United States protection. Soon afterward, the United States entered the boundary dispute between Costa Rica in a dynamic fashion. United States Chief Justice White awarded the territory in dispute to Costa Rica. However, permission to intervene and abiding by the results of the intervention are two different things. Panamanians refused to abide by Justice White's decision, and the award was not implemented until 1921 when Costa Rica forcibly seized the territory in dispute. The matter was then

24. McCain, p. 72.
25. *Ibid.* p. 81.
26. *Ibid.*

appealed to the League of Nations by the Panamanians who disliked the American decision. For some unexplained reason the United States failed to reiterate the tenets of the Monroe Doctrine to the League and permitted primarily European nations to render a decision affecting a hemispheric nation.[27]

Anti-American sentiment spread and in February of 1915 further demonstrations in Cocoa Grove were directed against the United States.[28] By April the demonstrations became endemic and spread to the port city of Colón. The Department of State investigated the situation in Panama and decided that the time was propitious for a new treaty with Panama. Negotiations were entered into but were quickly halted as World War I intervened.

The Great War did little to curtail Yankeephobia, and American troops were not diverted from their bases on the Isthmus. During the elections of 1916 United States troops were again in evidence, but the order that was preserved was not worth the ill will that was created. Panamanians sought every conceivable opportunity to criticize the United States. On April 17, 1917, Panama declared war on Germany, and nationalists stated that it was necessary only because of the close ties to the United States. Whether or not Panama entered the conflict out of a sense of obligation to the United States had no bearing upon public opinion, which indicated a fear of being pulled into a protracted international conflict on behalf of an unpopular protector. During the course of World War I the United States exercised her protective rights against citizens of belligerent nations domiciled in Panama.[29] Germans living in the nation were interned as

27. See Dexter Perkins, *A History of the Monroe Doctrine* (Boston: Little Brown & Co., 1963), p. 326.
28. McCain, p. 83.
29. See Norman J. Padleford, *The Panama Canal In Peace and War* (New York: Macmillan Co., 1942), p. 139.

the government of Panama cooperated fully with the United States in an endeavor to eliminate enemy sympathizers.

It was in the midst of the war that the American petroleum companies were first established in Panama. The exigencies of war compelled the Americans to seek potential sources of oil, and the existing involvement in Panama made it a natural site to search. The presence of additional Americans on their soil aroused the ire of Panamanians. Demonstrations against the Americans were widespread and clashes between members of the armed forces of the United States and locals during May of 1917 grew sufficiently dangerous to warrant the dispatch of American troops. United States Marines arrived in the Province of Chiriquí by July of 1918 and remained there for two years.[30] The sight of the Marines in Panama was now a common and unpleasant symbol of United States power.

With the termination of hostilities and the removal of the German submarine threat to the Panama Canal, the United States was again in a position to concentrate upon internal problems in Panama. By 1918, the Department of State decided to remove American political controls from the nation and let the people fend for themselves. In order to preserve order, the United States insisted that Panama create a national police force. Under the guidance of United States Army and Marine officers, the Panamanian police force was completely reorganized between 1918 and 1919. Henceforth the police were looked upon suspiciously as an appendage of the United States.

The era of Prohibition in the United States affected relations with Panama as the Volstead Act pertained to the Canal Zone. The traffic in liquor was difficult to control, and the Volstead Act precipitated numerous irritating diplomatic

30. McCain, p. 85.

incidents between the two nations. It might be added that all was not negative from the Panamanian point of view, as considerable profit was derived from the surreptitious sale of whiskey to Zonians.

United States relations with Panama were constantly hindered by incidents of one type or another. The Panamanians agitated for revision of the 1903 Treaty, and the United States continued to act unilaterally in matters affecting her interests in Panama. The treaty controversy was accelerated in 1922 when the United States required Consuls in the Canal Zone to obtain exequators from the United States, thus denying, in the Canal Zone, the validity of Panama issued exequaturs. Panama construed this as a measure expressly designed to derogate her sovereignty and another controversy ensued.[31] The government of Panama demanded that the matter be submitted to arbitration but the United States declined, for in essence an arbitral commission would be deciding upon the question of sovereignty in the Canal Zone, and this the Department of State felt was adequately spelled out by the Treaty of 1903. The United States preferred to cling to the concept of "Titular Sovereignty," which William Howard Taft had referred to as a "barren scepter" with a "poetic and sentimental appeal to the Latin mind."[32]

Panama assiduously demanded clarification of mutual problems existing between herself and the United States and requested that the 1903 Treaty be revised. Questions were raised concerning lands necessary to maintain and protect the Canal, the status of the Panama Railroad Company, land in the port city of Colón, water and sewage payments, taxation, freight rates, commissaries, vessel sales and service,

31. Manuel Garcia-Mora, "The Panama Canal Controversy," *Vital Speeches,* (April 15, 1964), p. 415.
32. Located in the Taft Papers.

private enterprise in the Canal Zone, cemeteries in Colón, warehouses, customs, passports, prohibition, communications, sanitation, postal services, money, extradition, hospitals and the coastal trade.[33]

Panama wanted the aforementioned problems rectified by a new treaty with the United States. The fact that the Panamanians desired a new treaty was a tacit admission that their nation could not endure without the United States. This was again corroborated in October of 1925, when Panama had to request formally that United States forces handle a mob of rent rioters.[34] This time Yankee troops with fixed bayonets were necessary to halt the violence. Again at election time, in 1925, Marines had to be brought in at the request of President Belisario Porras. The United States was thus often assuming the role of the undesired policeman.

As the official alliance between Panama and the United States was drawing closer, feelings between the two nations were becoming estranged. By the Kelly-Alfaro Pact of 1926, Panama guaranteed to participate automatically in all United States wars. This treaty brought objections from legal specialists in the League of Nations who stated that it violated the League Covenant which stated that nations should wait three months for an arbitral decision on disputes prior to entering a war.[35] Fortunately the Kelly-Alfaro Treaty was rejected, and United States relations with Panama did not have to bear the scrutiny of the League of Nations. In actuality, the abortive Treaty of 1926 was more restrictive than had been its 1903 predecessor.

33. McCain, p. 230.

34. See John L. Mecham, *The United States and Inter-American Security 1889–1960* (Austin: University of Texas Press, 1962), p. 89.

35. American University, Special Operations Research Office, *Area Handbook For Panama* (Washington, 1962), p. 315. (Hereinafter cited as SORO.)

Agitation, negotiation, and intervention were the order of the day as the 1920's drew to a close. In 1928 the United States felt obligated to take part in the Panamanian elections on the pretext of preserving order. The enmity of the Panamanians was aroused and again the two nations endeavored to renegotiate the 1903 Treaty. President Calvin Coolidge did not help when, on November 11, 1928, during the course of a speech he stated: "Our outlying possessions, with the exception of the Panama Canal Zone, are not a help to us but a hindrance."[36] Panama was offended by the implications of the American President, particularly in the utilization of the word "possessions." A formal complaint was lodged with the Secretary of State and relations between the nations deteriorated as the Panamanians demanded that their sovereignty be recognized.

The United States now approached a new era in Latin American relations. With the advent of the Clark Memorandum[37] and the Good Neighbor Policy, the question was would the policy of intervention in Panama persist? Was Panama to be unofficially regarded as a "possession," or was it to be afforded the same recognition extended to other Latin American republics?

THE GOOD NEIGHBOR

The Latin American policy of the United States changed during the 1930's. The era of non-intervention approached as the Hoover and Roosevelt administrations endeavored to allay Latin American fears of United States imperialistic de-

36. *For. Rel. of U.S.,* Vol. III, 1928, p. 679.

37. The Memorandum, prepared by Undersecretary of State J. Reuben Clark in 1928 and published in 1930, declared the "Big Stick" policy of Theodore Roosevelt to be unjustified by the terms of the Monroe Doctrine. Thus the U.S. was no longer to pursue a policy of unilateral intervention in the hemisphere.

signs. At the same time the State Department still dealt with the Canal Zone as it would an American possession. The number of complaints arising out of United States occupation of the Canal Zone would increase once the Panamanians sensed that the United States was trying to improve her image in the hemisphere.

Panama was involved in massive social and political struggles during the early 1930's. An internal revolt signaled the political defeat of the purely white aristocracy, which was replaced by a mixed aristocracy. Panama's national police force, which remained aloof from the social struggle, became the country's primary political arbiter. The middle class gained entrance into the political process. It was from this group that the preponderance of objections to United States policy had traditionally emanated. The white aristocracy, which often collaborated with the United States for the sake of financial gain, was no longer in a position to appease the masses. If anything, the political upheaval increased anti-Americanism in Panama.

Latin America's attention was now turned toward the Panama Canal by the Peruvian political theorist Víctor Raúl Haya de la Torre. The ideology of Haya's *Alianza Popular Revolucionaria Americana* (APRA) movement included goals of Latin American unity and internationalization of the Panama Canal. By 1931 the program of Haya de la Torre was known throughout Latin America, and the anti-United States stand of the *Apristas* was generally applauded in Panama. Although there was no consensus in Panama concerning the internationalization of the Canal, there was unanimity in the belief that this measure, although less desirable than nationalization, was superior to United States suzerainty.

Incidents continued to obstruct harmonious relations between the United States and Panama. The effects of the Volstead Act continued to be felt in the area. Panama opposed the sale of 3.2 per cent beer in the Canal Zone, as it competed directly with local brewing interests. So complicated did the controversy become that in 1932 Panama's press hinted that the government was seriously considering severing relations with the United States. It seems unlikely that such a trivial matter could cause so much dissension, but diplomatic breaks have been caused by even less serious provocation.

Striving to bring the grievances of Panama to the attention of President Franklin Delano Roosevelt, President Harmodio Arias journeyed to Washington in autumn of 1933. President Arias indicated to Roosevelt that his nation desired liberal revision of the 1903 Treaty. The Panamanians did not fully realize that the United States was on the verge of revitalizing her overall Latin American policy, and when Franklin Roosevelt granted insignificant concessions in the Canal Zone he became a minor hero in Panama.

The Memorandum of J. Reuben Clark, in 1928, modified the Roosevelt Corollary to the Monroe Doctrine. The military forces of the United States pulled out of Haiti, the Dominican Republic, and Nicaragua; and the Platt Amendment, granting the right to intervene in Cuba, would be abrogated by 1934. At the Seventh Inter-American Conference, in Montevideo, Uruguay, in 1933, Secretary of State Cordell Hull accepted the principle of nonintervention in the internal or external affairs of hemispheric nations. The prospects for better accord with Panama appeared bright.

A new treaty with Panama which would eliminate friction with the United States and the right of intervention along with guaranteeing Panama's independence was now conceivable. In 1934, President Roosevelt sanctioned the drafting of such a treaty. To Assistant Secretary of State Sumner Welles fell the task of negotiating the new pact. The Good

Neighbor Policy was now in effect, and Panama was to be one of its beneficiaries. The United States proposal to completely revise the existing 1903 Treaty was implemented by means of a new general treaty. In addition, two new pacts relating to radio communications in Panama and the Canal Zone were concluded, along with an agreement for the construction of a highway between Panama City and Colón. Panama was no longer a protectorate of the United States but an ally. Intervention was now supposedly a relic of the past. The Convention of Friendship and Cooperation, signed by Cordell Hull and Sumner Welles for the United States and Narciso Garay and Ricardo Alfaro for Panama, recognized the sovereignty of Panama. It should be noted that the promise not to intervene was opposed by the military in the United States which felt that it would serve to weaken American defenses on the Isthmus.

The new Pact known as the Hull-Alfaro Treaty was the first successful revision of the Hay-Bunau-Varilla Agreement which had caused so much consternation over the years. By the terms of the Pact, signed on March 2, 1936, a bilateral approach to foreign policy was initiated and the obligation to guarantee the independence of Panama was eliminated.[38] The United States relinquished rights over lands already occupied[39] and agreed to increase the annual rental paid to Panama for the Zone and Canal to $430,000, in order to compensate for devaluation.

Presidents Arias and Roosevelt concluded still another treaty. This one, entered into on January 20, 1936, guaranteed Panamanians equality of opportunity with Americans

38. Some assert that this treaty made Panama a virtual protectorate of the United States.

39. Almon R. Wright, "Defense Site Negotations Between the United States and Panama, 1936–1948," *Department of State Bulletin* (August 11, 1952), p. 212.

in the Canal Zone, a pledge which has never really been fulfilled. With the conclusion of these new pacts evolved a modicum of harmony and an intensified Panamanian effort to extract concessions from the United States.

In the spring of 1939, the United States Legation in Panama City was elevated to Embassy status, a move which delighted Panamanians as it enhanced their nation's prestige. As the war in Europe progressed it was feared that the Panama Canal was included in Hitler's conquest plans,[40] and the United States realized the importance of increased cooperation with Panama. In order to facilitate better Canal defense the United States began enlarging the Canal, started construction on a trans-Isthmian highway, and requested additional territory for military installations. The United States was confronted with the task of defending the Atlantic, the Pacific and the Caribbean, and the Panama Canal was a vital link in the defense program.

In order to protect the western approaches to the Panama Canal, the United States concluded treaties with Costa Rica, El Salvador, Gutemala, and Nicaragua. However, Panamanian politics precluded a similar defense arrangement. Both the British, who still had vast interests in the Caribbean, and the Americans would have preferred to subordinate Panama to their wishes, but President Arnulfo Arias was determined to preserve his nation's neutrality at all costs. Possibly this assertion of Panama's sovereignty was retribution for previous United States actions. Under no circumstances did President Arias wish to be known as subordinate to the Yankees. He listened attentively to Panamanians of German and Italian ancestry and steered a pro-Axis course. The

40. Subsequently it was proven that the fears of the United States were well founded; Hitler did formulate a plan for the conquest of the Panama Canal.

Panameñista Party of Arias espoused nationalism and xenophobia, and the United States was its major target.

In 1941 the situation in Panama was grave in the eyes of the United States. German controlled airlines were operating out of both Brazil and neighboring Colombia, and the Panama Canal was in jeopardy. By the end of the year the national police forced Arnulfo Arias out of power and the pro-Axis regime was supplanted by the administration of Ricardo Adolfo de la Guardia. On December 7, 1941, Panama offered full military cooperation to the United States and by May of the following year was rendering other types of aid as well. The government of Panama interned Japanese subjects, froze assets of the Axis powers, and began censorship of radio messages and cablegrams. On December 10, 1941, Panama declared war on Japan and two days later instituted similar action against Nazi Germany and Italy.[41]

During World War II Panama's support of the United States policies reached its apogee. The increased cooperation was predicated upon self-interest, rather than an emerging affinity for the United States, as Panama's very existence depended upon the successful prosecution of the war. Panamanian troops were being trained by United States instructors and the entire Isthmus assumed a carnival air during the war. Panama acquired all of the things generally associated with towns located near military installations. Saloons, shoddy merchandise, swindlers, gamblers and prostitutes were now commonplace in Panama City and Colón. Financially the nation prospered, as a result of the war, but prosperity was accompanied by signs of moral decay.

During the global conflict the greatest threat to Panama

41. See Edward O. Guerrant, *Roosevelt's Good Neighbor Policy* (Albuquerque: University of New Mexico Press, 1950), p. 125.

was the German U-Boat fleet which could destroy the effectiveness of the Canal with a single blow. Coastal patrols were ever vigilant, and the Panamanians cooperated fully, for failure to do so would lead to serious repercussions if the Germans penetrated the Canal's perimeter of defense. Still the government of Panama was alert to anything that might damage potential profit or infringe upon the nation's sovereignty. When in March of 1942 a few commercial aircraft landed at Albrook Field in the Canal Zone, Panama's Ambassador to the United States, E. Jaen Guardia, protested.[42] He averred that the planes had entered the Zone on business unrelated to the operation of the Zone, and thus the landings were detrimental to the economy of Panama. After due explanation the Panamanians were assured that the landings were precipitated by emergency conditions and that the United States would abide by her treaty obligations. Feeling that her economic interests in the field of commercial aviation were thus safeguarded, Panama refrained from further objections.

Panama agreed not only to participate in military defense but to permit the United States to use thirty-eight thousand additional acres of land for such installations as airfields, detection equipment and bombing ranges. By the end of the war, over one hundred-thirty installations had become operational in Panama. These were to be returned within one year after the peace.[43]

By 1945 Panama was one of only two Latin American nations not having Lend Lease agreements with the United States. Argentina, because of dictator Juan Perón's Axis sympathy, had been exempted from United States aid, but why Panama? The Panamanians were resentful of this obvi-

42. *For. Rel. of U.S.*, Vol. VI, 1942, p. 619.
43. By 1945, the United States occupied 134 separate areas in Panama.

ous neglect, and the American attempts to explain the lack of assistance were not convincing. The United States claimed that Panama was not a recipient of Lend Lease aid because supposedly aid had been forthcoming via the protection of the Canal Zone. This argument was inconclusive, in that such aid was indirect, and more beneficial to the United States than Panama. It seemed the United States had once again taken Panama for granted, and this oversight was not to be soon forgotten.

In an effort to rationalize the lack of direct aid via Lend Lease, one could say that the millions that flowed into the nation by way of the Canal Zone more than sufficiently compensated Panama for her efforts on behalf of the United States. Nevertheless, in order to reaffirm friendship with Panama the United States began to emphasize social and cultural relations. Specialists in vocational training, public health, and rural and special education were furnished to the nation by the United States.[44] However, the Panamanians thought this hardly adequate in view of the fact that during World War II 5,300 combat vessels and 8,500 troop transports had passed through the Panama Canal.[45]

After the war, United States attention was diverted from Latin America in general and turned toward Europe. The Inter-American Defense Board, in an effort to be prepared for further global conflicts, endeavored to strengthen military bases in Panama. However, Panama's Provisional President, Enrique A. Jiménez, agitated for the Americans' departure. Once entrenched, it was not easy to dislodge the United States, and in December of 1946, Ambassador Frank T. Hines tried to make wartime acquisitions permanent by requesting a twenty-year extension on the leases of thirteen

44. Guerrant, p. 125.
45. Tate, p. 132.

facilities in Panama. The request was denied, and the following May the United States announced that some ninety-eight sites were being returned to Panama, and only those required for defense would be retained.[46] By August of the same year eighteen additional sites were abandoned by the United States.

Violent anti-United States demonstrations broke out in December of 1947 when the Panamanian government agreed to permit the United States to retain a number of strategic bases for a period of five years, and a technical installation at Río Hato, seventy miles from Panama City, for ten years. The riots fostered the resignation of Panama's Foreign Minister Alfaro, who had been instrumental in permitting retention of the bases. Once again Panama concentrated upon extracting concessions from the United States. Anti-imperialist demonstrations became an integral part of the developing Cold War. The United States was to gradually acquiesce to more demands, with the first major concession coming in 1947 when the Civil Service Commission granted Panamanians permission to take the examinations necessary for employment in the Canal Zone.

As Panama began to make gains she increasingly pressured Washington. On December 23, 1947, Panama's National Assembly rejected an agreement granting the United States the right to occupy other bases in the nation and the populace was ecstatic. Communists, now beginning to take the initiative in the nation, claimed that the United States wanted to retain bases in Panama as she did in Europe. The Communist line decrying United States imperialism perfectly complemented nationalist sentiment.

A group of American businessmen approached the Panamanian government in 1948 and requested permission to establish a Panamanian airline. The Americans offered to

46. Mecham, p. 296.

provide the aircraft in return for the necessary airfields and nationality for the airline. The government of Panama interpreted this as a mutually beneficial attempt on the part of sincere Americans to create an essential transportation link in the country. Panama agreed to the proposition and before a contract could be formally entered into the American planes landed in Panama. The entire plan proved to be a hoax perpetrated by a group of ex-servicemen working with pro-Israeli Americans in New York. The Panama base was needed as a layover for the aircraft prior to departure for Israel, which was not as yet a sovereign state, for use in the war against the Arab nations. When the Panamanian officials arrived at the airfield to inspect the aircraft, they found them missing and immediately held the United States responsible. Although this was an unfortunate experience which did not have the authorization of the Department of State, it was credited by the Panamanians as another United States subterfuge designed to exploit their nation.

The removal of United States bases from Panama proved costly to both nations. For example, the abandonment of an airfield outside of the Canal Zone in 1948 cost the United States more than one million dollars,[47] and not even affluent nations relish the idea of financial loss, no matter how minimal. On the other hand, the closing of United States bases adversely affected Panama's economy. By 1949 businesses and merchants, who had thrived on American dollars which flowed from the temporary military installations, were now in critical financial condition. Panama's economy was slipping, and in order to refurbish the treasury the government would have to reopen negotiations for the lucrative United States bases.

47. J. Fred Rippy, "The U.S. and Panama, Endless Appeasement," *Modern Age* (Summer, 1964), p. 279.

In order to bolster Panama's crumbling economy the United States dispatched Monnett B. Davis, a specialist in Latin American affairs, as Ambassador to Panama. Under the direction of Ambassador Davis the United States negotiated an aviation treaty with Panama on March 31, 1949. By the terms of this pact the United States agreed to assume some responsibility for the construction of Touceman National Airport to service Panama City and the Canal Zone. Despite this service rendered to Panama, 1949 was not a year to express gratitude to the United States. The nation was preoccupied by internal problems emanating from diverse sources. Activities by the international communist movement had been accelerated on the Isthmus. At the same time Wilson Walter Brown, a former United States Air Force officer, was implicated as an arms peddler in a plot to overthrow the government of Panama. Nationalists as well as subversives immediately resumed attacks upon the United States, and the era of the Good Neighbor merged with the Cold War as United States relations with Panama deteriorated.

CHAPTER
THREE

Panama In The Cold War

With the advent of the Cold War, Panama's role in world affairs became increasingly more important. Panama, in relation to her size, would receive a disproportionate amount of attention from the Soviet Bloc and thus would be given additional consideration by Washington. Whether or not Panama would use her geographic position, with regard to the communists, as a bargaining point in dealings with the United States would depend upon what was to be gained from the respective world powers. The atomic age had diminished the military and strategic value of the Panama Canal, but the Department of State was not thoroughly convinced of this, and the Soviet Union was cognizant of the fact that one atomic bomb could destroy the Canal. The Russians desired the elimination of all western controlled ocean links such as Suez, Gibraltar and Panama, which in the event of limited conflicts would be of strategic importance. The Korean conflict then increased the prospects of future limited encounters.

In the post World War II era Panama witnessed a middle class growth. At the same time the prosperity of the Zonians increased. Many of the Zonians were newcomers and ignorant of Panama's heritage and traditions. Misunderstandings with Panamanians were frequent, and anti-United States violence increased. Panama's Chief of Police, José Antonio Remón, now had at his disposal some two thousand well drilled men as anti-United States rioting became a daily way of life.

When post World War II differences over military bases were temporarily resolved, other factors exacerbated anti-United States feelings in Panama. For example, during the early 1950's the *Peronistas* spread their brand of Yankeephobia. Although the adherents of Juan Perón's "third position" theory of *Justicialismo* were few and far between, they still had a negative affect upon United States relations with Panama. Panamanians did not desire owing allegiance to Argentina or Perón any more than to the United States, but they were quick to grasp at anything that implied sovereignty and a weakening of ties with the United States.

Increasing anti-United States sentiment led to "Operation Sovereignty," a movement initiated by students at the University of Panama who had been inspired by numerous communist infiltrators. Although violent Yankeephobia did not auger well for relations with Panama, the communist threat was not as serious as the House Un-American Activities Committee indicated. From this juncture onward, riots and demonstrations persisted.

When the "Police Action" erupted in Korea and the Cold War threatened to escalate, Panama immediately joined with the United States to secure her own interests. As the communists made greater inroads in Asia, Panama deemed the time propitious to extract concessions from the United States. Panamanians figured that a United States desirous of garnering allies would be susceptible to proposals of a compromising nature. As Mao Tse-Tung took over in China and Chiang Kai-Shek was ousted, Panama supported the United States position in the United Nations and hoped that the United

States would reciprocate by granting concessions in the Canal Zone. Panama offered the United Nations a small contingent of volunteers, training sites, merchant marine facilities, and access routes to Asia. Although these offerings were nominal insofar as the Korean War was concerned, the Panama Canal was important to the transportation of troops.

During July of 1951, a vital reorganization in the structure of the Canal Zone government took place. The Canal Zone government became an independent agency of the United States, as the powers governing the Canal and Zone were separated. Although the Panama Canal Company ran the Canal as a non-profit making organization, the Governor of the Zone still held the position of President of the Panama Canal Company. During the same period Zonians were displeased as the graduated income tax was extended to the Canal Zone, giving rise to legitimate complaints of taxation without representation.

Panama's National Assembly in November of 1952 passed a resolution declaring that the $430,000 received as annual lease payment from the United States in accord with the 1936 Treaty was insufficient. Immediately the communists, together with the *Peronistas,* began to agitate for revision of the 1936 Treaty. By April of 1953 President Remón announced that the United States and Panama were about to enter into negotiations designed to revise the 1903 Treaty. President Remón claimed that his nation was seeking neither millions nor alms, only justice. Whether or not justice would be forthcoming would ultimately be decided in Washington, not Panama City.

In August of 1953 a simulated forty kiloton atomic bomb was exploded by the United States some five hundred yards from the Miraflores Locks. This was part of "Operation Jackpot," an attempt to train a defense crew in the Canal in the event of disaster. This exercise instilled fear in the hearts of many Panamanians and illustrated the necessity of United States defense forces in the region and served to temporarily quell some demands that the Americans pull out of Panama entirely.

The negotiations concerning the Treaty of 1903 began on September 10, 1953. Panama demanded higher rental fees, better employment opportunities for her citizens in the Canal Zone and on the Canal, fairer treatment for Panamanian workers employed by the United States, and restrictions on the use of commissary facilities used by civilian citizens of the United States. In essence Panama was protesting discrimination against her nationals and the concurrent privileges granted to American civilian employees in the Canal Zone. In the midst of the negotiations Panamanian extremists accused the United States of aggression in Korea, and a damper was temporarily placed upon the bilateral discussions.

The negotiations with Panama were soon overshadowed by the immediacy of the impending communist threat to the hemisphere emanating from Guatemala. In June of 1954, Panama was among the first of the Latin American nations to support a United States proposal for an emergency meeting of the Foreign Ministers of the Organization of American States members to discuss the spread of communism in Guatemala.

Simultaneously the United States and Panama endeavored to negotiate a treaty to revise the 1903 pact. Treaty negotiations bogged down when the United States requested that the contemplated new revisions of the 1903 Treaty be made permanent. Before Panama could raise objections and submit counter proposals, President José Antonio Remón, who was directing the diplomatic talks, was assassinated on January 2, 1955. When a new treaty was subsequently signed, it did not really reflect Remón's or Panama's demands.

Enlightened Panamanians realized that the United States was not on the verge of departing from the Isthmus. Pursuing a more pragmatic approach toward the United States, Panama began to utilize the Americans presence to best advantage. In 1954 the 3,000 man *Guardia Nacional* was elevated to military status in order to avail itself of United States military training facilities that were available in the Canal Zone. Panama's resignation to the presence of the Americans stimulated immediate United States responses. For example, American shipping interests now pressed for reduction in Canal tolls under the guise of pretending to encourage coastal shipping. Both nations vied for concessions, and as soon as one nation relaxed its vigil, or tempered its demands, the other took the initiative.

Panamanian nationalism was on the upswing and pressures began to mount rapidly by 1955. Anti-United States riots and violence were commonplace. The Remón-Eisenhower Treaty, alluded to above, was felt to be dualistic by many in Panama. Under the terms of the pact concluded on January 25, 1955, Panama received the equivalent of thirty-nine million dollars, some twenty-nine million dollars in real estate and the remaining ten million dollars in diverse forms.[1] The treaty was designed to be implemented by July, 1958, but was retarded severely by failures in the power structure of Panamanian politics. After eight years of agitation for its conclusion, the treaty only served to alter the old one. In particular, Panama resented the retention of the "perpetuity clause" whose elimination had been the primary objective in her negotiations.

Panama was still in a state of shock over the race track assassination of President Remón when Vice President Richard M. Nixon visited in February of 1955. Mr. Nixon was

1. See J. Fred Rippy, *Globe and Hemisphere* (Chicago: Henry Regnery Co., 1958), p. 110.

well received and spoke at length with President Ricardo Arias about mutual problems. Primarily the two discussed rising unemployment and ways of rectifying this problem.

The talks were inconclusive, but opened the way for the ratification of the new treaty. In March of 1955, after sixteen months of foot dragging, the Remón-Eisenhower Treaty was ratified. Panama's demands for a higher rent were granted and the nation was to receive $1,930,000 annually. In return the United States received some twenty thousand acres at the Río Hato airbase site rent free for fifteen years, with the provision that she would consult with Panama prior to utilizing the land.

Panama was soon reconciled to the fact that the new treaty was inadequate. But further negotiations were complicated by another international crisis, when in September of 1955, the exiled Argentine dictator Juan Domingo Perón sought refuge in Panama City. The presence of Perón gave renewed impetus to a few followers of *Justicialismo* and courage to many previously unrevealed leftists and Yankeephobes who now stepped up their propaganda. The government of Panama felt Perón to be potentially detrimental to negotiations with the United States and did not make the deposed President of Argentina welcome. Ultimately Perón found it difficult to establish a successful base of operations on the Isthmus and departed for a more congenial sanctuary.

In order to propitiate the Panamanians after the departure of Perón, the United States government ruled that American businesses in the Canal Zone could not compete with Panama's enterprises. This ruling, although never implemented, indicated that this might be the beginning of United States assent to the demands of Panama, and the Panamanians were hopeful. By 1956 full scale agitation for nationalization of the Panama Canal was resumed under the direction of President

Ernesto de la Guardia. Support was forthcoming from the increasingly vocal Communist Party which was headquartered at the University of Panama. *Peronistas* and Communists, whose credos were basically inimical to each other, now were allied to gain strength. This alliance, together with support from Panamanian nationalists, increased the tempo of anti-United States agitation.

To commemorate the one hundred and thirtieth anniversary of the first Inter-American Conference in Panama, the Organization of American States planned a celebration for July, 1956. The Americans were invited to send a high level delegation to Panama for the festivities; and the government in Panama City, being fearful of an international incident, spirited Perón and followers off to Nicaragua. The celebration was concluded without serious incident, and the consensus was that the atmosphere for negotiations was clearing. Unfortunately another diplomatic crisis was precipitated and precluded immediate harmony between the nations.

United States Secretary of State John Foster Dulles, in July of 1956, persuaded Great Britain to exclude Panama from the twenty-two nation user's conference to discuss the dangerous Suez crisis. The controversial Secretary of State logically felt that any association which would cause world opinion to find similarities between the situation in Suez and that existing in Panama would eventually prove harmful to United States interests on the Isthmus. On August 15, 1956, Panama officially protested her exclusion from the Suez parley and expressed the opinion that the actions of the United States were contrary to her best interests. Five days later, in a formal statement, Panama stated that she would never accept international control over the Canal. Only nationalization of the Canal would be acceptable to the Panamanians, who now endeavored to imitate Nasser, but they forgot the one real difference between Panama and Egypt. Their Canal was constructed by the United States, while the Suez Canal was built by Egyptians.

During and after the Egyptian nationalization of Suez, Panama was restive. Constant complaints about British and United States failure to include Panama in the conference to discuss the problem of Suez were heard from Panama City. When John Foster Dulles stated that the United States represented the interests of Panama, the Panamanians objected on the grounds that they had never relinquished sovereignty over the Canal and Canal Zone. Secretary of State Dulles erred in his opinion of Panama's position in reference to the Canal, but as a practical matter he steered the proper course for his nation. His actions were designed primarly to preclude Panama's emulation of the Egyptian action in regard to the Suez Canal.

Egypt offered little consolation to Panama insofar as the position of the United States was concerned. The Egyptian press derogated the treatment afforded Panama, which after all was a prime user of the Suez Canal.[2] When Egyptian sponsored Suez Canal talks were convened, Panama was invited to participate by President Nasser. Hostility toward the United States increased immediately and *El Dia* reported: "What Panama wants is better treatment from the United States."[3] The events that transpired in Egypt raised Panamanian nationalism to a higher pitch.

A series of disparate events then occurred which served to do further damage to relations with the United States. In August of 1956, one Manuel José Hurtado and eighteen fol-

2. Although Panama's merchant fleet is small, many of the nations of the world find it financially advantageous to register their ships in the Isthmian nation. Thus, technically numerous vessels of Panamanian registry pass through the Suez Canal.

3. *El Dia* (Panama), September 6, 1956.

lowers initiated a guerrilla war in the jungles adjacent to Balboa. Señor Hurtado ironically had received his military training at the United States Fort Sherman in the Canal Zone, and now was expressing his brand of Yankeephobia. Although the insurrection was abortive, it was a portent for the future.

So frustrated were the Panamanians by the intransigence of the United States in matters relating to the Canals, both Suez and Panama, that the government often reacted ludicrously. The height of absurdity was reached when Panama, in an attempt to eliminate vestiges of United States influence, requested that American garbage collection in Panama City and Colón be terminated. The citizens of the terminal port cities protested vehemently against the action of their government as a serious sanitation problem developed. Panama had reached an impasse in her dealings with the United States and knew not where, or to whom, to turn for deliverance.

The spirit of the late President Remón remained alive in his often repeated words: "*Ni millones, ni limosnas, queremos justicia*—neither millions, nor alms, we want justice," as Panama pressed for renegotiation of the 1955 Treaty. In March of 1957, a seminar on International Law was held at Panama's National University. Some of Latin America's finest legal minds attended and the consensus was that the "perpetuity clause" in the 1903 Treaty was illegal. The lone dissenter among the international jurists was the Cuban Francisco V. García Amador, who felt that Panama had no right to denounce something she entered into openly. There can be no doubt how a delegation from Castro's Cuba would now view the problem in light of the existence of the Guantanamo Naval Base. The United States occupies this territory under the terms of a treaty which Cubans believe approximates the "perpetuity clause" of the 1903 Treaty with Panama.

The 1957 experimental war games, "Operation Caribbean," revealed that the Panama Canal was entirely defenseless from nuclear attacks. Because of this the United States petitioned Panama for sites, outside of the Canal Zone, on which to construct missile bases to protect the Canal. Panama reluctantly agreed to take the matter under advisement. But Panama feared that construction of missile sites to protect the Canal would be an open invitation to disaster and contended that the Canal could be adequately protected from the Canal Zone; she expressed a reluctance to relinquish any more terrain to the United States.

In the meantime, President Eisenhower authorized a United States bill to provide for a high level bridge to be constructed over the Canal at Balboa.[4] Three quarters of a million dollars were allocated for this purpose to implement the 1955 Treaty. At this point United States relations with Panama were in a state of flux and for the next six or seven months there was a notable absence of Panamanian rancor. However peaceful spans in relations between the two nations rarely endure and the usual crisis occurred when American evangelist Billy Graham held what Archbishop Francis Beckman called "heretical revival meetings" in Panama in February of 1958.[5] Catholics were warned to stay away from the revival sessions but disobeyed the instructions of their bishops, and Reverend Graham's productions played to capacity houses. Once again extremists were provided with ammunition to launch a massive propaganda assault against the United States, which was now portrayed as desirous of undermining Panama's Catholicism.

In an attempt to restore harmony and absolve the United

4. "Implementation of Treaty with Panama," *Department of State Bulletin* (September 16, 1957), p. 477.

5. "Panama," *Hispanic American Report* (February, 1958), p. 83.

States of complicity in the Billy Graham meetings, President Ernesto de la Guardia, in March of 1958, proclaimed "Point Four Week."[6] This was designed to pay tribute to the United States for its assistance in the realm of "leadership preparation."

It is difficult to understand the motivation of President de la Guardia, but it does not take extensive knowledge of human behavior to be skeptical of "Point Four Week." Had it not been only a few years since Panama severely criticized United States concentration of post war rebuilding efforts in Europe rather than in Latin America? Was President de la Guardia heaping praise upon the Americans in the hope that this would be a step leading to desired treaty negotiations? If this were de la Guardia's intention, then he failed to follow up his line of pointed diplomacy. A month after the superficial festivities of "Point Four Week," Panama began to press the United States on the sovereignty issue. Although obvious to the Department of State, the renewed pressure to renegotiate the existing treaties was primarily a political move fostered by the impending 1960 presidential elections in Panama. The liberals, who forced the government of Panama to take a definite stand on the sovereignty issue, were damaging long range relations.

Even President de la Guardia was caught in the attempt to impress the electorate. In response to the United States request for permission to construct rocket bases outside the Canal Zone, the President stated that the sites could not be made available until the flag of Panama was flown along with the Stars and Stripes in the Canal Zone. Panamanian students were seized by the idea of affording their flag equality and began to demonstrate. They vented their wrath not only upon

6. "President of Panama Proclaims Point Four Week," *Department of State Bulletin* (March 31, 1958), p. 522.

the Americans, but upon their own *Guardia Nacional* as well. In the series of melees that followed nine lives were lost, as were possibilities for negotiations with the United States.

Dr. Milton Eisenhower, in July of 1958, completed a special report to Washington on the state of relations with central America and singled out Panama as a danger spot. He spent considerable time there with President de la Guardia and other public officials. The Panamanians received him with little enthusiasm and even picketed the United States Embassy during his visit, carrying placards reading "The Canal is Ours." Upon returning home Dr. Eisenhower recommended that Panama's sovereignty in the Canal Zone be officially recognized by permitting her to fly her banner alongside that of the United States. Unfortunately this suggestion was opposed by the Secretary of the Army, who objected on the grounds that this might be the first step toward complete Panamanian control of the Canal Zone. The Secretary of the Army had the last say, and his decision would subsequently trouble him.

After the United States rejection of the request that the flag of Panama be prominently displayed in the Canal Zone, Panama retaliated by passing a law which extended her sovereignty over coastal waters from the traditional three-mile limit to a twelve-mile limit. Thus Panama declared herself in control over an additional nine-mile stretch between both of the Canal entrances and international waters. Panama was now beginning to assert herself against the powerful United States and, for the moment, events on the Isthmus simulated another Berlin confrontation. Panamanian nationalists as well as the usual contingent of leftists and Communists were pleased by the apparent affront to the United States. Panama's press intimated that the nation would not be satisfied until the United States agreed to an even split in Canal profits. Politicians in Panama, in order to win popular favor, exploited to the hilt the position of their nation in relation to the United States. By 1959, it was obvious that it was time for the United States to take the initiative away from Panama.

Anti-United States incidents were now so commonplace in Panama that local officials believed something to be awry when a day passed without one. The next step was taken by the United States on January 7, 1959, when a note was dispatched to the Panamanian Ambassador stating that Panama's claim to wider territory on the high seas would not be recognized. The American stand on this matter was shared by both Japan and Great Britain, who dispatched similar notes of protest over Panama's extension of her territorial waters. By this time anti-American sentiment had reached violent proportions and Panama's National Assembly officially voted Representative Daniel J. Flood, Democrat of Wilkes-Barre, Pennsylvania, the most staunch American critic of Panama, "Public Enemy Number One."[7] An aura of antagonism pervaded the atmosphere of both nations' Congresses.

Latin Americans were conscious of the impending danger and the serious consequences of a United States confrontation with Panama insofar as the Organization of American States was concerned. Former President José Figueres of Costa Rica suggested that a new conference on the Canal be held under the auspices of the OAS. However, Panama maintained that this might lead to Inter-American controls, and she was unalterably opposed to anything short of complete sovereignty over the Canal and Canal Zone.

Panama continued to complain to the United States through diplomatic channels, charging failure to comply with the 1955

7. The name Daniel Flood still evokes the wrath of enlightened Panamanians who feel that this man has labored continuously to undermine nationalism on the Isthmus.

Treaty provisions for equal treatment and opportunities for Panamanians in the Canal Zone. President Ernesto de la Guardia wrote directly to President Eisenhower suggesting that the United States live up to her obligations. The matter was turned over to the Department of State, but Panama insisted upon discussing the situation on the Chief Executive level. For decades the Department of State had controlled relations with Panama City, and President de la Guardia was determined, once again, not to be a victim of the diplomatic runaround.

Panama's refusal to deal with the Department of State did not yield immediate results, as subsequent chapters show, but would eventually prove beneficial. On June 24, 1959, the United States Atomic Energy Commission, together with the Department of State, and Panama formally agreed to cooperate in research designed for peaceful uses of atomic energy.[8] This was an agreement to exchange materials vital to nuclear fission. Nevertheless this temporary respite in mutual antagonisms did little to alleviate the basic differences between the nations. By July, nationalist sentiment against the United States was on the rise and demonstrations mounted. *Voz Universitaria,* the newspaper of the National University, continuously called for the government to revise all existing treaties with the United States. Veteran correspondent Ralph K. Skinner of the *Christian Science Monitor* reported that Panamanian nationalists were desirous of an international incident to force the United States and Panama to arbitrate their grievances. The seriousness of the situation was emphasized the following month when the American Foreign Ministers met in Santiago, Chile. At that time Panama's Foreign Minister Miguel J. Moreno, Jr. stressed the friction

8. "United States and Panama Sign Atomic Energy Agreement," *Department of State Bulletin* (July 13, 1959), p. 45.

between the United States and his nation and averred that the United States violated the 1955 Treaty. Señor Moreno announced that his nation was retaliating by lifting tariff exemptions on liquor consumed in the Canal Zone, which he stated caused his government to lose one million dollars annually in taxes.

Foreign Minister Moreno, again in September of 1959, aired his nation's grievances against the United States. This time he told his tale of misfortune to the General Assembly of the United Nations. Obviously Señor Moreno did not desire anything more than publicity, as he never requested United Nations help. The Panamanian attack gained momentum in October of 1959 when President de la Guardia stated that the United States was blocking his country's rightful demand for more Canal benefits. Señor Moreno urged international arbitration for the Canal dispute and was supported by Ambassador Ricardo Arias, who argued that Panama's relationship with the United States was not similar to Algeria's relationship with France. Both men contended that Panama was sovereign in the Canal Zone. At the same time President de la Guardia predicted that eventually a sea level canal would fundamentally change Panama's relations with the United States, as Panama could successfully operate a lockless canal. The soundness of de la Guardia's judgement was questionable, for it was tantamount to an admission that Panama could not operate the Panama Canal under present conditions without the assistance of the United States.

International friction continued into November of 1959 as Panamanian nationalists were stirred to action by an elite group of politicians led by the newspaper magnate Harmodio Arias. The followers of Señor Arias threatened to invade the Canal Zone to raise their national flag and proclaim Panama's sovereignty in the region. Foreign Minister Aquilino

Boyd, with an eye on the presidency, on November 3, 1959, led a march on the Canal Zone requesting recognition of Panamanian sovereignty. The Communists quickly picked up the tempo and involved themselves in a fight with the Canal Zone Police. United States combat troops were brought in to support the Zone authorities and quell the rioting. At the same time that violence was erupting in the Canal Zone, a mob attacked the United States Embassy and desecrated an American flag. Students claiming to be commemorating the fifty-sixth anniversary of Panama's independence turned the celebration into a blood bath. During five hours of rioting some eighty persons were injured, most of them in a futile attempt to plant a Panamanian flag in the Canal Zone. An estimated two thousand persons took part in the demonstration, and Canal Zone Governor William Potter had to order the use of tear gas to disperse the unruly mobs.

Although Panama City bore the brunt of the disorder, the chaos spread throughout the nation. In Colón, the United States Consulate was viciously attacked and damaged. Relations between the two nations were at low ebb as the United States criticized Panama's failure to prevent or halt the wanton destruction. Meanwhile, Panama's National Assembly censured Governor Potter's reprisals and continued to demand that the Panamanian flag be flown in the Canal Zone.[9]

From the riots of November 3, 1959, until the time of this writing, United States concessions to Panama have increased. The fact that the United States placed a border fence between the Canal Zone and Panama City caused many to feel that the situation was analagous to that existing in Germany with regard to the famous Berlin Wall. The traditional demands were not altered as Panama requested equal

9. Traditionally the propaganda value of such censure moves has had a profound effect upon United States policy in Panama.

pay for native workers in the Canal Zone and recognition of her sovereignty in the Canal Zone and Canal. The demands were often repeated after the riots, and on subsequent Flag Days and Independence Days similar demonstrations occurred. The library in the United States Information Service building together with the American flag became targets for rioting Panamanians. Panama objected to American use of bayonets and fire hoses to defend what did not belong to the United States. American Ambassador Julian F. Harrington protested to Foreign Minister Miguel J. Moreno, Jr., repudiating the desecration of American flags and the unprovoked attack upon the Chancery of the United States Embassy by a group of a hundred and fifty persons. Eventually Panama expressed her regrets and requested that high level diplomatic talks be commenced.[10]

If the November 1959 riots did nothing more, they emphasized the need for discussion between the nations and led to talks on the highest diplomatic levels. Secretary of State Christian Herter dispatched Under Secretary of State Livingston T. Merchant to Panama to speak with President Ernesto de la Guardia. De la Guardia stated that it was imperative that the United States recognize Panama's sovereignty in the Canal Zone. The United States relented and intimated that it was willing to recognize Panama's "titular sovereignty" in the Canal Zone. Although this concession did not fulfill the desires of the Panamanians, it was a step in the right direction. By December of 1959, Panama was calmer as Ambassador Ricardo Arias and Assistant Secretary of State for Inter-American Affairs Roy R. Rubottom, Jr., began discussion over the status of the flag of Panama in the Canal Zone.

10. "U.S. & Panama Exchange Notes on Anti-American Demonstrations," *Department of State Bulletin* (November 23, 1959), p. 795.

Panama's request to fly its flag in the Canal Zone came under heavy fire in the United States and little was done about it immediately. The House of Representatives, in February of 1960, rejected by a 380–12 vote a bill which would permit Panama to fly her flag in the Canal Zone. The majority of Congressmen felt that by permitting Panama's flag to fly in the Canal Zone the United States would be abdicating some of her rights in the area, and that this should not be done unless a new treaty was enacted for that specific purpose. The negative action on the part of the United States Congress resulted in minor reverberations on March 1, 1960, Panama's Constitution Day, when a small and non-destructive demonstration was staged.

Psychologically, relations between the United States and Panama were steadily deteriorating. In order to halt the apparent breakdown in communications between the United States and Panama, President Eisenhower, on April 19, 1960, announced a nine-point program for the improvement of relations with Panama. In an effort to recoup lost prestige in Panama, President Eisenhower indicated that Panamanians would now have greater access to supervisory jobs in the Canal Zone, in addition to more unskilled and semi-skilled positions. Salaries of Panamanian employees of the United States were now to be raised to levels commensurate with those received by United States civilians holding similar positions. The construction of new homes for Panamanians residing in the Zone was promised along with other benefits which would raise their standard of living. President Eisenhower also promised to eliminate housing discrimination in the Canal Zone. However, to the dismay of the Panamanians the comprehensive program designed to improve relations neglected the flag question entirely.

President Eisenhower, in a concerted effort to improve

relations, removed Ambassador Harrington who had not endeared himself to the people of Panama with his outward attitude of indifference. To replace Ambassador Harrington, Washington nominated Joseph S. Farland of Morgantown, West Virginia, a man who was able to create good will on the Isthmus. Ambassador Farland, in order to reduce tension, inaugurated *Operación Amistad* (Operation Friendship), a scheme designed to encourage friendly contacts between United States military personnel, Zonians and their Panamanian neighbors. The task of implementing Operation Friendship fell to Major General Theodore F. Bogart, commander of the United States Army Caribbean Command. There can be no doubt that the efforts of both Ambassador Farland and General Bogart were successful in eliciting more sympathy from the Panamanians. Ambassador Farland, in particular, far exceeded the normal bounds of diplomacy in the process of promoting understanding and won a place for himself in the hearts of the people of Panama.

Although some feared that United States action in Panama during mid-1960 would lead to further concessions and was possible submission to diplomatic blackmail, the future for relations between the nations looked brighter. Foreign Minister Miguel J. Moreno, Jr., while attending the Organization of American States Foreign Ministers Conference in Costa Rica, spoke extensively with Secretary of State Christian Herter. While the American and Panamanian top diplomats discussed their nations' mutual problems, the Eisenhower administration was apparently confused and under the illusion that the 1903 Treaty had been revised twice and indicated sufficient revisions had been made in the recent pact with Panama. At this juncture a breakdown in communications between the Department of State and the Chief Executive was accidently repaired, when during the course of a press conference President Eisenhower was queried about the flag issue; he indicated that in his estimation Panama was the rightful owner of the Canal Zone. Now that the Department of State fully understood the previously nebulous point of view of the President, the road was clear to steer another course in United States diplomacy. On September 17, 1960, President Eisenhower ordered the United States and Panamanian flags to be flown together in Shaler Triangle in the Canal Zone. Ambassador Farland released the news to the people of Panama who rejoiced, and within four days the two banners flew side by side.

If nothing more, the raising of the flag of Panama next to that of the United States marked the official recognition of Panama's "titular sovereignty" in the Canal Zone. However, the initial raising of the two banners was not carried out without incident, as an American non-commissioned officer was wounded during the ceremony by a knife-wielding Panamanian nationalist. Whether or not the decision to fly the Panamanian flag in the Canal Zone was a wise one or not has been the source of considerable controversy. The concession created good will in Panama and raised American prestige. Time eventually would prove that President Eisenhower's conciliatory action with regard to the flag stimulated the Panamanians to demand further concessions. Within less than four years Panama's desire for sovereignty in the Canal Zone would give rise to an irreconcilable conflict with the United States and ultimately result in an outbreak of hostilities leading to the severance of diplomatic ties. Piecemeal concessions are obviously not the answer, as Panama will settle for nothing short of complete sovereignty.

CHAPTER FOUR

Communism

An account of the Cold War, as it relates to Panama, would be incomplete without a study of the International Communist movement on the Isthmus. Although Panama has not been a primary target of communism in Latin America, as have been Guatemala, Cuba, Venezuela and Peru, the threat of subversion close to a waterway as vital as the Panama Canal has caused considerable consternation for the governments of both Panama and the United States. Certainly Panama as a crossroads of the world is of strategic value to the communists.

The inherent dangers of sabotage to the locks of the Panama Canal were realized even before it was built, and this vulnerability has always necessitated special security measures. The existence of the Canal and the controversy over sovereignty have provided fertile ground for communist propaganda. With anti-Americanism running rampant on the Isthmus, the communist primary objective of embarrassing the United States has been enormously abetted. Moscow, Peking, and Havana have endeavored to capitalize upon and promote the ideas of Yankee imperialism in Latin America, and American occupation of the Canal Zone has presented a ripe target. Continuously the communists ask, "What benefits have over a half century of association with the United States brought to Panama?" The Marxist-Leninists stress that the United States must release the bonds that restrain Panama.

In attempts to propagate their beliefs the communists constantly allude to the benefits of a 1917 type Russian Revolution, as opposed to the United States model of government which has been so harshly imposed upon the Republic of Panama. This approach is meaningful to the Panamanian middle and lower classes which find it difficult to advance easily. It is only logical that Panama, a nation controlled by an oligarchy, is going to provide fertile ground for the development of overtly compassionate ideologies. The communists in Panama insist that there is no future except with the destruction of the existing social order. Primary among their goals are the breakup of the large *fincas* or *haciendas* and the distribution of land to the Panamanian peasants, as well as equal distribution of the nation's wealth.

In Panama's trade union movement where some modicum of organization exists there has been considerably more violence and susceptibility to foreign propagandizing. Ever since the end of World War II Panama's National Department of Investigation, an organization roughly comparable to the United States' Federal Bureau of Investigation, has frequently located subversive elements in one trade union or another.

Despite the fact that the Communist Party is an illegal political entity and precluded from the ballot in Panama, it has managed to maintain itself, and even grow, over the past decade. Even though Panama has never diplomatically recognized the Soviet Union and has never considered it in the national interest to do so, communist sympathizers have continued to appear in the nation.[1] The Communist Party has

1. Even the Soviet Satellite States have had little strength on the Isthmus. For example, the Polish Minister to Mexico is also accredited to Panama, but Poland has no diplomatic post on the Isthmus.

always been small and never a major force in Panamanian politics, but it has been organized into efficient cells. In proportion to the number of communists in other Latin American nations, Panama's contingent has been diminutive. However, one must bear in mind that the communists in Panama have no immediate programs for ascending to power but, rather, have a long range projection for gaining control of the Isthmus.

In lieu of the existing Sino-Soviet split it is interesting to note that, with reference to Panama, both the Soviet Union and Communist China are in accord. Although Panamanian listeners to Radio Moscow and Radio Peking are immediately cognizant of the divergence of opinions, they also realize that although disparate means for achieving power in Latin America are advocated, the ultimate goals of these nations for Panama are identical. Certainly the existence of a strong pro-Moscow or pro-Peking party in Panama would be of inestimable help to their respective programs. Currently there is no evidence of one faction being stronger than another in Panama, although it is obvious that those who favor the Chinese Communist line are more militant.

Historically, communists have not been adverse to contracting alliances with any group that might advance their cause, and nowhere has this been more true than in Panama. Although there are no precise connections between the ruling families in Panama and the Communist Party, on occasion the oligarchy has used communist support, and in all probability will do so again to accomplish selfish rather than ideological objectives. Panamanian nationalists and the communists share a mutual foe, the United States. Both groups are confronted by the difficult problem of de facto United States sovereignty over the Canal and the Canal Zone. In this respect the Panamanians are not the only Latin Americans who share the communist sentiments; even such staunch anti-communist governments as those in Mexico and Venezuela have similar beliefs with regard to the Canal and environs.

THE EARLY DAYS

Organized communism entered Panama via the United States during the early 1920's. During this era the Communist Party of the United States was entrusted with the task of directing the activities of communism on the Isthmus. It was not until 1925 and the founding of the *Partido Laborista* (Labor Party) that the communists were able to gain a foothold in Panama. The *Partido Laborista* affiliated fraternally with the Communist International but was not wholly communist.[2] Politically the *Partido Laborista* had little influence as support for communism grew slowly during the 1920's, and the Labor Party was exceedingly weak. In 1925 the Communist Movement in Panama organized with the Tenant's League and the General Syndicate of Panamanian Workers founded by Cristobal Segundo and Eliseo Echévez. For the first four or five years these organizations strove to gain membership, but the going was not easy as Panamanians did not eagerly join organizations whose credos were often incomprehensible and ludicrously idealistic.

It was not until the Congress of the *Confederación Sindical Latino Americano* was convened in Montevideo in May, 1929, that any attention was focused upon the communists in Panama. At this conference labor representatives from Panama and fifteen other Latin American nations joined together in the *Federación Sindical de Obreros y Campesinos* (CSLA), a communist run central labor organization. The membership was composed primarily of journalists, painters, cobblers,

2. See Robert Alexander, *Communism in Latin America* (New Brunswick: Rutgers University press, 1957), p. 392.

dockworkers and a few farm hands and carpenters. The new organization's affiliate on the Isthmus was known as the *Confederación Sindical de Obreros y Campesinos de Panamá.* Fourteen small unions banded together to comprise this first affiliate of the Latin American regional arm of the Profintern.

By 1930 communist control over the *Confederación Sindical de Obreros y Campesinos de Panamá* waned, and an official Communist Party was created under the direction of the Moscow trained revolutionary Eliseo Echévez. By June of that year the workers and peasants bloc aligned itself with the communists for political purposes. For the next three long and frequently bankrupt years, the Communist Party of Panama struggled to maintain its existence and in 1933 linked itself with the Comintern. But a serious blow was dealt Panamanian communism when a conflict developed between the nation's Socialist Party, led by Demetrio Porras, and the Communist Party. The rivalry severely cut into communist membership and retarded its progress.

When communist membership was declining in the late 1930's the Party allied itself with a political faction led by Arnulfo Arias. Although the party of Arias was essentially pro-facist, it was also nationalistic, and the alliance was in keeping with the times, the era of the Nazi-Soviet Pact. New life was breathed into the communist movement in Panama, at least until Hitler attacked the Soviet Union and Panama was forced to ally with the United States.

During World War II the Communist Party officially became the *Partido del Pueblo,* or People's Party. With the advent of the United States—Russian alliance for the prosecution of the war against the Axis, the People's Party grew. After the noted Mexican Marxist Vicente Lombardo Toledano, chief of the *Confederación Trabajadores de America Latina,* visited the Isthmus in 1943 and publicly advocated

Panama's control of the Canal, communist membership rose sharply.

In October of 1944, the National Labor Congress in Panama City founded the *Federación Sindical de Trabajadores de Panamá,* led by the Communist Efraim Morel.[3] This new organization (FSTRP), though small, proved to be vocal and aggressive, as its able Secretary Señor Morel was a dynamic organizer and administrator. Comrade Morel instituted a campaign against the United States among members of Panama's most nationalistic group, the middle class.

With the termination of global hostilities in 1945, defense of the Canal was no longer assigned strategic priority, but with the inauguration of the Cold War, subversion was now the serious concern of those entrusted with the security of Panama. Communists in Panama immediately altered their tactics, as the United States became aware of the impending dangers. To counteract the influence of Lombardo Toledano in Panama in 1946, a rival labor union, the United Public Workers of America (UPWA), an affiliate of the CIO, was established.[4] It was hoped that the existence of this new organization would detract from the membership in communist dominated unions. Unfortunately the United States assessment of the role of the new organization was totally inaccurate as its membership of some ten thousand workers was controlled by known communists.

In the years following World War II both communists and Panamanian nationalists voiced strong objections to United States foreign policy. The first violent anti-United States reaction came in 1947 when the Americans proposed to negotiate a treaty with Panama for the retention of Air Force bases

3. *Ibid.* p. 393.

4. See George W. Westerman, *Blocking Them At The Canal* (Panama City: May, 1952), p. 47.

constructed outside of the Canal Zone during World War II. The Panamanian communists were expertly conforming to the Moscow line and their anti-Yankee stand was marked by demonstrations on numerous occasions. For all of its vociferousness the Communist Party remained only a viable propaganda outlet. Politically the Party could not get off the ground as evidenced by the election of 1947 when the Communist presidential candidate, Cristobal Segundo, received less than a thousand votes.

In the United States the House Un-American Activities Committee was beginning to grow suspicious of communism in Latin America by 1948. The Committee's Chairman indicated that communists were infiltrating the Canal Zone under the very noses of the Americans and envisioned a Panama overrun by Stalinist agents. This assessment was typical of the unfounded beliefs that were so prevalent during the McCarthy era. In actuality the communists were finding it difficult to operate successfully under the watchful eye of the demagogic Arnulfo Arias. The communist labor movement in Panama suffered severe setbacks at the hands of ORIT *(Organización Regional Interamericana de Trabajadores),* the AFL-CIO sponsored organization in Latin America.

A crack-down on Communists began on March 19, 1949, and Panama's Foreign Office expelled Max Brodsky, regional director of the United Public Workers Union, because of his Moscow ties.[5] Although Brodsky had not been permitted in the Canal Zone, he had operated effectively from Panama and was quite influential in labor circles. President Harry S. Truman, on July 22, 1949, signed a bill to compel employees

5. Lawrence O. Ealy, The Republic of Panama in World Affairs 1903–1950 (Philadelphia: University of Pennsylvania Press, 1951), p. 168.

in the Canal Zone to take loyalty oaths.[6] Of course the existence of such oaths is absurd, as the communist cell leader is often the first one to affix his signature. But at least the action was indicative of United States concern over the growth of communism in Panama and gave the communists something to ponder.

PASSING MID-CENTURY

Relations between the United States and Panama improved by 1950 as President Arias went along with the anti-communist movement sponsored by the United States. The government of Panama placed under close surveillance CTAL, the Lombardo Toledano led organization. The close scrutiny of President Arias contributed significantly to CTAL's failure to gain membership as rapidly as was desired by the communists. As communism lost support, Russian allegations against the United States increased. Constantly the USSR charged the United States with discrimination in the Canal Zone, and pro-Moscow Yankeephobes were continuously harassing American servicemen on the Isthmus.

It was the expulsion of the communist dominated United Public Workers, a Zone Union, from the CIO, on February 16, 1950, that initiated a temporary decline of communism in the nation. Communist support dwindled decisively as only a few bus drivers, tailors and metallurigical workers remained loyal to the unions with Moscow affiliations. Panamanians were now more conscious of the inherent dangers in communism and, led by the newspaper *The Panama Star,* fought to eliminate this threat.

A Presidential Decree issued on April 29, 1950, outlawed communism in Panama. This action, with which the Cabinet

6. *Ibid*. p. 170.

concurred, was aimed directly at the People's Party, but was never really implemented. The communists claimed that the outlawing procedure was not predicated upon ideological grounds but was really a political move on the part of Arnulfo Arias, who desired to unleash an attack upon all opposition to his dictatorial rule. President Arias contended that, on the contrary, this was not a political move, but a necessary action to thwart subversion on the Isthmus. In this respect President Arias aligned himself with the point of view of the United States and thus came under nationalist criticism for being pro-Yankee.

Subsequently the Communist Party was declared unconstitutional and its overt activities abated. In actuality the outlawing of the Communist Party drove it underground where it would be more difficult to watch. Nevertheless, 1950 was a year of genuine concern for the communists in Panama. In May, Party headquarters were raided and all records confiscated.[7] Even persons in high positions were not immune from Panama's intensive search for fellow travelers. In October Cristobal Segundo, an alternate Judge of Panama's Supreme Court, was publicly assailed as a leader of the Communist Party.

Panama's Congress undertook an investigation of subversion in the nation. In January of 1951, after a thorough investigation, the majority leader of the Justice Committee of the National Assembly expressed the opinion that there could be no doubt that communists had infiltrated the government of Panama. Ultimately this disclosure led to the passage of legislation against crimes of sabotage and sedition. President Arias felt that the communists were endeavoring to disrupt the not-too-harmonious relations with the United States and

7. *New York Times,* May 5, 1950.

by May of 1951 construed the problem to be of serious proportions. In an effort to combat the communist threat, the government of Panama decreed that private ships of Panamanian registry could no longer deliver cargoes to communist nations or communist dominated states. As a result many ship owners changed their registries and Panama lost considerable revenue.

Another incident came to the fore and shed light upon the communists in Panama. Jules Dubois, the Latin American correspondent of the *Chicago Tribune,* a man with an uncanny knack for self-involvement, was attacked by the *Partido del Pueblo* as a spy when he was involved in the showing of pictures depicting People's Party members with their hammer and sickle banners. Considerable publicity ensued and the People's Party headed by Hugo Victor, a young teacher, received an abnormal amount of adverse criticism in the press. However, while Hugo Victor was bearing the brunt of this journalistic attack as a front man for the communists, the most successful communist operator in Panama, Secretary General Rubén Darío Souza, continued to agitate covertly.[8]

With the election of former security chief José Remón to the Presidency in 1952, a concerted effort was made to curtail all communist activity in Panama. The communists, however, had different ideas. The Moscow Congress of October 1952 launched "Operation Latin America," a plan to accelerate ideological revolution in the hemisphere. Although "Operation Latin America" began with Guatemala, it obviously included such nations as Cuba and Panama. The task confronting President Remón was formidable, and his police began to tighten security. Propaganda films, smuggled in from behind the Iron Curtain, were confiscated by the hundreds.

8. Herbert Matthews, "Communist Party in Panama Is Deemed Potential Threat," *New York Times,* March 3, 1952.

At the same time a Peking oriented movement was growing on the campus of the National University.

The seriousness of the communist threat necessitated a Conference of the Foreign Ministers of the American States. At this conference held in June 1953 Panama expressed fear of communism's spread from Guatemala throughout the Caribbean. By September of the same year Panama's Chief of Security Police, Jorge Luis Alfaro, voiced apprehension regarding subversive activities on the Isthmus. The government arrested two communists, Isaac Argentino Vainikoff and Rubén Darío Souza, for trying to arouse anti-United States sentiment. The communist scare spread rapidly in Panama, and by December a bill was introduced in the National Assembly to outlaw totalitarian, communist, Falangist, and fascist organizations. This bill, which prohibited communists from holding public office or doing business with the government, was initiated primarily because of the fear of communist influence spreading in Panama's schools. However, the legislation was ineffective as it failed to provide penalties for its violation. Less than three hundred communists were known to be in Panama by November, 1953, and a good portion of them directed their venom against President José Antonio Remón. When President Remón was subsequently assassinated, the communists were accused of masterminding the murder, but the charges were dropped for lack of evidence.

The communists began to envision Panama as a base for subversive aggression against Latin America. The threat to Central America was real by 1954 when Guatemala's government was openly sympathetic to the communists. With Guatemala as a beachhead it was entirely feasible that Panama, because of its strategic location, would become the next dissemination center for communist propaganda in Latin America and Communist literature from Guatemala inundated Panama. When the French liner *Wyoming* was detained at Cristobal, under suspicion of transporting arms from European Bloc nations to Guatemala, Panama again became cognizant of the communist threat.[9]

On May 25, 1954, Guatemala received from Poland 1,900 tons of arms valued at an estimated ten million dollars.[10] The existence of these military armaments just eight hundred miles away from the Canal Zone caused fear of Guatemalan and communist domination in Central America. Apprehension spread the summer of 1954 when the communists fomented a bus drivers strike. The government thought that this might be the first actual step toward a communist take-over. However, the bus drivers strike was of short duration and not connected with the Guatemalan revolution, which did not spread to Panama.

From 1955 until 1959 communism in Panama received few headlines. Panama relaxed her vigil briefly, just as the communist revolution in Latin America became a reality with the take-over in Cuba by Fidel Castro. Communism *Fidelista* style became the basic problem confronting the free nations of Latin America, and Panama was in the midst of the turmoil.

In May of 1959, Cuban invaders landed in Panama and a series of incidents, which will be elaborated upon in a subsequent chapter, occurred. Communism in Panama was no longer dormant, and the nation braced itself for a new barrage of agitation. Allen Dulles, Director of the United States Central Intelligence Agency, warned that at the Twenty-First Party Congress in Moscow in 1959 the Latin American Com-

9. Martin B. Travis and James T. Watkins, "Control Of The Panama Canal: An Absolute Shibboleth?," *Foreign Affairs* (April, 1959), p. 414.

10. *New York Times,* May 26, 1954.

munists were instructed to pursue nationalistic propaganda lines. When the next United Nations Economic Commission for Latin America meeting was held in Panama City, Soviet, Polish, Hungarian and Czech observers were present. Obeying their orders to exacerbate nationalism, the Soviet delegates offered Panama aid in the form of development loans. Although these loans were rejected, the fact that they were offered was indicative of future communist attempts to garner friends in Latin America. Panama became the hub of contraband trade in arms headed for communists in Colombia and Venezuela. This illegal traffic was abetted by the sympathy of Panamanian nationalists who could see no farther than their quarrels with the United States and would do anything to cooperate with others who harbored similar antipathies for Americans.

The communists made a concerted but futile effort in the 1960–1962 period to gain control of nationalist groups which were engaged in trying to elicit government aid to Panamanian citizens of low income groups. Early in the 1960's the communists attempted to capture the Chiriquí Land Company through its pro-communist legal advisor Carlos I. Zuniga. Señor Zuniga had long desired to infiltrate the hierarchy of this plantation giant, hoping that the disgruntled proletariat would band together with dissenting managerial elements to foment an insurrection. Precisely what type of rebellion was planned is difficult to ascertain as the movement was never launched.

With the election of Roberto Chiari as President in 1960, the incursions of the communists in the banana plantation area were halted. President Chiari listened attentively to Secretary of State Christian Herter's plans for keeping the communists from gathering support in Panama. Secretary Herter and the United States were not the only ones who were uneasy about a rise in communist activity in Panama. Generalissimo Rafael Trujillo, dictator of the Dominican Republic, expressed concern over communist objectives in Latin America. The communist threat was emphasized by Trujillo in order to justify the existence of a military regime, which he claimed was an anti-communist bastion in the hemisphere. Señor Trujillo, in world councils, continuously accentuated the fact that the Panama Canal was a major communist objective and was being contested for by propaganda, not direct revolt.

Communist propaganda leaflets flooded Panama, and in June of 1960 the police confiscated eight air freighted packages of communist inspired printed matter.[11] In November of the same year, Andrés Galván, President of the Mixed Trade Workers Union, spent twenty-eight days in Cuba and returned full of praise for the Cuban revolution. Señor Galván also traveled behind the Iron Curtain in Europe and became enamored of the communist way of life. His colleague Eugenio Barrera spent seven months in the People's Republic of China and returned to Panama swayed completely by communist thought. The exposure of these Panamanian labor leaders to communist ideologies and the training they received in Marxist—Leninist lands was to prove significant.

Late in 1960 and early in 1961 the banana plantations on the Chiriquí Land Company property were subjected to communist led labor strikes. The communists hoped that these uprisings would lead to the secession from Panama of the Provinces of Chiriquí, Veraguas and Bocas del Toro. The plan was for the newly separated provinces to federate and create a Soviet Bloc nation called the *República de Occidente.* At this point news about communism in Panama dwindled and the lack of reports gave rise to the speculation that the government surpressed such data. Details about communism

11. *New York Times,* June 25, 1960.

and Cuba were being avoided because the government was genuinely concerned.

An effort to combat subversion and communist inspired guerrilla warfare in Latin America was initiated in April of 1961 by the United States with the establishment of a school for counter-insurgency in the Canal Zone. The creation of this instructional facility was an aftermath of the abortive Bay of Pigs invasion. This illustrated to the United States that it was not adequately prepared to train individuals to engage in anti-guerrilla tactics.

Panama's reaction to this attempt by the United States to thwart communism was unprecedented. Panamanian students, with the urging of President Chiari, demonstrated against the communists. They demanded that Panama immediately break diplomatic relations with Cuba and asked for stricter enforcement of Law 43, which prohibited communism. An anti-communist campaign was begun by wholesale confiscation of subversive propaganda materials. The communists tried to combat these attacks by launching a counter propaganda offensive which spread the false rumor that Panama was about to enter into diplomatic relations with the Soviet Union.

By October of 1961, the communist threat in Panama was sufficiently serious for Minister of the Interior Marco A. Robles to bring the problem to the attention of the National Assembly. In formal testimony before the legislature, Minister Robles stated that there were too many communists and fellow travelers in government circles. He particularly noted that the nation's public education system harbored numerous workers with Marxist—Leninist leanings. Minister Robles spoke in generalizations, as the exact number of communists involved in government work was impossible to determine. Accuracy was not possible, and the best estimates establish the strength of the Communist Party in Panama at this time at about five hundred to a thousand members.

The communists responded to President Chiari's crackdown by endeavoring to steer clear of urban areas, concentrating their efforts upon the agricultural sectors of the nation. On November 13, 1962, the banana workers on the Chiriquí lands demonstrated. This disorder was Communist led and inspired and indicated that, temporarily, they were seeking an alternative plan of action.

United States concern over Soviet military power in Cuba compelled the strengthening of forces already in the Canal Zone. In February of 1963, the United States Army stationed a permanent company of anti-guerrilla paratroopers, trained as commandos in the Canal Zone. This elite cadre occupied quarters at Fort Gulick and was on immediate call for duty anywhere in the hemisphere. This force supplemented the permanent troops in the Canal Zone and Fort Gulick. By February of 1963 the Inter-American Police Academy had graduated 12,400 Latin American officers and men.[12] In November Panama's *Guardia Nacional* arrested Juan Bautista Chavarría, a Costa Rican communist, for smuggling propaganda, explosives and weapons into Panama. A formidable front was now being constructed against communism on the Isthmus.

SPECIAL SCHOOLS AND SPECIAL FORCES

At both Forts Gulick and Sherman, in the Canal Zone, considerable attention is still given to anti-guerrilla, anti-terrorist and counter-insurgency tactics. Extensive courses are offered in the area of community development projects or "civic action," as it is felt that military might alone is insufficient to

12. By 1964, this number had increased to 13,700.

deter communist efforts to promote social unrest in Latin America. In addition to the troops required for the day by day protection of the Panama Canal, special forces are maintained by the United States to serve in an advisory capacity. The Canal Zone also houses a school for jungle warfare, the Inter-American Police Academy and a Tactical Officers School.

The School of the Americas was founded in 1949 for the purpose of training United States personnel, but by the 1960's the majority of its graduates were Latin American military men. Based at Fort Gulick, the School of the Americas teaches how to employ effectively counter-insurgency tactics and techniques in Latin America and how to combat guerrilla wars such as that which Castro launched in Cuba. Included in the curriculum are courses in military police work, deployment of infantry in jungle operations, paramilitary work, and political, sociological and psychological defense. The intelligence aspect of the School's work is of particular importance since it affords the United States an opportunity to observe Latin American military men in action and to assess their potential in terms of future hemispheric crises.

Courses at the School of the Americas range from two to forty-week sessions of intensive training. Instruction is offered at the command, cadet and staff levels, designed to build internal stability and counteract Communist sponsored or supported insurrections. The American instructors speak Spanish in over thirty courses and generally are chosen from the best of the military.[13]

Since its establishment, the School of the Americas has

13. The training in Spanish and Portuguese that they receive at the Language School in Monterey, California, is excellent, and the fluency of these instructors is surprising.

been subject to perpetual denunciation from leftists and Communists who see it as an imperialistic Yankee beachhead in Latin America. Despite this, the School has played an important role in giving to the military people of Latin America and the United States a more thorough understanding of each other.

Panama's *Guardia Nacional* is the nation's second line of defense after the United States, and it derives considerable benefit from the existence of the School on the Isthmus. A number of guardsmen are trained in the Canal Zone and the rest in Panama. The influence of the *Guardia* cannot be minimized in assessing Panama's foreign policy and internal politics. It was in the *Guardia* that José Ramón made his niche and from there ascended to the presidency in 1952.

The *Guardia Nacional,* a national police force, consists of three platoons of trained paramilitary troops, no tanks or anti-aircraft and one airplane. In the event of invasion the effectiveness of the *Guardia* would be negligible as far as repelling invaders is concerned. However, Panama has preferred to utilize her finances for things other than defense and permits the United States to assume the burden of protecting her frontiers and boundaries.

It is in the maintenance of internal stability that the *Guardia* excels, and this is accomplished with nothing more than rifles and tear gas. With the increase of Communist activity during the post World War II era, the *Guardia's* job has become more difficult. Demonstrations have to be handled continuously, and sporadic crime waves have kept the *Guardia* on twenty-four hour duty. Not the least of the chores of the *Guardia* is the protection of tourists who contribute greatly to Panama's economy and are frequently the targets of xenophobicly motivated attacks. In the summer of 1966, *Guardia* patrols were very much in evidence on the streets of Panama

City in an effort to present a physical and visual deterrent to violence. Unfortunately this 3,500 man force is too small to safeguard the entire nation effectively, and it has been forced to concentrate its efforts on the major urban areas where most of the populace is located.

THE CONTEMPORARY SCENE

Obviously the situation in Panama is subject to the variegations of Moscow's, Peking's and Havana's foreign policy, and what tack it will take is uncertain. However, of one thing one can be sure; communism will not lessen or be eliminated overnight.

Toward the middle of the 1960's the official Soviet Government News Agency's organ *Tass* referred to the build up of United States forces in Panama as a return to the Theodore Roosevelt policy of the "Big Stick." If the Communist propagandizers were consistent, they would realize that by using the term "return" they are implying that imperialism has at least temporarily abated, an admission, they would never consciously make. Be that as it may, the communists still demand that the Panama Canal be nationalized. They backed the Committee for Redemption and Defense of National Sovereignty in order to ally with the strongest anti-United States movement in the nation.

Just how successful the communist alliance with nationalistic groups has been will be illustrated. The half century of discord between the United States and Panama culminated in the January, 1964, riots. The Communists seized every opportunity to inflame the situation, and communist communications media did nothing to prevent the violence. Three known Communist orators were instrumental in organizing the march on the United States school in the Canal Zone which precipitated the hostilities. Floyd Britton, a fellow traveler whom the police had implicated in numerous anti-United States demonstrations, was among those at the forefront during the uprising. In addition to Britton, at least seventy known communists and *Fidelistas* were identified by local police during the course of the fighting. Communists distributed arms and primitive weapons to the demonstrators and instructed them to kill Americans. Communist complicity in the January, 1964, flag riots in Panama was eventually corroborated after investigation by United States Secretary of the Army Cyrus Vance.[14]

Guerrilla wars of national liberation are the goal of the hemisphere's communists as emphasized at the 1964 winter meeting in Havana. At this conference it was agreed to abandon the *vía pacifica* policy of non-violent penetration in Latin America. The communists planned to engage in Castro-like guerrilla operations from the eastern provinces of Panama and to direct an offensive against neighboring Colombia. Documents seized in Davíd alleged that the Communists in Chiriquí had completed plans and even assigned a "D-Day." They were about to step up activity designed to win support among farmers in the area. Arms and propaganda smuggled in from Costa Rica were seized affirming the belief that the communists had stepped up their activities after the break in diplomatic relations in 1964, between the United States and Panama. But the Communist inspired outbreaks in these regions were well handled by the *Guardia Nacional* and little if any subversion was achieved.

The people of Panama hear little about communism as it exists in their nation. For the most part, the news of seizures of caches of communist propaganda and arms as well as incarcerations of communists is kept quiet. In fact, rumors of

14. Moscow loudly proclaimed "International law is on the side of Panama." International Affairs (Moscow), March, 1964.

burgeoning Panamanian sympathy for Fidel Castro and the growth of *Fidelista* bands are generally more prevalent in the United States than in Panama. The government has halted the influx of Cuban, Chinese, and Russian propaganda, and the communist line is rarely heard on Panama's radio or television. What little seeps in is completely overshadowed by materials distributed by the United States Information Service, which apparently is on the inside track to the nation's communication media.

Panama presently enjoys freedom of the press, and numerous journals exist free of government control. One is subject to criticism if he claims that news pertaining to Communism is surpressed. What would be more accurate is to state that the newspapers themselves diminish the truth by keeping the Communist threat out of the headlines. One odd reason for the lack of news coverage of Marxist—Leninist activities is the fact that Communism is most appealing to "illiterates."

The nation's leading evening journal *El Panamá America,* and its English language version *The Panama American,* are published by the Arias family, a pro-United States and violently anti-communist faction. The leading morning journal, *La Estrella de Panamá,* and its English version *The Star and Herald,* have also traditionally opposed all forms of communism.

Despite the fact that journalists tend to play down communism in Panama, there is evidence attesting to its existence. Communist activity is most noticeable in Panama City and Santiago, the capital of Veraguas Province, where Molotov cocktails are occasionally tossed by the communists. They also erect their own propaganda signs and tear down ones designating United States projects and particularly delight in defacing signs demarcating Alliance for Progress projects.

The advocates of the Peking line have vociferously

denounced the United States. On January 12, 1965, in Peking, the All-China Students Federation expressed its support for Panama's struggle to gain sovereignty over the Canal Zone. The group announced: "The joint struggles of the peoples of Panama had inspired the people of other countries in Latin America in their struggle for national liberation to call for victory against United States imperialism."[15]

The crisis in the Dominican Republic in April of 1965 brought renewed communist activity to Panama. In an attempt to avail themselves of the situation, Party members in Panama began to analogize the United States intervention in the Dominican Republic to that existing in the Canal Zone. The communists stressed that the sovereignty of Panama was jeopardized by land hungry Americans waiting for an opportunity to conquer the Isthmus by force of arms. Only the vigilance of the *Guardia Nacional* prevented the Dominican crisis from stimulating an adverse reaction in Panama. When on May 18, 1965, the leftists called for three thousand demonstrators to march upon the United States Embassy to protest United States intervention in the Dominican Republic, only thirty-one marchers turned out with anti-United States placards.[16]

In commenting upon the state of communism in the area, the Most Reverend Marcos G. McGrath, Bishop of Santiago de Veraguas in Panama's interior, commented: "Marxism is very divided and has lost a lot of impetus in Latin America. But the danger is still great as long as the economic imbalance continues to exist."[17]

It remains difficult to properly assess communist member-

15. "China & Panama," *Survey of China Mainland Press* (January 18, 1965), p. 37.
16. James Whelan, "Calming the Storms Spawned by Violence in Panama Canal Zone," *The Latin American Times,* July 6, 1965.
17. *Star & Herald* (Panama), July 1, 1965.

ship, as the Party is outlawed in Panama and anyone who admits affiliation cannot procure decent employment. However, leading officials in the Republic of Panama believe that communists or sympathizers occupy minor posts in the bureaucracy. In fact, many ranking government officials are reluctant to root out the communists, whom they believe assist the causes of nationalism.

In many instances it is extremely difficult to distinguish communists from the nationalists. For example, one ardent nationalist, trained in the United States and holding an important government post, was questioned by the writer about the possible demonstrations on July 4th. He replied, "I hope that all hell breaks loose, and the Communists are successful in advancing our endeavors to obtain our just sovereignty."

THE NATIONAL UNIVERSITY

Currently the communists have not infiltrated any well organized large middle class group. The only viable outlet for their actions is the National University. The University functions with nominal autonomy in contrast to other Latin American universities which possess a great deal more latitude and freedom from governmental control. Although Panama's Minister of Education is on the University's Executive Council nothing is done about the communists who seek sanctuary within the confines of the campus. The Ministry of Education justifies this lack of control on the premise that to stifle the communists on the University campus would be to curtail freedom of expression.

In analyzing the situation on the campus of the National University, more is there than meets the eye. In Panama, with its undiversified economy, few employment opportunities exist for those individuals who have obtained a higher education. This lack sometimes results in riots, and students vent their frustration by violently opposing the United States and its policy in regard to the Canal and Canal Zone. Thus, at times it is extremely difficult for the casual observer to differentiate between these supernationalists who distribute anti-United States literature on the University's campus and professional agitators who do likewise.

In conversing with self-professed radical youths, who abound on the campus, one is immediately struck by their lack of knowledge of Marxist—Leninist ideology. Their knowledge of Maoism and Castroism, insofar as militancy is concerned, far surpasses their comprehension of basic communist philosophy. Actually the professionals have not taught theory but have striven to turn them into activists.

Frequent rifts and fissures occur among the members of the leftist *Union de Estudiantes Universitarios* (Union of University Students). For example, the *Movimiento Revolucionario Universitario* (Revolutionary University Movement) advocates an unruly kind of anti-United States policy, which is never specifically spelled out. Members of this group disseminate communist literature, much of which is incomprehensible, and leave the false impression that they are in control of student activities at the University. Other groups stress diverse goals ranging from the promotion of *Fidelismo* to the support of Egyptian style Canal nationalization.

In the realm of lower education Panama far surpasses many of the nations of Latin America, but higher education and the National University need strengthening in many areas. The physical needs of the University are apparent; three or four classes are conducted simultaneously in a single classroom. The academic standards of the University are low, even by Latin American standards. Qualified professors are not readily available. Thus, a great part of the faculty is part-time. Many of these Professors hold degrees equivalent to a United States bachelors degree. The equivalent of the American Masters degree appears to be the highest held by a majority of University faculty members, and Ph.D.'s are rare.

The libraries of the National University are inadequately stocked, and a thorough examination of the types of reading material available revealed that neither pro-communist nor pro-United States literature is dominant. Materials ranging from Marxist thought to documents published by the United States House Un-American Activities Committee are available for student use and reflect no inherent bias or conscious attempt to influence the students toward one sphere of influence or the other.

Conversely, students are generally one-sided in political outlook. Sons and daughters of wealthy Panamanian conservatives attend schools in the United States as do honor students who receive government scholarships. Thus the campus of the National University is devoid of representative opinions and the students are inclined to be somewhat left of center. Students come from social classes that have not been afforded all of the advantages of life and are susceptible to envy and propaganda. The most bitter among these are selected to attend Friendship University in Moscow, where they do not devote their efforts to scholarship, or even learning the Russian language, but to receiving the communist philosophy in their native tongue.

The student body at Panama's National University seems younger now than at any time in the last decade and most of the youths do not support the prevailing governmental structure. However, few will go so far as to embrace communism. This was illustrated in 1953 when the Panamanian Federation of Students broke with the International Students Union, a direct result of the ISU's proposals that Panama establish commercial relations with the Soviet Union.

Over the years a concerted effort has been made to identify all communists associated with the faculty of the University as well as those in the student body. In August of 1952, out of one hundred faculty members only one communist professor could be located, and out of 1,749 students only eight professed to be communists. In 1962, when the student body had grown to 5,056 and the number of professors had increased to 193,[18] there was no commensurate increase in the number of card-carrying communists on the campus.

The reputation for propagating communism and harboring communists on the campus of the National University has been grossly exaggerated. It is true that a preponderance of all of the posters which are plastered on the walls of the University buildings contain anti-United States slogans and propaganda, but this does not indicate a communist orientation. The fact that nationalistic Panamanian students share similar aims with communists does not make them fellow travelers. The American who strolls through the campus immediately notices the absence of pro-United States literature, but his experiences are not unpleasant.

In actuality the Christian Democrats at the National University, who are exceedingly militant, create more disturbances than the communists.[19] Intellectual autonomy of the University is still sacrosanct and the government has adhered

18. Inter-American Development Bank, *Social Progress Trust Fund Fourth Annual Report* (Washington: Inter-American Development Bank, 1965), p. 414.

19. Panama's Christian Democrats are more militant than the Christian Democrats in Chile who have recently become prominent under President Eduardo Frei.

to the liberal traditions of this institution by not interfering with the small radical groups which exist within its confines.

A FINAL NOTE

Down through the years, Panamanian nationalists have not only allied themselves with the anti-United States position of the communists but nonetheless many such as Arnulfo Arias have staunchly resisted communism. Communist Bloc nations have been excluded from conducting business in the Canal Zone as well as in Panama.[20] Since World War II Panama has only elected two avowed leftists to its National Assembly and official communist representation in the nation's government has been negligible. The Socialist Party in Panama has traditionally been impervious to communist penetration and thus potential support for the international conspiratorial ideology has been reduced. Currently there is little possibility of a communist take-over in Panama; the center of subversive activity, Panama City, is closely watched over by President Robles and the security police. Communists have found it difficult to infiltrate urban labor which is protected by such patriotic watchdogs as George Westerman, publisher of Panama's *Tribune*. For the most part, Panamanian proletarians are reluctant to engage in subversive activities because of the peril of losing their positions. The only segment of organized labor into which the communists have made significant inroads is the *Federación Sindical de Trabajadores de la República de Panamá* (FSTRP), a communist dominated organization led by Congresswoman

20. The Canal Zone is prohibited, by law, from selling petroleum products to ships flying Russian, Communist Chinese, or their satellite's flags, except under special Commerce Department permits which are rarely issued.

Thelma King. The FSTRP now has a membership of less than two hundred and possesses little political influence.[21]

Communism in Panama had increasingly become the province of full time professionals, and part-time advocates have disappeared. The few true communists that exist are exceptionally able and their cells are well organized. The handful of well disciplined Party members had at its disposal one thousand marginal fellow travelers who could just as easily reject as embrace the Marxist—Leninist ideology. The communists take a charismatic approach to Panama and endeavor to capitalize upon the United States divergence between alleged liberalism and de facto segregation in the Canal Zone. There can be no doubt that when the United States implements the policies it has heretofore paid lip service to, communism in Panama will be dealt a serious blow.

"Dual Communism" is the method the communists employ as they work both sides against the middle in order to be certain of representation in all sectors of Panamanian life. Fear that Panama's government tolerates communism are unfounded, and recent newspaper accounts of increasing communist guerrilla offensives in the interior of the nation are fallacious. With the ideological split between Peking and the "revisionists" in Moscow, communism has been badly fragmented rather than strengthened. So chaotic is the state of communism in Panama that unity among its factions appears improbable. The fact that during the summer of 1965 the Italian Communist Party had to supply funds necessary to maintain propaganda campaigns in the nation is indicative of further fragmentation. Currently the communists are accom-

21. Aside from the FSTRP and its affiliates, only the Syndicate of Topographers and Graphic Arts Workers has been a stronghold of Communism, and this is attributable to Secretary General Pablo Ríos, who has allied with the *Unión General de Trabajadores de la República de Panamá.*

plishing nothing more than the creation of confusion and embarrassment to the governments of both the United States and Panama.

CHAPTER
FIVE

Fidel Castro And International Relations

Fidelismo has had a much greater appeal to the people of Panama than has international communism. Panamanians have seen many similarities between traditional *personalismo,* coupled with nationalism, and the successes of Fidel Castro's revolution with its anti-Yankee overtones. From the inception of the Cuban Revolution Panamanians depicted Castro not as a representative of Sino-Soviet Marxism, but as the successful eliminator of dictator Fulgencio Batista's United States oriented, oppressive socio-economic system.

Basic parallels can be drawn between Cuba and Panama. Both nations achieved independence as a result of United States action. Both have repeatedly been subjected to United States intervention in their governmental affairs. A valid analogy can be drawn between the Platt Amendment, under which Cuba was virtually subservient to the United States until 1934, and the Treaty of 1903 which has subordinated Panama. Panama and Cuba have been economically dependent upon the United States. Cuba's market for her primary crop, sugar, was guaranteed by the United States, while Panama relied upon the Panama Canal as a primary source of revenue. Geographically both nations have played a strategic military role and have been of considerable value to the United States in times of war. Above all, down through the years both nations have built up an intense nationalism which has diametrically opposed United States policy.

Throughout Castro's early days in the Sierra Maestra he had the support of Panama, as well as most of the nations of the hemisphere. Castro was looked upon as a genuine idealist, who embodied the needs and aspirations of all of the peoples of Latin America who clamored for social revolution. Every time Fidel succeeded in extracting a concession from the United States or dealt it another blow, Panama cheered jubilantly. Panama has construed each subsequent elimination of United States influence in Cuba as a step closer to the fulfillment of her own desires.

The United States has tended to disregard the uplifting effect of Castro's success upon the morale of the other nations in the hemisphere. Instead, the United States has been primarily concerned with Castro's pledges to help liberate other Latin American nations from the alleged imperialistic rule of the United States. Havana has repeatedly denounced United States territorial control in Latin America, with specific references to the Guantanamo base in Cuba, Puerto Rico, the Virgin Islands and Panama. Cuban propaganda directed against the United States for supposedly coveting territory occupied by *Latinos* has been instrumental in allying many of Panama's nationalists with the communists.

Since the advent of Fidel Castro, the communists have found sympathy in those who resent the United States in the Canal Zone. The *Fidelistas* have criticized the United States for practicing racist policies in the Zone, and many Panamanian Negroes see their own reflection in the Cuban egalitarian revolutionary espousals. Fertile ground sowed by communist infiltration has been tilled by the Cubans, who have gone all out to win converts in Panama. Panamanian leftists are being schooled in the rudiments of subversion and guerrilla tactics in Havana, while approximately two tons of Castro's propaganda is confiscated and burned each month on the Isthmus.

When Fidel Castro came to power in 1959, his followers took over a Communist Party in Panama that had been relatively weak. Soon propaganda began to flow into Panama through the publication *La Justicia,* a daily put out by the Chinese community in Panama City.[1] By 1959 *Prensa Latina,* the Cuban Press Agency, had its releases used widely on Panamanian television and radio, and an intensive campaign was inaugurated to enlist Panama in Cuba's cause and the cause of international communism. So aggressive were the Cuban diplomats in Panama City that they frequently offended the Panamanians, who were accustomed to a more genteel manner of persuasion. Nevertheless, the emissaries of Fidel Castro were successful in creating dissatisfaction in Panama.

On April 19, 1959, Ruben Miró, the Panamanian revolutionary leader, stated in Havana that an armed group of insurgents would invade Panama and overthrow the government of President Ernesto de la Guardia.[2] On April 25, a force of ninety-one Cubans led by Major César Vega, sailed to Panama.[3] This group landed at Nombre de Dios, a town of a thousand people, twenty miles northeast of Colón and fifty miles north of Panama City, where they were immo-

1. This was not indicative of a general sympathy for Castro among the sizeable Chinese population in Panama as their two other newspapers *Yin P* and *El Vocero* violently assailed Communism.

2. *New York Times,* April 20, 1959. This is the same Ruben Miró who had been jailed as a suspect in the assassination of President José Remón.

3. The precise number of those in the landing party has never been ascertained. Some observers state that only 86 landed in Panama.

bilized on May 1 and compelled to surrender. This abortive invasion caused apprehension in Panama but not mass hysteria. Panama protested this violation of her sovereignty to the Organization of American States and an investigation was initiated.

When interrogated, César Vega, the Havana nightclub owner and revolutionary, stated that he had hoped to ignite a spontaneous rebellion of the oppressed masses in Panama. He sincerely believed that there was sufficient resentment toward the de la Guardia government to cause a rebellion. However, popular support was not forthcoming, and this episode proved a dismal failure, and the invaders were quickly dispersed. Precisely what motivated the abortive landing and what transpired after it was intiated are subject to many interpretations. There has been little agreement about the exact objectives of the invaders. Reports were that upon landing the Cubans stated, "Fidel sent us," but others denied Fidel was in any way connected with the venture.

The government of Panama was convinced that the Cubans intended to occupy part of the Canal Zone in order to cast doubt upon the ability of de la Guardia government, which had been unable to assert Panama's sovereignty in the area. The Panamanian Chief Executive accused his countryman Roberto Arias of masterminding the expedition. Panama City charged collusion between Arias, who was desirous of gaining a political foothold in the nation, and Castro's Cuba which believed that any type of confusion might spread its revolution. Many in Panama City were of the opinion that Major César Vega willingly engaged in the operation in order to further the political aspirations of Roberto "Tito" Arias, the husband of the famous British ballerina Margot Fonteyn. In fact, the sequence of farcical events combined with speculation led the affair to be known popularly as the "Aquatic Ballet."

Eventually Major Vega admitted that the expedition had been sanctioned by Havana as part of the overall scheme to spread *Fidelismo* throughout the hemisphere. In order to publicly disavow any role in the uprising, Castro jailed the returned Cuban participants.

Although the Cuban invasion was inconsequential insofar as direct results were concerned, it did illustrate a key point. The weaknesses of the government of Panama and the *Guardia Nacional* became more apparent when Panama appealed to the Organization of American States for assistance. In reality this was the first time since the implementation of the Rio Treaty of Reciprocal Assistance of 1947 that a member nation of the OAS was accused of armed intervention. However, since the aggressor nation was not specifically designated, the treaty could not legally be invoked. The Council of the OAS, with Cuba's compliance, voted to apply the sanctions of the Rio Treaty to the situation, and an investigating committee was dispatched to Panama. The United States, Guatemala, Costa Rica, Ecuador and Colombia sent air and sea patrols to check into the matter, but concrete evidence was impossible to accumulate.

By May of 1959, the invaders were acquitted of charges that they conspired to overthrow the government of Panama, and Roberto Arias, who had sought refuge in the Brazilian Embassy, was granted safe conduct to Brazil. Later in the year, when Castro's forces attacked Nicaragua, Haiti, and the Dominican Republic on the pretext of opposing dictatorships, Panama's original conviction that the April invasion was Castro instigated was confirmed.

In November of 1959, Gregorio Ortega, a Cuban communist, was arrested in Chiriquí Province along with Rogelio Caparrós, a Cuban trained diplomat, on charges of fomenting riots. The *Fidelistas* were doing their utmost to exacerbate Panamanian nationalism, and the proof of their success came with the anti-United States riots which broke out in the nation on Independence Day, November 3, 1959.

The government of Panama feared that the support of the *Fidelistas* would create a revolution in the nation, and immediately embarked upon a campaign to eliminate Cuban propaganda. Whether or not this campaign was successful is difficult to assess. Originally the *Fidelistas* were strong only in Chiriquí's capital city of Davíd, but their influence began to spread. The United States Central Intelligence Agency reported that by 1960 Cuban funds were being disbursed throughout Panama as well as in Guatemala and El Salvador. Several pro-Castro tabloids and radio stations sprung up in Panama in 1960. However, much of Fidel's appeal was erased when the Cuban dictator stated that he was, and would always be, a Marxist-Leninist.

The First Congress of University Students of Central America and Panama, a leftist oriented group, met in May of 1960. For four days numerous speakers condemned the economic imperialism of the United States and pledged support to Castro. At this Congress the Panamanian student group affiliated with the Prague directed International Students Union (ISU), a communist oriented organization.

Now that Castro had successfully engendered a feeling of sympathy among the students of Panama, he would focus his attention upon Panama's labor movement. During June of 1960 members of the Cuban diplomatic corps were caught training Panamanian workers in the techniques of sabotage and propaganda distribution. On June 24, 1960, eighteen packages of communist propaganda materials were found aboard an incoming *Aeropostal de Cuba* airplane. Panama's Foreign Minister Miguel J. Moreno, Jr. called in the Cuban Ambassador José Antonio Cabrera, and a series of reciprocal accusations and denials ensued. George B. Allen, Chief of the United States Information Agency at this time opined that this was a part of Cuba's overall anti-United States campaign and possibly not directed primarily toward Panama.

By August of 1960, the government of Panama accused Cuban Ambassador José Antonio Cabrera of soliciting anti-United States agitators to organize demonstrations. One noteworthy *Fidelista* failure was the demonstration held on August 16, when the Organization of American States convened in Costa Rica. The Cubans made no attempt to conceal their attempts to create antagonism in Panama during the OAS meetings, and the events were clearly documented in *Revolución,* the official organ of the Cuban Revolution. The Cuban Ambassador to Panama was directing his propaganda to the people of Panama to the dismay of the government.

It was the intention of the Cubans to antagonize the government of Panama and thereby win popular support on the Isthmus, and they were mildly successful. The support for Fidel did not increase greatly, but the government of Panama was infuriated. In November, the government declared the Cuban Consul, Adolfo Martí Fuentes, *persona non grata.* By January of 1961, Panama recalled her Ambassador to Cuba, Alberto Obarrio, and Havana reciprocated by recalling Ambassador José Antonio Cabrera Villa, who had served in Panama City for a year and a half. A rupture in diplomatic relations between the two nations was imminent. Cuba's persistent intervention in the internal affairs of Panama had gone too far. Soon Fidel would be deprived of a viable Panamanian outlet for his diatribes against the United States.

Christian Democratic elements in Panama, led by the Cuban exile Luis Manuel Martinéz, demonstrated against Castro and advocated a break in diplomatic relations. The government of Panama, although in sympathy with Señor Martinéz, preferred to remain neutral for the time being but eventually deported him on grounds of being too reactionary.[4] In an effort to tighten internal security Internal Justice Minister Marco A. Robles barred the importation of the Cuban edition of *Bohemia* and the propaganda sheet *Revolución*, and the *Fidelistas* in Panama began to feel uneasy.

In April of 1961, Panama supported the action of the United States at the Bay of Pigs as necessary to quell the fires of nationalism, which were being fanned by the *Fidelistas* in the country. The government officially condemned Castro's regime in an effort to demonstrate that all pro-communist riots would be thwarted. However the Bay of Pigs failure severely damaged the prestige of the United States in Panama and served to throw more communist coals on the fire. When Fidel emphasized the fact that the United States was prepared to go to war to recoup her lost property and investments, a note of accord was struck. Panamanian nationalists, now more than ever, were certain that the United States would not relinquish claims to the Canal Zone.

On May Day 1961, the FSTRP paraded in Panama City in order to gather support for Castro. Panama's relations with Cuba rapidly deteriorated as President Chiari depicted Castro as an ever present menace. The preponderance of *Fidelista* activity in Panama, by July of 1961, was now centered around the *Vanguardia de Acción Nacional* (VAN). On the fourth of July, VAN headquarters were raided by government officials and Cuban propaganda and machine guns were found. VAN terrorism spread, but not on a wide scale. The Cuban chargé d'affairs was soon ordered out of the country, and the Supreme Court of Panama upheld a governmental decision to close the pro-Castro VAN building in an effort to curtail *Fidelismo*.

4. One wonders whether these are adequate grounds for deportation in a democracy.

By December, 1961, the government of Panama had initiated a campaign leading to a break in diplomatic relations with Cuba. Top officials in the government were now convinced that the only answer to the revolution Fidel Castro was exporting was complete severance of diplomatic relations. There was very little official opposition to the rupture with Cuba. Only Assemblywoman Thelma King, who had made numerous journeys to Havana and was an ardent Castroite, and Aquilino Boyd, a constant critic of the United States, desired retention of relations with Cuba.

Castro stepped up his denunciations of the government of Panama and on December 9, 1961, referred to Panama and Colombia as "tools of United States imperialism."[5] Fidel made numerous false accusations against President Chiari, and diplomatic relations between the nations were severed. The factor which caused the formal break on December 14, was a speech by Dr. Castro on December 9, in which he challenged Panama as a "government of traitors and accomplices of the imperialist Yankees." Panama's National Assembly voted on December 11 to cut all trade with Cuba, and the result was almost unanimous.[6] Castro's legal entry into Panama was eliminated and *Fidelista* operations would thereafter be surreptitious.

By January of 1962, communism, Havana style, was a clandestine movement in Panama and Panama's Committee for the Defense of the Cuban Revolution, led by Edgardo Nathaniel Hill Arboledo, was driven underground. In order to prepare the region both defensively and offensively against possible invasion originating in Cuba, Finance Minister Gilberto Arias proposed the creation of a common front against Castro, which would include Guatemala, El Salvador, Nica-

5. *New York Times,* December 9, 1961.
6. There was one abstention and two negative votes.

ragua, Haiti, Honduras, Colombia, Costa Rica, Venezuela and Panama. In essence the plan was designed to strengthen the area in which the OAS had proved weak.

Panama became increasingly more militant in her anti-Castro attitude and during the 1962 Punta del Este Conference she threatened to join the Central American nations and bolt the OAS if that body did not expel Cuba. Throughout the Inter-American Foreign Minister's Conference, Panama voted with the United States and took every occasion to condemn Castro and Cuba. When Foreign Minister Galileo Solís returned from the Eighth Meeting of the Foreign Ministers at Punta del Este, Uruguay, he inferred that Secretary of State Dean Rusk told him that the United States not only appreciated the stand of the Panamanians, with reference to Castro, but also that the Department of State was interested in revising the existing treaty governing the Canal and Canal Zone. Thus the mutual antipathy for Cuban communism was a definite step toward the resolution of Panama's problems with the United States.

A *Fidelista* movement was uncovered in the Soná area of Veraguas Province in November, 1962. Communist instigators were promising small farmers parcels of land if they contributed twenty-five dollars to their land distribution and agrarian reform movement. The *Fidelistas* were hitting hard at the United Fruit Company which they contended dominated seventy per cent of Panama's foreign exchange. Certainly the magnitude of the United Fruit holdings was more than sufficient to arouse the ire of nationalists and cause rebellion among the agrarian sectors which felt crushed by the weight of United States capital.

The contentions of the *Fidelistas* with regard to the United Fruit holdings contained a modicum of validity. The United Fruit plantations are reminiscent of the South during the pre-Civil War era. That is not to say that United Fruit has not brought advances to the region, for the banana plantations have undergone considerable improvement. In the realms of sanitation and hygiene the plantations have made enormous strides forward. However, considerable progress can still be made, as United Fruit continues to be known as "*El Pulpo*" (The Octopus). The very fact that United Fruit has no local stock holders, provides superior housing for employees who are United States citizens, practices segregation, and has made no genuine attempt to acquaint American employees with Spanish, is sufficient to embitter Panamanians. Even more vital to the *Fidelista* propaganda is the fact that the United Fruit Company was guilty of the same malpractices in Cuba which were eliminated by the Cuban Revolution, and only then by confiscation of its holdings. Similar occurrences would not be unwelcome in many sectors of Panama.

The plantation uprising caused Justice Minister Marco Robles to place Castro oriented activities under closer surveillance as he feared Havana directed sabotage. Between 1962 and 1964, approximately two hundred Panamanians were trained in Cuba or the Soviet Union and were fully capable of instigating minor insurrections in the country. President Chiari ordered measures to prevent further communist penetration as Castro purported to sabotage Panamanian railroads and other transportation facilities.

The United States was also concerned about the degree to which communism was taking hold in Panama. On February 28, 1963, Congressman Donald Rumsfeld, Republican of Illinois, asked that all shipping bound for or from Cuba be banned from the Panama Canal. This immediately evoked a violent reaction from Panama. The nationalist newspaper *La Hora* asserted that "the Canal was for the benefit of the World" and that the curtailment of Cuban shipping would place enormous hardships on Panama.[7]

Meanwhile subversion continued, and on March 7, 1963, the *Departamento Nacional de Investigaciones* (DENI) arrested Cuban trained subversives with ties to the outlawed *Partido de Pueblo*. The arrests were made as the *Fidelistas* advocated a popular democratic revolution in the Puerto Arnuelles area along the Pacific coast where recent terrorist activities had been widespread. Cuban exiles in Miami reported that Castro was dispatching saboteurs who were landing at sites on the Bocas del Toro Peninsula and Chaquín beach along the Atlantic coast of Panama.[8] At the same time Cuba was air dropping subversives into the hinterlands of Venezuela, Colombia, Bolivia and Panama in anticipation of beginning a hemispheric wave of guerrilla warfare. As rapidly as the communists poured their resources into the nation, they were stifled by the forces of Panama. For the balance of 1963 Cuba endeavored to build strength in Panama and President Chiari diligently tried to reduce the capabilities of the dedicated *Fidelistas*.

Numerous *Fidelistas* were implicated in the Flag Riots of early 1964, which took place while Cuban Premier Fidel Castro was in Moscow conferring with Russian Premier Nikita Khrushchev. While the Cuban and Russian Chiefs of State conducted friendly talks, Thelma King, the Panamanian legislator and erstwhile Castroite, led a mob of 750 to 1,000 to Panama's *Guardia Nacional* headquarters and demanded weapons to use against the Yankee imperialists. At the same time the King operated radio station urged mob violence directed against the forces of the United States. Both General Andrew P. O'Meara, who ordered United States forces to

7. February 28, 1963.
8. November, 1963.

quell the riots, and Secretary of State Dean Rusk agreed that Castro's influence was felt in the area. If Castro agents were not present the Flag Riots might never have reached fever pitch.

Interestingly, *Pravda,* on January 14, 1964, drew an analogy between Panama and Cuba in reference to the United States.[9] Panama's leftist Student Federation supplied many of the activists in January of 1964, among them Victor Avíla, Adolfo Ahumada and César Arosemena, all Havana trained, and Eligio Salas, the communist leader at the University of Panama, a known protégé of Fidel. The events of 1964 are indicative of the volatile situation in Panama. As long as social inequities exist, revolution Castro style shall continue to appeal to the people. Communists trained in Cuba will continue to agitate and propagandize. Walls of schools, churches and public edifices will continue to display pro-Castro signs and slogans. The spread of *Fidelismo* has been, and will continue to be, well planned, if not well financed. A recent Central Intelligence Agency report noted that Castro had spent only thirty thousand dollars in Panama to foment revolution in contrast to a million in Venezuela and a quarter of a million in Guatemala.[10]

Presently the United States occupies four military installations in Latin America; the Guantanamo Naval Base in Cuba, the Canal Zone and its environs, a missile tracking station in the Dominican Republic, and a similar base on Fernando de Noronha Island in Brazil. The Soviets, towards whom the Cubans lean, are intent upon exploiting anti-United States sentiment to the point that the Americans will be expelled

9. In recent years *Pravda* has increasingly paid attention to United States involvement in Panama.

10. *Latin American Times,* July 29, 1965.

from these Latin American sites, and they have agreed to help export Fidel's revolution.

Panamanian Communists claim the Organization of American States has no jurisdiction in their nation's disputes with the United States. On the other hand, the United States and Panama both consider Castro an agent of the international communist conspiracy and thus feel that he should be dealt with by the proper agencies of the Inter-American system. Panamanians also contend that if it were not for the presence of the United States in their land, the Cubans would not repeatedly intervene in their internal affairs, and this contention is difficult to refute.

One cannot envision a large following for Fidel in Panama. Even the existence of a Cuban sympathizer in the nation's National Assembly has not enhanced the prestige of the *Fidelistas*. The *Guardia Nacional,* with guidance by the United States, is geared to maintaining order in the nation and has become vehemently anti-communist and anti-*Fidelista.* Hostility toward Cuban type leftist students has been increasing and anti-guerrilla warfare training has made Castro's revolutionary task more difficult. Panama's National Unity Front, a conglomeration of leftists who have merged to form a communist oriented political organization, presents no viable threat because it cannot even meet the minimum requirements to qualify as a political party.[11]

Rumors about contraband arms, to be used for revolt, entering the country from Cuba are rampant, but the government has been and is ready to meet such subversion. What the future holds is difficult to predict. On July 29, 1965, Panama's

11. The National Unity Front does not include among its membership 2% of the nation's electorate, or approximately 22,000 members, which is necessary to qualify to run a slate of candidates in a national election.

Minister of Interior, José D. Bazan, stated that the government had no specific knowledge of Cuban subversive movements in the nation, but expects a rise in *Fidelista* activities.[12] The threat from Cuba has to date been successfully defeated but Fidel Castro has not abandoned the thought of exporting his revolution to Panama.

INTERNATIONAL RELATIONS

When dealing with international movements such as communism and United States relations with Latin America, it is worthwhile to make a cursory examination of Panama's other international commitments and relations.

Panama's relations with Central and South America have traditionally been ambivalent. Certainly Panama borrows freely from the cultural, economic and social aspects of both regions which have at times claimed her. For the most part, Latin Americans feel the Canal Zone and the Treaty of 1903 to be the Berlin Wall of the hemisphere, and the Latin American nations are almost unanimous in their denunciation of United States policies toward Panama, which they view as an obstacle to hemispheric harmony.

Panama's relations with her bordering neighbors are to a degree indicative of the nation's place in the region. Relations between Panama and Colombia have usually been amicable. This is strange since Panama is a child born of internal Colombian dissension. The only formal conflict with a neighbor was the dispute with Costa Rica in 1921 over the Coti zone, which is now a part of Costa Rica. But this conflict inflicted no permanent damage and relations between Panama and her northern neighbor are pervaded by an atmosphere of calm and harmony.

12. *Latin American Times,* July 30, 1965.

Although there has been sympathy in Latin America for the problems of Panama, no nation has ever really offered to render assistance. Perhaps this is due to their own problems, inherent weakness or the unique situation with regard to the United States on the Isthmus. The five Central American nations realize that their independence depends upon defense of the Inter-American system, and if that fails, upon the United States. Thus Panama, which has traditionally been excluded from their political and social programs, has always been included in their security plans.

Panama and her Latin American neighbors traditionally adhered to the doctrine of non-intervention, along with the precepts of Luis Drago and Carlos Calvo.[13] In the attempt to assert her sovereignty and protect against incursions by foreign powers, Panama joined both the League of Nations and the United Nations. Panama has maintained the legal fiction that all nations are juridically equal, a basic credo of the Organization of American States. So vehement has Panama's advocacy of juridical equality been that she blamed the United States for the collapse of the League of Nations, an organization in which she contends the Americans sought to differentiate between the inferior and superior powers of the world.

Yet in both the United Nations and the Organization of American States, Panama has generally found it advantageous to support the interest of the United States. When Panama entered the Inter-American system after World War II, she

13. The Doctrine of Luis M. Drago, Argentine Minister of Foreign Affairs, was announced in 1902 and stipulates that there can be no territorial expansion in the Americas by a nation seeking to collect on financial obligations owed to it by an American State. The Mexican Carlos Calvo averred that under no condition does an alien have the right to request that his government intervene on his behalf (absolute sovereignty concept).

did so with the hope that juridical equality afforded by the organization would enhance her position in relation to her quarrels with the United States. This hope was obviated when Panama became a signatory to the 1947 Rio Treaty of Reciprocal Assistance, as she knew that without the support of the United States she was exceptionally weak and vulnerable.

Despite the OAS principle of non-intervention, the United States has been granted this privilege in Panama by the Treaty of 1903. This paradox has evoked criticism from Panamanians as well as other Latin Americans. Panama sincerely believes in the equality of nations, as it is in her best interests to do so, while the adoption of such a policy by the powerful United States would be foolhardy. Panama claims a deep respect for international law, while maintaining that it is the United States which at times does not.

Panama maintains diplomatic relations with all western hemisphere states and European nations except Cuba and, for reasons previously mentioned, does not have ties with Soviet Bloc nations. She has given lip service to the idea of maintaining a neutrality of the Egyptian or Indian variety, and upon occasion a Panamanian delegate has been sent as an observer to conferences of neutralist powers. But Soviet Bloc influence has not been sufficiently effective to convince Panama of the advisability of neutrality. The overriding influence of the United States has made it impossible for Panama to seriously entertain thoughts about neutrality, but the nation endeavors to retain relations with as many nations as is politically and financially feasible. For example, Panama maintains relations with Israel, Lebanon and the United Arab Republic, but does not engage in relations with the new emerging nations of Africa, with whom such connections would be too costly.

It is amazing that in view of past difficulties with the United States, Panama has not gravitated toward the Soviet sphere. During and after the 1964 disputes which culminated in a rupture of diplomatic relations with the United States, no specific overtures toward Moscow or Peking were made. The government of Panama has remained a staunch and loyal supporter of American foreign policy with regard to world ideological struggles.

Panama, as a member of many international organizations,[14] is vitally interested in the Latin American Free Trade Association (LAFTA), which was inaugurated by the Treaty of Montevideo in 1960 and encompasses an area populated by 150 million people. She has recently expressed an interest in the Mercado Común Centroamericano (MMC), (Central American Common Market), but mere "association" with the Central American Common Market is not desired. Rather, direct participation is coveted, as Panama does not want to be a member dictated to by the other member nations.[15] In fact, the Panamanians would like to make their nation the banking center for the MMC, but it is possible that half a loaf may be better than none, and Panama might have to settle for "associate" status. This is a new tack, for prior to 1965 and before talks concerning the MCC, Panama never expressed great interest in joining this Central American association. This change of position is indicative of Panama's optimism, as

14. Food and Agriculture Organization, (FAO), the United Nations Educational, Scientific and Cultural Organization (UNESCO), the International Monetary Fund (IMF), the International Bank for Reconstruction and Development (IBRD), the International Finance Corporation (IFC), and the International Development Association (IDA).

15. Stated Ramon H. Jurado, President of Panama's National Economy Council on June 23, 1965.

the government envisions more sovereignty in the future and less reliance upon the United States.

Panama has definite commitments and obligations to international policies and possesses no isolationist tendencies. She would definitely prefer to work exclusively through the United Nations and Organization of American States and relinquish any ties with the United States, which connote overlordship. However, American interests in Panama are so vast and diverse that it is unlikely that Panama will ever be able to completely divest herself of United States influence. As long as international communism is present Panama will continue to work with and through existing international organizations and the United States in order to attain her economic, social and political objectives.

CHAPTER
SIX

Kennedy And After

Political changes took place in both the United States and Panama in 1960 when Roberto F. Chiari and John F. Kennedy were elected as Chief Executives. President Chiari staked his political prestige upon his ability to gain concessions from the United States, and in order to prevent public outbursts of Yankeephobia, Chiari urged his people not to become obsessed with the Canal conflict. He worked diligently and quietly to affect some basis of accord with the United States in regard to the question of sovereignty in the Canal Zone. The United States was primarily motivated by the desire to afford protection for its citizens in Panama and also promote commercial progress on the Isthmus. When President Kennedy was inaugurated in January, 1961, there was an aura of hope for progress in relations between the two nations.

In 1961 President Chiari's government was blaming all terrorism in the land on the communists as nationalism, for the time being, was played down. Even leftist Assemblywoman Thelma King's proposal to eliminate all contacts between Panamanian officials and United States authorities, except through respective Foreign Ministries, was immediately condemned. But President Chiari's attempt to de-emphasize anti-United States sentiment was repeatedly negated by the actions of various groups. For example, in May of 1961 a meeting of intellectuals at the University of Panama ended in a request for official condemnation of United States relations with Panama and stimulated the Panamanian press to begin its xenophobic demands anew.

On November 2, 1961, a letter from President Kennedy assured President Chiari that the United States was trying to give Panama the full benefits of the Canal and was intent upon resolving the existing differences between the two nations. President Kennedy indicated that the United States was cognizant of the fact that the 1903 Treaty was not satisfactory to Panama. The American Chief Executive stated that a re-evaluation of Panama's needs and demands would be forthcoming.[1] This communication gave further incentive to Panama's Assembly which unanimously passed a resolution abrogating all treaties with the United States. Although such action was meaningless since it lacked mutual consent, it was a portent for the future.

When President Kennedy, in June, 1962, indicated the desire to settle the protracted dispute with Mexico over sovereignty in the Chamizal area, he raised Panama's hopes for a similar settlement regarding the Canal and Canal Zone. Kennedy intimated that he was aware of the difficulties with Panama and was contemplating a treaty revision. President Chiari then journeyed to Washington to speak with the youthful Kennedy for the better part of a week.[2] At the conclusion of their meetings the usual joint communique was issued. The two leaders agreed upon the need for discussions of the 1903 Treaty, arranged for the flying of Panama's flag in the Canal

1. "President Kennedy Replies to Letter From President Chiari of Panama," *Department of State Bulletin* (December 4, 1961), p. 932.

2. June 12–14, 1962.

Zone, and reaffirmed their respective beliefs in the Alliance for Progress.[3]

Although President Kennedy made no definite commitments to President Chiari, a year and a half later, after his death, Panama was to claim that he promised to revise the Treaty of 1903.[4] The Department of State denied any such Kennedy promise, saying the Panamanians had misconstrued the promise to discuss mutual problems as an agreement to revise the existing treaty.[5]

For the balance of 1962, few problems arose between the two nations, and on October 12 the Thatcher Ferry Bridge across the Canal was dedicated as a symbol of unity between the United States and Panama. Panamanians demonstrated against the name of the bridge on the grounds that it should rightfully be called the "Bridge of the Americas." This incident revealed the temperament of Panama, whose people objected to anything connected with the United States. In order to satisfy the Panamanians, on October 29, 1962, dual flags were raised at the Canal Zone Administration Building at Balboa Heights. A few days later the banners of both nations were raised at the Administration Building at Cristobal, but symbolic concessions are rarely satisfactory.

The reaction to the flying of the Panamanian flag in the Canal Zone was considerable. Zonians believed this to be a step closer to eventual United States relinquishment of control in the area. However, a citizen of the United States, Gerald A. Doyle, instituted court actions to prevent the flying of the Panamanian flag in the Canal Zone. In January of

3. "President Chiari of Panama Holds Talks with President Kennedy," *Department of State Bulletin* (July 9, 1962), p. 8.

4. J. Fred Rippy, "The United States and Panama: The High Cost of Appeasement," *Inter-American Economic Affairs* (Spring, 1964), p. 92.

5. February 10, 1964.

1963 a group of Canal Zone employees formed the Gerald A. Doyle Flag Fund Committee, and ten thousand dollars were raised by members of Government Employees Lodge 14, the Veterans of Foreign Wars of the Canal Zone and the Federation of Federal Employees.

On July 8, 1963, U. S. District Court Judge Guthrie F. Crowe dismissed the motion of Gerald A. Doyle, Jr. to end the flying of Panama's flag in the Zone. In arriving at his decision, Judge Guthrie ignored the philosophical and theoretical aspects of the sovereignty issue, which he felt to be confusing, and declared that Panama had the legal right to fly her flag to the left of that of the United States. The court intimated that it believed the flying of the two flags side by side in the disputed territory to be purposeless and might lead to further complications.

Despite the mutual antagonisms between the privileged Zonians and the natives, Panama continued to prosper from the existence of the Canal Zone. In 1963 alone, the income flowing into the Republic of Panama from the Canal Zone amounted to $91,849,000.[6] This sum could not be overlooked by those in Panama agitating for the abandonment of the Zone by the United States.

On April 25, 1963, Foreign Minister Galileo Solís stated that unless significant advances were made by July of that year President Chiari was ready to dissolve the joint United States-Panama Committee formed to settle differences. In reiterations of this sentiment the Foreign Minister asserted that he was particularly disturbed by the fact that after a year of fruitless talks the American representatives still had no authority to negotiate a new treaty. While Minister Solís castigated the United States, President Chiari revealed that he had been conferring with Ambassador Joseph Farland

6. *New York Times,* July 5, 1964.

and had discussed the possibility of the construction of a sea level canal across Darien Province.

President Chiari demanded, in May of 1963, that the United States pay a fifty million dollar sum as interim compensation until such time as a new treaty with the United States could be concluded. At the same time, Panama's Director of Economic Planning, David Samudio, was engaged in discussions with the Department of State, seeking a new treaty replacing the one of 1955. Samudio also discussed the possibility of a new sea level canal in Darien Province. Relations between the United States and Panama improved as Panama was reluctant to press existing problems and risk the loss of a new sea level canal and its potential profits.

Panama softened her approach to Canal problems and on June 19, 1963, Foreign Ministry Counsel Eloy Benedetti, appearing on television after a tour of Egypt and Suez, urged Panama and the United States to enter into a partnership venture with respect to the Canal. Temporarily, Panama abandoned the demand for complete sovereignty and indicated that sharing in the operation of the Canal would be acceptable. For a month or so an air of harmony appeared to develop as, for the moment, the major conflict between the nations was a disagreement over the use of Panamanian postage stamps in the Canal Zone.

The joint United States-Panama Commission met for the last time in July 1963.[7] Some accord had been reached, but in proportion to the length of the deliberations the results were negligible. It was then decided to form a bi-national labor advisory committee to take jurisdiction over disputes in the Canal Zone. As a result of this committee's action, the United States agreed to withhold and pay to Panama income taxes of Panamanians employed in the Canal Zone.

7. On July 23, 1963.

Hereafter Panamanians in the Zone were to be given the same health and life insurance benefits as American employees. Also, Panama requested jurisdiction over a corridor including Ancón's Fourth of July Bridge, Thatcher Bridge over the Pacific end of the Canal and the road to Arrayán, giving the nation continuous jurisdiction from the Panama Canal to the land west of the Canal. Slowly, the United States was relenting, and Panama's long suppressed quest for sovereignty was being granted in piecemeal fashion.

On August 2, 1963, the resignation of United States Ambassador Joseph S. Farland, whom the Panamanians trusted and who was instrumental in solving many problems, resulted in irreparable damage to relations between the nations. Many, often contradictory, reasons for Ambassador Farland's departure have been offered. It was common knowledge that Farland saw basic defects in the Alliance for Progress. He felt that too great emphasis was being placed, by the *Alianza,* upon economic development and not enough upon social welfare. It was his belief that the programs of the Agency for International Development (AID), in conjunction with the Alliance, were not acceptable to the Panamanians and were far too costly for Panama and could not be guaranteed by the United States.

This was not the first time that an Ambassador in Latin America has been forced to resign by Washington for disagreeing with the manner in which the Alliance for Progress was being implemented. Dissatisfaction with the *Alianza* was not the only factor leading to Ambassador Farland's resignation. This affable diplomat had been appointed by President Eisenhower and had served in Panama since June 28, 1960. He incurred the wrath of Canal Zone officials who believed him to be a pro-nationalist and opposed to their basic position. They even contended that Ambassador Farland was liked by the Castroites who felt that he should be retained because he unconsciously aided nationalist policies. Thus the departure of Joseph Farland was to be a serious drawback for the government of Panama, which now more than ever was convinced that the United States was devoid of idealism and that all American foreign policy was predicated upon the "what is in it for me?" attitude. Certainly it was not desirable to remove a man who was so desperately needed by the Panamanians. Foreign Minister Galileo Solís stated that he found it "difficult to find an American Ambassador with better understanding of Panama's problems."[8]

The love and respect that the people of Panama built for Ambassador Farland is difficult to describe. He is still spoken of frequently by the man in the street, and he has made it a point to visit the nation regularly to renew old friendships. The common folk felt that José Farland cared, while those in the government of Panama believed him to be neecssary. As in all such cases, there are two sides of the coin. The Panamanian intelligentsia referred to Ambassador Farland as "Smilin' Jack," while numerous others agreed that he was well liked, but ineffective on the important issues. This gives rise to the contention that the genial ambassador is not always the best man for the job. In any event, the mystery surrounding the Farland case will continue to be argued by those in the Department of State who point to the fact that Ambassador Farland was never given the usual debriefing when he resigned. Officially the story has been denied, but the public will never be certain.

After the Farland episode, Panama was disheartened, as evidenced by Foreign Minister Solís' talk, in September of 1963 before the General Assembly of the United Nations.

8. "Panama," *Hispanic American Report* (August, 1963), p. 767.

He stated the existence of the 1903 Treaty would continue to cloud relations between the two nations. In the course of his speech he referred to John Hay's alleged admission that the Canal Treaty was "very satisfactory and advantageous to the United States, and not so advantageous to Panama."[9] Although he offered no documentary proof of the Hay statement, this nonetheless expressed Panama's feelings. While Minister Solís was criticizing the United States before the United Nations, Canal Zone Governor Robert Fleming was assuring the House Appropriations Committee that relations between the United States and Panama were at their best. Still the Committee was displeased as Panama pressed for economic and political concessions.

The government of Panama continued to warn against anti-Yankee campaigns which it felt opened the door for subversive elements. Also the Panamanians were cognizant of the fact that overt actions against the United States might imperil the possible construction of a sea level canal across Darien. The government fully realized that a decision by the United States to construct a sea level canal in an area outside of Panama would seriously jeopardize the economy of the nation.

Disregarding the government's admonitions, in October of 1963, leftists and nationalists demonstrated their hostility by throwing a few Molotov cocktails at the United States Embassy. Anti-United States riots and demonstrations were expected to follow when suddenly the word of President Kennedy's assassination reached Panama. Panamanians paused in tribute and various Kennedy rites were held, and throughout the Isthmus flags were flown at half mast. This was a supreme tribute to the man whom most Latin Ameri-

9. "Panama," *Hispanic American Report* (September, 1963), p. 862.

cans deemed *muy simpatico,* as in the past only deceased Panamanian Presidents had been accorded this honor.

Another ramification of the Kennedy assassination was the confusion concerning the nomination of Ambassador Farland's successor. At the time of the death the nomination of Frank M. Coffin, a Deputy Managing Director of the Development Loan Fund, and Administrator in the Agency for International Development, was on the President's desk. Mr. Coffin had been named to the post on the 16th of November, and now the nomination was temporarily in limbo. The problem of proper diplomatic representation and the delays caused by the Kennedy assassination later played a significant role in relations with Panama.

As 1963 drew to a close, Canal Zone Governor Robert J. Fleming, a Major General in the Army Engineer Corps, announced that the United States and Panamanian flags would fly jointly at numerous sites throughout the Canal Zone. The brief Kennedy era had drawn to a tragic close, but the myth of the man lingers. John F. Kennedy furthered numerous programs in Latin America, but on the whole it is too early to assess his accomplishments. Despite the blunder of the Bay of Pigs, Kennedy had been off to an auspicious start. For lack of other criteria he will be judged on that, and for years to come the Kennedy image will endure in an aura of semi-sanctification.

THE UNITED STATES INFORMATION SERVICE

During the tenure of President Kennedy the United States Information Service reached its pinnacle in Panama in terms of notoriety as its headquarters became a frequent target for xenophobic attacks. Since the inauguration of Lyndon B. Johnson it has received considerably more attention than in the past. It is the function of USIS to counteract the propaganda propogated by the Communists and *Fidelistas* and to promote the United States line. Specifically the United States Information Agency endeavors to acquaint Panamanians with United States life, institutions and programs such as those carried out by the Agency for International Development and the Alliance for Progress. The USIS library is used frequently by Panamanians, but one wonders whether or not those who congregate there (primarily students) do so because of its air-conditioned reading rooms and padded seats, which provide a refreshing interlude from the oppressive heat and humidity of the Isthmus. Certainly the staff of the USIS in Panama is well trained and when this was written appeared to be more competent than its counterpart staffs in other Latin American nations. This is, no doubt, attributable to the fact that Panama is considered a "hot spot" by the Department of State and also the fact that President Johnson's first foreign policy crisis involved that nation.

THE ALLIANCE FOR PROGRESS

Panama was a recipient of Point Four Assistance from the United States until 1960 when the program was supplanted by the *Alianza para el progreso* (Alliance for Progress), an outgrowth of former Brazilian President Juscelino Kubitschek's proposed "Operation Pan America." Between July 1, 1945, and June 30, 1963, Panama received direct fiscal aid from the United States amounting to one hundred sixty million dollars, and indirect aid of about twenty million dollars. The figures do not accurately indicate the amount of United States aid flowing into the Republic of Panama since funds were received from various other sources. For example, the Pan-American Highway project alone brought in forty-one million dollars in United States gifts and an additional thirteen million dollars in loans.[10]

Panama has long been in need of assistance in order to create another "Operation Bootstrap" such as that which evolved in Puerto Rico under the guidance of Governor Muñoz Marín. In addition to the domestic need for a rehabilitation program, there is a need to contain Castroism and communism which flourish in underdeveloped areas. The Alliance for Progress was designed to meet both needs. Essentially it is an economic program serving to raise the standard of living and simultaneously eliminate one of the basic elements upon which communists rely for support. The psychological aspects of such a program, inaugurated by the United States and implemented together with the government of Panama, will go a long way toward combating communism in the nation.

In March of 1961, President Chiari expressed Panama's first official approval of the *Alianza.* The idea of a self-help program had enormous appeal on the Isthmus. The more the program could appear to be Panamanian and the less the United States was involved, the better it would be. Panama's General Planning and Administrative Department had been established in 1959 under the direction of the Office of the President of the Republic, and this department which guided the economic and social development of the nation was a natural outlet through which the Alliance for Progress could function. To Planning Director David Samudio fell much of the burden of implementing the *Alianza.*

The Alliance, together with Planning Director Samudio, planned to raise the nation's gross national product from $560.5 million in 1964 to $719.1 million by 1970. It was hoped that in the same period the per capita income could be

10. Rippy, "The United States and Panama: The High Cost of Appeasement," p. 90.

raised from $470 to $560. Numerous Panamanian agencies are taking part in the development plan along with counterpart agencies in the United States Government. Although the above goals are not excessive, in terms of Panama's past record achieving them will be a monumental task.

The Alliance for Progress has not been the easiest project to sell to Panama's entrepreneurs. Native capital has been and continues to be reluctant to invest in the nation's economy when more secure and lucrative areas for investment are available in Europe and the United States. Panama has experienced adminstrative difficulties in utilizing *Alianza* funds, and graft and corruption have at times not permitted sufficient money to filter down to the level where it can do the most good.

A Panamanian Economic Mission visited the United States in October of 1961 to discuss a projected five year plan. The United States was informed of the Alliance aid desired by Panama and was asked to make an effort to stimulate American private investment on the Isthmus. Since it is impossible to completely administer an economic program such as the Alliance from Washington, the local responsibilities were primarily entrusted to the United States Agency for International Development, which is housed in the bullet-marked Panama Cement building across from Panama's National University.

Many United States AID people are involved in *Alianza* programs which are concerned with regional and sectoral planning, taxation, fiscal revision, and administrative assistance. The employees of AID are exceptionally dedicated and desirous of helping the Panamanians to help themselves. Enlightened Panamanians are conscious of this and speak of them with high regard. The Agency for International Development has delved into every aspect of Panamanian life except politics, in order to supplement and implement the Alliance for Progress. It is impossible to dichotomize between the work of the *Alianza* and AID, and thus we shall dwell on some of the more clearly defined AID programs in Panama.

AID has concentrated some of its efforts upon high level manpower and labor development, to provide Panamanians with higher education and high level manpower training necessary for supervisory employment. AID has endeavored to improve government administration, as well as to provide fiscal reform in the nation. Rural development has not been neglected, with emphasis upon natural resources surveys, agrarian support, rural road development training, integration of health facilities, mobile rural health programs, and national school construction. Financial institutional and private enterprise development in Panama have been assisted by the creation of housing credit institutes and self-help housing projects, as well as the actual persuasion of nationals to invest in these projects and their nation's future. The list of AID projects is impressive and includes such additional features as nursing education, trade and industrial education, public safety program support, scholarship programs at the Canal Zone College, and a rural library project. One could go on, but the result would be the same, conscientious work, pursued by capable and diligent representatives of the United States who are too frequently misunderstood and disliked.

The Alliance for Progress in collaboration with AID has undertaken other programs. Panama's census, which by Latin American standards was good, has been improved. Statistics are being compiled accurately and in a sophisticated fashion. Unpublicized work on birth control studies, always highly controversial in Catholic countries, is being pursued clandestinely by Panamanian medical and governmental officials, who are guided by United States technicians. Progress on water supply and sanitation projects is visible everywhere in a nation that, despite being surrounded by water, has had a filthy and insufficient supply of potable water. Despite some conflict of interest difficulties, housing projects are being completed, although at a rate slower than desirable.

Tax reform, a phrase which for years has sent chills down the spines of affluent Panamanians, has been attacked in a sensible manner. Both the Act of Bogota and the Charter of Punta del Este call for tax reforms and collections, but traditionally the Panamanian corporation has been taxed at an extremely low rate, when taxed at all. In order to obtain economic progress in the nation, people will have to be made to assume their fair share. No longer can the vulnerable member of the lower classes be compelled to pay taxes from his substandard wages while the corporate giants and big businessman evade the tax collector. A system of exemptions, exclusions, deductions, payments and penalties, and filing of returns has to be devised if the nation is to go forward. Teams of economists, supported by the OAS, the Inter-American Development Bank and the United States Internal Revenue Service, have been laboring to place Panama's internal economic structure in order.[11]

The results of these and many Alliance for Progress programs are as yet inconclusive, but even the untrained observer can see improvement. New laws are going on the books, and what is more important they are being enforced. The communists too, are worried by the accomplishments of the *Alianza* as is evident by attempts to hinder its projects. To date *Fidelista* or communist activities have not seriously impeded progress. Subversion has been negligible, signs have

11. An OAS advisory team led by Professor Milton Taylor of Michigan State University has rendered Panama valuable assistance in this realm.

been defaced, a few bombs tossed, but little real damage has been done. In fact security measures have been enhanced by United States assistance, as the agency for International Development has endeavored to strengthen the *Guardia Nacional* and the nation's security police.

In order to further the Alliance for Progress there is still need to gain the confidence of the Panamanians. The motives of the United States are still questioned on the Isthmus, but aid is desired. Nationalists still ask why in the past such remote nations as Laos received huge sums while Panama's allotment was minimal. There is a question as to whether or not the Alliance will eventually make progress sufficient to permit Panama's own running of the Canal. In reference to the *Alianza* and United States aid the question of who profits most, the deprived or the oligarchy, is frequently asked. One must conclude, both profit to a degree. Panamanian economists feel that even more United States and *Alianza* aid is necessary if the nation is ever to reach a level of development which will provide for a better way of life for all citizens. The United States is just beginning to comprehend what the Alliance for Progress really entails and concerted efforts are being made to succeed.[12] Now that the initial planning phase has been completed, the second phase, or period of implementation, is underway.

THE PEACE CORPS

One of the most successful programs launched during the Kennedy Administration was the Peace Corps. Of all the Kennedy projects the Peace Corps has made the most significant impression in Latin America. Over two-thirds of all the

12. Between October of 1965 and 1967 the United States expects to contribute some $51.1 million to the *Alianza* in Panama.

Peace Corps volunteers are in Latin America, and Panama has the largest contingent on the Central American Isthmus. The initial Peace Corps contingent in Panama numbered eighteen and by the summer of 1965 had grown to 132.

To the knowledge of the writer there has not been a single blemish on the record of the Corps in Panama. The splendid job turned in by the volunteers is particularly significant in light of the fact that the nation has been involved in adverse diplomatic interplay with the United States. From the outset the Peace Corps has been an unqualified success in Panama. This is attested to by the fact that more workers are being continuously requested by the government of Panama. The volunteers who serve in Panama receive their training at the University of Arizona, and the manner in which they have adapted to and have been received in Panama is a credit to the institution and personnel who have assisted in their preparation.

Much of the success is attributable to Jack Hood Vaughn, Director of the Peace Corps, who formerly served as Latin American Director of the Peace Corps, Ambassador to Panama and Assistant Secretary of State for Inter-American Affairs. As ambassador, he gave strong support to the Peace Corps program on the Isthmus.

The entire atmosphere pervading Peace Corps operations in Panama differs markedly from that of other branches of the United States government in foreign lands. Peace Corps headquarters are located in an unpretentious Spanish style home in a quiet residential section of Panama City. The unmarked building, just off Avenida Cuba, which one has difficulty in locating, has attracted little or no notoriety. Unlike the structure housing the Agency for International Development, the Peace Corps headquarters are unknown to the entire populace and are not a target for demonstrations.

Upon entering the Peace Corps headquarters one is immediately struck by the absence of air-conditioning, which is standard equipment in United States installations on the Isthmus. The workers, and even the Director, are casually attired and the "official air" which frightens many Panamanians is absent.

One derives the impression that the Peace Corps has been carefully used in Panama. The organization goes out of its way to disassociate itself from the American community, and in no way desires to be identified with the splendor which is attached to Embassy life in Panama City. Although the Peace Corps Director maintains close contact with the United States Ambassador, whose duty it is to coordinate all American activity in Panama, the Corps maintains an air of autonomy. Even volunteers do not regularly socialize with fellow Americans in the nation. Because of their close identification with the Panamanian community, the Peace Corpsmen are accepted as *compadres,* rather than Yankee interlopers. It is noteworthy that during the 1964 Flag Riots the corpsmen were not personally attacked nor too adversely affected.

Volunteers are not permitted in the Canal Zone, nor do they have the commissary privileges that are so deeply resented by the Panamanians. The Peace Corps makes a conscious effort to refrain from publicity of the type that sheds a dim light on the United States. Never is the Peace Corps criticized in the Panama City press and only rarely have the communists been successful in having the Peace Corps criticized by the press in the interior of the nation.

The Peace Corps works exclusively with Panamanian agencies such as the Ministry of Labor, Social Welfare and Public Health and Ministry of Education and thus avoids controversy. The program in Panama embraces an extensive teaching curriculum, and volunteers serve on every level of education from elementary school to the National University where they offer courses in history, physics, English and social welfare, as well as performing administrative functions.

However the primary involvement in the nation is in community self-help projects. In these endeavors the volunteers with local assistance attack long-standing problems which the populace is well aware of, but whose existence they have been fatalistically reconciled to in the past. The volunteers move right into the heart of the slum or community in which they are going to work and live alone, with partners or in close association with a local family.

The most striking successes of the Peace Corps in Panama have been in slums adjacent to the Canal Zone. In this area, where poverty and poor sanitary conditions are evident and their existence blamed on the United States, volunteers have been able to overcome nationalistic antagonisms and work in complete safety. While the Yankee Zonian, who resides on the other side of the street, is in constant jeopardy, the Peace Corpsman can be virtually free from harm.

The work of the Peace Corps complements the programs of the Alliance for Progress and the Agency for International Development, as all three have similar goals, but differ in their modes of implementation. For example, housing projects and school and bridge constructions are often served by representatives of all three agencies performing diverse tasks aimed at a common end.

The rendering of medical treatment for persons inhabiting outlying districts has been a recent project of the Peace Corps. Natives who ordinarily would pass through a shortened life without exposure to a physician or dentist are now being afforded modern medical care. Medical teams composed of one Panamanian doctor for each United States doctor have been organized to aid people in inaccessible regions, such as the Indians living in the San Blas Islands. The success of these teams is incredible in view of the lack of sophistication of those with whom they work. Even more impressive is the manner in which the workers manage to learn such exotic languages as Guaymi which enable them to converse with natives who have no knowledge of Spanish.

One can be relatively certain that the Peace Corps will continue to expand its activities in Panama and hopefully undo generations of anti-United States sentiment. Perhaps the finest tribute to the Peace Corps is the fact that it is beginning to be emulated by others. In the future, Panama will undoubtedly receive Peace Corps types from more fortunate nations of the world such as Japan and West Germany. If for nothing else, President John F. Kennedy will always be remembered in Panama as the innovator of the Peace Corps, which hopefully will fulfill the function of its name.

CHAPTER
SEVEN

The Johnson Era—The First Foreign Policy Crisis

The shock of the Kennedy assassination wore off rapidly in Panama, and by December, 1963, relations with the United States began to deteriorate. Flags in the Canal Zone were still flying at half mast when the Panamanian bus drivers in the Canal Zone went on strike for higher wages. Little incidents plagued the Americans in the Zone and mutual antagonisms were restored to a state of normalcy. Adversity in Panama was now accelerated at a pace almost too rapid to cope with the human element. After more than a half century of dissension, relations between the United States and Panama reached their lowest ebb.

On January 7, 1964, a student at Balboa High School, encouraged by his parents and in defiance of the Canal Zone Governor's orders, raised a United States flag on a pole in front of the school. The flag was removed by Zone authorities, who contended that its presence violated an agreement with Panama and aroused nationalist ire. The flag was subsequently replaced by other students who posted a twenty-four hour guard to make sure that it was not removed. At 4:30 P.M. on January 9th, 150 students from the *Instituto Nacional,* the nearest Panamanian high school, marched on the Balboa High School with a Panamanian flag in hand. American students immediately attempted to thwart the Panamanians, and the Canal Zone police had to intercede. Police Chief Gaddis agreed to permit the Panamanian flag to remain at the bottom of the flag pole, but in the confusion it was damaged. The crowd that congregated around the site was then dispersed and moved en masse to Panama. Enroute they tried to remove the United States flag that was flying alongside the flag of Panama in front of the Canal Zone Administration Building.

This series of events took place less than seven weeks after Lyndon B. Johnson became President of the United States and caught him with his diplomatic guard down. What began as a semi-serious prank by a group of overly emotional adolescents escalated into President Johnson's first foreign policy crisis. How the newly inaugurated President would handle the situation in Panama would be highly significant to the nations of the world. President Johnson would be forced into the unenviable position of having to reach a decision. The immediacy of the problem, and the lack of United States's preparation for it, would reflect the foreign policy capabilities of the Johnson administration and have a direct bearing upon relations with other nations of the hemisphere. The United States would be compelled either to capitulate or compromise, and in any event to establish a precedent. Lyndon Baines Johnson's first big test in international affairs came at a time when the United States was not represented by an ambassador in Panama City and had not been represented there since the preceding August, when Joseph Farland had resigned from the post. The negotiating skill of the Department of State was about to be tested, and in particular the Assistant Secretary of State for Inter-American Affairs, Thomas C. Mann, was placed in a precarious position.

Reports circulated throughout Panama that the national

flag had been defiled and trampled upon. Crowds began to form around the entrances to the Canal Zone. Eventually 3,000 Panamanians entered the Zone and, despite the efforts of the eighty-five man Zone Police Force, burned and sacked the Ancón freight house, a railroad station and a train.[1] While this initial attack upon the Zone was being made the area was under the command of Colonel David S. Parker, substituting for (General) Governor Fleming who had departed for Washington. Governor Fleming heard the news while stopping in Miami and immediately returned to Panama. Colonel Parker requested that the United States military Commander in the area, General Andrew P. O'Meara, assume command in the Zone. General O'Meara complied in order to provide adequate protection for the 36,000 United States personnel in the Zone.

Jules Dubois of the *Chicago Tribune* stated that the January 9, 1964, explosion was plotted by the communists and Castro as a diversion from their subversive activities in Venezuela.[2] There can be no doubt that the communists in the nation allied with the nationalists in an effort to indicate displeasure with the United States policies. Regardless of the real motivations of the communists, whether they were diversionary or not, the threat was genuine. Rioting and demonstrations spread throughout the nation and even in Colón United States citizens and business enterprises were harassed.

On January 10, 1964, Foreign Minister Galileo Solís informed Secretary of State Dean Rusk that Panama was severing diplomatic relations with the United States. The decision was that of President Chiari and was actually opposed by his Minister of Foreign Affairs. President Chiari evidently was

1. January 9, 1964.
2. See Jules Dubois, *Danger Over Panama* (Indianapolis: Bobbs Merrill Co., 1964), p. 11.

displeased by the United States' repeated refusal to formulate some mutually satisfactory agreement concerning the status of the Canal Zone. The time was now propitious, while the popular support was present, to force the hand of the Americans.

THE ROLE OF INTERNATIONAL ORGANIZATIONS

Panama invoked the 1947 Treaty of Reciprocal Assistance (Rio Treaty) and accused the United States of aggression. In an emotional outburst President Chiari denounced the American actions and pledged never to resume diplomatic relations without a definite United States commitment to renegotiate the 1903 Treaty. President Johnson, being a novice in the realm of international relations, broke diplomatic protocol and phoned President Chiari directly in order to try to resolve the dispute. Latin Americans generally do not appreciate informality, but fortunately the Panamanians over the years have become acquainted with United States ways, and this attempt to by-pass proper diplomatic channels was not greatly resented. However, it may be noted that in April of 1965, when President Johnson again tried to circumvent protocol in the Dominican Republic crisis, he incurred severe criticism in Latin America.

President Johnson ordered Assistant Secretary of State for Inter-American Affairs Thomas C. Mann to go to the Canal Zone. On January 10, 1964, a United States mission headed by Secretary Mann, Secretary of the Army Cyrus Vance, Edwin Martin, formerly holder of Mann's position, and Ralph Dungan, a Presidential Assistant for Inter-American affairs, was dispatched to Panama. At the same time the Security Council of the United Nations met at the request of

Panama to discuss charges of United States aggression.[3] Señor Aquilino Boyd, Panama's representative at the United Nations, charged the United States with a long history of aggression in Panama and cited the November 3, 1959, riots as a specific example. Señor Aquilino Boyd did not confine his remarks to the floor of the United Nations but in a public statement at Kennedy International Airport asserted that he was ashamed of American democracy. However he remained mute when an inquisitive journalist asked whether Boyd Bros. Inc., the Panamanian agent of the American Express Company which his family controlled, would sever connections in the United States.

Chief Delegate Boyd told the United Nations that the Canal Zone had never been sold, ceded or rented to the United States, and that Panama retained sovereignty in the area. He contended that the United States had only limited rights necessary for construction, maintenance and sanitary protection and servicing of the Canal.[4] He then proceeded to recite the grievances of Panama against the United States. In rebuttal, Adlai E. Stevenson, the United States Ambassador to the U.N., expressed the distress of his nation over the accusations of Panama, and promised an all-out effort to restore order.

On the same day (January 10, 1964) William Sanders, the Assistant Secretary General of the Organization of American States, told the United Nations that the OAS would review the case. Meanwhile in the UN's Security Council, Nikolai Fedorenko of the U.S.S.R. stated that the situation in Panama was the result of a great power attack upon a small Latin American nation. He expressed the belief that the gravity of the situation exceeded the competence of the

3. "Panama," *United Nations Review* (February, 1964), p. 6.
4. *Ibid.,* 10.

Organization of American States and should be examined by the United Nations. Simultaneously the President of the Inter-American Peace Committee ordered a special meeting at the request of Panama and the United States.[5] The standing committee composed of members from Argentina, Colombia, the Dominican Republic, the United States and Venezuela could not very well approach the problem. Thus Chile was elected to replace the United States, which was a party to the dispute.[6]

While the matter was being considered by both the United Nations and the Organization of American States, mobs in Panama were burning buildings and attacking the Canal Zone. With the assistance of trained agitators they inflicted considerable damage in the area. Four United States soldiers were killed as were twenty-three Panamanians. The magnitude of the battle over the Canal Zone is emphasized by the fact that United States ballistics experts retrieved over 2,000 bullets from the walls of the Tivoli Hotel, the major American bastion which was under fire for three and a half days. Destruction was not solely confined to Panama City and its environs; attacks were reported as far away as the farm center of Davíd, some 314 miles to the west.

To what extent this was an all-out war has not been ascertained by the Panamanians. But those who viewed the matter objectively realize that it would be difficult to accuse the United States of little more than defending its position. At no time during the battles did United States military personnel or police forces leave the Canal Zone for Panama. The hostilities were not as widespread as initial press reports indicated, and accounts of United States citizens being helped by Panamanian friends and neighbors are numerous. However,

5. "The Situation in Panama," *Department of State Bulletin* (February 3, 1964), p. 152.

6. *Ibid.*

matters were not enhanced when President Chiari led the demonstrations which accompanied the funeral procession for the Panamanians who perished.

On January 12, 1964, the United States was assured by the OAS Peace Committee Chairman that the matter would be given urgent attention. It was then proposed by Chairman Enrique Tejera-Paris that a joint cooperation Committee, composed of a civilian and a military representative of the Inter-American Peace Committee be established. The United States accepted this proposal on January 13, and the wheels were set in motion. The following day the White House issued the statement that President Johnson had received a full report on the situation from Secretary Mann, whose primary concern was for the security of the Panama Canal.

In conjunction with the Organization of American States Peace Committee, Edwin Martin of the United States and Galileo Solís of Panama, on January 15, 1964, agreed to engage in "*negociaciones formales*" or talks.[7] The topics of these talks were not specified, and many Americans and Panamanians misconstrued this as an attempt to negotiate the existing treaties regarding the Canal and Canal Zone. A semantical argument ensued over the translation of the Spanish word *negociaciones,* which the Americans felt meant "discussions" and the Panamanians interpreted to mean "negotiation." Both governments released the news of agreement to the public in its most appealing nationalistic form, which resulted in a good deal of confusion.[8]

The Inter-American Peace Committee urged the re-estab-

7. Allan & Sherman, *The Reporter* (February 27, 1965), p. 28.

8. The real problem was whether or not the word "*negociaciones*" in the Spanish text was equal to the English word "discussion" or the word "negotiation." There is no Spanish word for "discuss" in the context in which it is generally used in the United States, and the closest one can come is the word *discutir* which connotes a verbal conflict.

lishment of diplomatic relations between the nations since without formal channels of communication, it would be extremely difficult to reach an accord. On January 15, 1964, the OAS Committee announced the two nations' willingness to begin formal discussions. The Committee stated that discussions without limitations would be held on any and all existing problems that affected relations between the United States and Panama. In a subsequent statement to the press, President Johnson indicated that the United States had assumed the role of a nation resisting aggression in the Canal Zone, but was willing, without preconditions, to resume peaceful discussions. He further indicated that the United States was prepared, within thirty days after the restoration of relations with Panama, to discuss all existing mutual problems.[9]

Once the United States indicated a willingness to discuss grievances, Panama's demands grew by leaps and bounds. Panama took the initiative and was not about to relinquish a strategic advantage. The more the United States could be embarrassed before the watching world, the sooner concessions would be forthcoming. On January 27, 1964, the Canal Zone publication *Spillway* indicated that Panama was now demanding dual flag flying at military as well as civilian locations on the Isthmus. Various journals in Panama City exploited nationalist sentiment and tried to force the United States to relinquish the Canal Zone.

By the end of January, United States Ambassador to the OAS Ellsworth Bunker stated that his nation welcomed an investigation of the purported aggression, in order to get at the crux of the matter. However, he seriously questioned

9. "President Restates U.S. Position on Panama and Canal Zone," *Department of State Bulletin* (February 10, 1964), p. 195. Statement was made on January 23, 1964.

whether or not invocation of the Rio Pact of Reciprocal Assistance was the proper approach to the subject, since it could in no way achieve Panama's desire to revise the 1903 Treaty.[10] Ambassador Bunker expressed regret that Panama chose to terminate direct talks with the United States, and he also indicated his nation's sorrow at Panama's reluctance to deal with the United States through the Inter-American Peace Committee. The United States believed it was ludicrous for Panama to complain about aggression in 1964 when the 1903 Treaty was the cause of the problem.

Chile's Ambassador Manuel Trucio agreed with the United States assertion that the facts did not warrant the use of the Rio Treaty. Punitive measures were not needed at this juncture, but rather there was a need for understanding. Panama remained intransigent, and threatened to withdraw from the OAS if the Rio Pact were not invoked. Chile abstained on an OAS proposal to investigate the situation on the grounds that it was illegal to do so since no aggression or even aggressive intent existed. However, Chile was biased by the fear that a discussion of the 1903 Treaty between Panama and the United States might lead to discussion of the 1902 pact between Bolivia and Chile which landlocked the former.

Both Panama and the United States charged that no member of the OAS desired to become involved in an investigation. The OAS investigation team was stalemated because no nation wished to offend either disputant. The efforts of the Inter-American Peace Committee only illustrated that a tremendous amount of distrust existed between the United States and Panama. The OAS effort was too weak to be of great value, and the attempted truce arrangement failed because

10. "OAS Council Moves to Assist in Solving U.S.—Panama Dispute," *Department of State Bulletin* (February 24, 1964), p. 300.

of the semantic argument previously detailed. The OAS substantiated the fact that the communists in the Republic of Panama were not the instigators of the riots, but this did not explain the degree of their involvement once the demonstration had commenced.

After protracted discussions, on February 4, 1964, the Council of the OAS resolved to convoke the consultive machinery as provided for by the Treaty of Rio, communicate on the matter with the United Nations, and investigate the situation.[11] Panama was still charging aggression, and the United States denied the allegations, asserting that American personnel were not even armed during the conflict (only tear gas was used.)[12] Seventeen members of the OAS, excluding the United States, Panama and Bolivia which withdrew, recognized that the United States troops had used a disproportionate amount of firepower, but refused to find the United States guilty of aggression. Thus the OAS acted as an organ of consultation attempting to heal the breach, and its mediating efforts proved futile.

FOREIGN REACTION

The United States readily admitted that world opinion and reaction were on the side of Panama. Latin Americans did not judge the situation in Panama objectively, but rather on historical perspective, which in light of past United States actions in the area is a dangerous thing to do. Mexico, one of Latin America's foremost exponents of complete and equal sovereignty, indicated a willingness to mediate the dispute. The Mexican daily, *Excelsior,* generally a pro-United States

11. *Ibid.,* p. 303.
12. *Ibid.,* p. 302.

organ, blamed the Americans[13] and intimated that the hostilities might have been the beginning of political or social revolution in Panama, instituted by Communists playing on leftist sentiment. The Mexicans advocated international control over the Canal, rather than continued United States domination. Both the Cuban and Mexican press correctly pointed out the inequities of the impoverished conditions of those in Panama as compared to the Zonians.

Costa Rican students demonstrated against United States policies in Panama and the Costa Rican government offered to handle Panama's diplomatic relations in the United States. Colombian leftists offered their services to President Chiari to fight for Panama's freedom. Colombian leftist sentiment was expressed in *La Voz Proletaria,* which decried United States imperialism and condemned President Valencia for his silence on the Panama question, which was felt to be tantamount to favoring the United States. In actuality the Colombian President was compelled to remain impartial since it was common knowledge that the United States was contemplating a new sea level canal and Colombia was a potential site.

Other American nations voiced their opinions of the Panama situation in various ways. Nicaraguans demonstrated against current United States policies and against the existing Nicaraguan-United States Treaty which guarantees the Americans the perpetual right of way through their nation. In El Salvador, *La Prensa Gráfica* advocated Panamanian sovereignty in the Canal Zone. Guatemala, laboring under press censorship imposed by the military, commented that the explosion in Panama was to be expected.

European journals recalled the intervention of France and

13. *Excelsior,* February 2, 1964.

Britain in the Suez controversy of 1956. In light of the Suez situation one might have expected the Europeans to defend the stand of the United States. But for the most part the Western Europeans were critical of the United States and even alluded to the American presence in Panama as "colonialism." To Europeans it seemed that if France and England must permit independence in their colonies, then the United States is obliged to do likewise. Radio Moscow denounced the imperialism of the United States, as was to be expected. Premier Nikita Khrushchev sided with the contentions of the Panamanians and urged that the United States be dealt with by the proper authorities. Somehow the Russians neglected to define what they meant by "proper authorities."

THE AFTERMATH

The riots that took place in Panama in January of 1964 were but the culmination of fifty years of protest. Any observer of the Panama scene could have foreseen the explosion. However, the United States, as has so often been the case in Latin America, was caught off guard by the hostilities and the adverse reactions of the Panamanians. Certainly there should have been an awareness of the dissension in the area by the authorities in the Canal Zone. If they were cognizant of the explosive situation in Panama they should have been prepared to cope with the consequences, if the sources of dissatisfaction were not eliminated. The Flag Riots, per se, were superficial insofar as they did not hinder the operation of the Canal, but were merely indicative of the explosive nature of the whole hemisphere. Demonstrations of this type, while not communist inspired, play into the hands of agitators who exploit them for all they are worth. In this instance injured national pride was a perfect tool for the Havana,

Moscow and Peking oriented agents. Many of the incidents during the period of rioting were obviously not merely the work of emotionally upset people, but were well calculated and executed by professionals trained to take advantage of such situations. Investigations proved that the burning of the Pan-American Airways Building was the work of professional arsonists, and numerous Molotov cocktails thrown at United States owned or operated enterprises were made by trained individuals, not by reckless amateurs.

Of the thousands of people who attended the funeral ceremonies for the victims of the riots many were investigated and few were found to be communists. In the final analysis local dissension far outweighed foreign influence during this period of turmoil. Panama's press was totally biased in favor of the cause of nationalism, while the press in the United States pleaded its own case. A key question to be decided was whether or not Governor Fleming was to blame for permitting the situation to get out of hand. Or did the *Guardia Nacional* fail to maintain order? It was strange that during the struggles the *Guardia,* which is usually equipped with pistols and clubs, was unarmed.

The ideals and development of the Alliance for Progress were struck a severe blow by the rioting of January 1964. It was impossible to conceive of United States-Panamanian cooperation when throughout the Isthmus pictures of the dead, considered as martyrs, were displayed. Panamanians changed the name of the recently named President Kennedy Avenue to the Avenue of the Martyrs, and the Zonians retaliated by boycotting the Republic of Panama.[14] American citizens and capital returned to the United States, and Panama's economy suffered. Even impartial foreign investors in Panama

14. From January 1964 until March 1964, 95% of the Zonians did not set foot in Panama.

withdrew their capital fearing that the economy might drop to a percentage insufficient to keep pace with the population growth and inflation. Potentially more disastrous was the fact that Panama, in order to avert a recession, was forced to open trade to the Soviet Bloc nations. On the other hand, Panamanians continued to enter the Canal Zone in order to work, as the loss of their wages would greatly retard Panama's already stagnating economy.

Panama's Bar Association requested that the International Commission of Jurists, a Geneva based private organization of judges and lawyers from the non-communist world, investigate and rule whether or not the United States violated three articles of the United Nations Declaration of Human Rights. Under scrutiny were Article 3, individual right to life, liberty and security of person; Article 5, the right to freedom from torture; and Article 20, the right to peaceful assembly and association.[15] The Commission acquitted the United States on all three counts and indicated that American action, while at times harsh, was nevertheless justified. The jurists also criticized the indifferent Zonians who have not, over the years, induced harmony with the Panamanians. Washington too was criticized by the Commission for not reorienting the Zonians. The government of Panama was taken to task for failing in the early hours of the conflict to control the violence of the mobs. Even the news media were condemned for inciting instead of curtailing violence.[16]

In the United States the episode of January 1964 was not a closed book. The Senate Foreign Relations Committee criticized the administration for not having an Ambassador in Panama for some four months prior to the hostilities. Senator

15. *New York Times,* January 29, 1964.

16. "Panama," *Hispanic American Report* (August, 1964), p. 509.

Everett Dirksen, leader of the Republican minority, blamed the United States for the incidents. He indicated that the difficulties originated with the concession permitting the Panamanian flag to fly in the Canal Zone. Dirksen implied that after nearly sixty years the Democratic Johnson Administration was capitulating to the Republic of Panama.[17] Professor J. Fred Rippy, a respected Latin Americanist, opined that the violence in Panama in January 1964 illustrated "the high cost of appeasement, if not the futility of foreign aid in the case of new nations characterized by political and economic underdevelopment."[18] Dr. Rippy implied that the Panamanians were ungrateful for all of the United States help over the years and are still endeavoring to gain additional concessions from the Americans. Future developments proved Professor Rippy's analysis to be both perspicacious and cogent.

The question still remains, to what degree were the Flag Riots premeditated or spontaneous. Only those involved can answer this with some modicum of accuracy. The entire episode is confusing and filled with paradoxes. A Panamanian engineer, in July of 1965, attested to this when he averred: "I was one of the very first to shout aggression, and do you know, it was six or seven months later before I had even a fair idea of what really happened on January 9th. I'm still not completely sure, I am sure that it wasn't as bad as we were given to believe at that time."[19]

As soon as some of the clamor died down, Governor Robert J. Fleming attempted to mollify the Panamanians by announcing that he would hire Panamanians as Zone Police.

17. Dubois, p. 356.
18. Rippy, "The United States and Panama: The High Cost of Appeasement," *Inter-American Economic Affairs* (Spring, 1964), p. 87.
19. Whelan, *The Latin American Times,* July 6, 1965, p. 2.

United States citizen members of the existing force were furious. This negative reaction by the American police was absurd in the light of the fact that for years Panamanians had served as Zone firemen. In actuality the security of the Zone might be enhanced by the addition of Panamanian police whom fellow nationals might be reluctant to attack. Despite the additional concession, the attacks on the United States by the Panamanian press did not abate. The United States was criticized for not paying sufficient rent for railroad facilities in Panama City and for selling water to ships passing through the Canal. In arguing for a greater share of the profits from both of these enterprises, the Panamanians neglected to realize that the United States built all of the appurtences involved and supplied their services to both Panama City and Colón.

On February 14, 1964, Secretary of State Dean Rusk, in an interview with the Voice of America, indicated that the United States would not be bullied into a new canal commitment.[20] Panama began to feel the effects of the riots, and although Canal traffic did not decrease, many tourist ships no longer docked at Panama City or Colón. Those that stopped did not disembark passengers for fear of violence. As a result the economy of the nation was thrown into a mild depression.

In early March, 1964, hearings before the United States House of Representatives brought denunciations of Panama's action during the previous January. Panama's government was labeled irresponsible for not calling out the *Guardia Nacional* when violence broke out, and for failing to arrest left wing agitators who took advantage of the situation. In mid-March a decision involving the White House, the Secretary of State, and Under Secretary of State Thomas Mann

20. "Secretary Rusk Interviewed on Voice of America," *Department of State Bulletin* (March 2, 1964), p. 335.

was announced. The United States disavowed its acceptance of the truce, which Panama had announced earlier. The United States predicated its action on the grounds that the Panamanians had rewritten President Johnson's statement regarding the truce. Thus endless caviling ensued. On the 16th of March, President Johnson, in an address to the delegates of the OAS commemorating the third anniversary of the Alliance for Progress, stated that he did not believe he and President Chiari had arrived at any genuine agreement. Actually, he was making a plea for some accord on the basis that the disagreement with Panama could prove detrimental to the purpose of the *Alianza* insofar as other Latin American nations were concerned. At the same time the President indicated that the United States was not about to be forced to rewrite the 1903 Treaty with Panama just to insure hemispheric solidarity. In other words, the United States would not be coerced for the purpose of preserving OAS unity.

It was not until April 3, 1964, that the United States and Panama agreed to designate special Ambassadors with sufficient powers to seek prompt elimination of the causes of friction between the two countries without limitations or preconditions of any kind. Noticeable in this agreement was the absence of phrases containing the words "discuss" or "negotiate," and even the Canal was not specifically mentioned. Also on April 3, 1964, through a White House press release, President Johnson informed the President of Panama that former Secretary of the Treasury Robert B. Anderson was being designated as Special Ambassador to carry on discussions with the Panamanians, and that Jack Hood Vaughn was being appointed regular Ambassador to the Republic of Panama.[21] Mr. Vaughn, formerly Regional Director for the Peace Corps in Latin America, assumed this post on April 17, 1964.

21. "United States and Panama Re-establish Diplomatic Relations," *Department of State Bulletin* (April 27, 1964), p. 655.

At the same time, President Chiari appointed Jorge Illueca, editor of *El Panamá American,* president of Panama's Bar Association, and former delegate to the United Nations, to begin talks with the United States.

The Republican Citizens Committee Critical Issues Council, under the direction of Dr. Milton Eisenhower, President of Johns Hopkins University, released a report on Panama in April 1967. The Committee's report recommended the following:[22]

1. Improve the present Canal at a cost of seventy-five million dollars.
2. Increase tolls by 30 per cent and Panama's annuity to fifteen million dollars.
3. Pay off the Canal debt of four hundred sixty million dollars to the United States Treasury.
4. Rotate American civilian personnel in the Canal Zone every two years where possible.
5. Train more Panamanians for technical positions in the Canal.
6. Extend the United States aid program in Panama.
7. Agree to negotiate a new treaty for a sea level canal within twenty-five years.

The Democratic administration did not react immediately to the Republican recommendations, but many of the ideas were subsequently incorporated into the administration's thinking. Certainly the Panamanians could find little to criticize in the proposals. The measures would stabilize the economy of the nation, reduce the United States claims to the territory in dispute, eliminate sources of individual friction, and begin to create a new image for the United States on the Isthmus.

22. See *The Panama Canal Its Past and Future* (Washington: American Enterprise Institute for Public Policy Research, 1964), p. 54.

In May of 1964, Ambassadors Anderson and Illueca began formal negotiations to eliminate the causes of friction between their respective nations. At this time Panama indicated that it would no longer push for treaty revision, but preferred economic benefits instead. Specifically Panama was desirous of eliminating the Zonian's commissary privileges, thus compelling the force of 36,000 to make their purchases in Panama. Also Panama desired equal job opportunities for its citizens in the Canal Zone. When President Johnson, on May 6, 1964, received Miguel J. Moreno, Jr., the new Ambassador from Panama, a new era in Panamanian relations with the United States was inaugurated, a period of protracted discussion and negotiation.

INTERNAL POLITICS

Unfortunately 1964 was an election year, and at such times the United States has traditionally been Panama's whipping boy. Panama's active political parties all had Presidential candidates, but Arnulfo Arias, representing the *Panameñistas,* was an overwhelming favorite. Dr. Arias ran on a platform which avoided connection with anti-United States propaganda. Immediately he was labeled a tool of the Yankees, but this had little to do with his defeat. Actually, Dr. Arias was unable to repudiate his past record, which linked him with the Nazis during World War II, and he was defeated by a slight margin at the polls by Marco Aurelio Robles.

Robles, a cousin of President Chiari, was the choice of a small ruling oligarchy which has controlled Panama since its independence. Marco Robles had the backing of Chiari, the *Partido Nacional Liberal* and a government coalition of eight parties. The new President was a humorless man, an unimpressive orator called "The Rifle" because of his toughness, and less chauvinistic than his predecessor. This banker-politician lacked the dynamism that Latin Americans love, but was a hardnosed law enforcer who, in order to preclude a repetition of the violence of the previous January, would press for and obtain the enactment of an anti-terrorist law.

The Robles government knew that it must obtain concessions from the United States in order to maintain power. As early as May 1964, Robles demanded that the United States revise the 1903 Treaty. His campaign advisor, David Samudio, head of Panama's National Planning Institute, proposed specific points to be raised with United States Special Ambassador Robert B. Anderson. The following points were integrated with the Liberal Party's platform.[23]

1. Panamanian partnership in the administration of the Canal.
2. Increased Canal tolls.
3. Increased amounts of income from the Canal accruing to Panama.
4. Return to Panama of all the territory in the ten mile by fifty mile zone not used in the operation maintenance or sanitation of the area.
5. Requirement that all Zone residents pay income and property taxes in Panama.
6. Relinquishment of the thriving ports of Cristobal and Balboa to Panama.

Although this was a prodigious request, it was not out of the realm of possibility.

Throughout the 1964 presidential campaign in Panama the Canal Zone was not a major issue, since all seven candidates favored negotiating a revision of the 1903 Treaty. Other issues prevailed such as tax reform, as recommended by the Alliance

23. "Panama," *Hispanic American Report,* (September, 1964), p. 608.

for Progress and advocated by Señor Robles. This turned out to be an unpopular move because those with influence in Panama are also those with affluence. When Robles subsequently emerged victorious, the rival factions, and the *Panameñistas* in particular, claimed fraud. The defeated opposition feared reforms would be wrought and accused the Liberals of perpetrating illegal acts at the polls. Bombs and Molotov cocktails were hurled in prominent public places, and at the home of ex-President Chiari, in protest. Some *Fidelista* and communist sympathizers took part in the minor hostilities.

In June of 1964 President-elect Marco A. Robles spent ten days in New York resting and conferring with David Rockefeller, president of Chase Manhattan Bank, and other industrialists. He made a plea for United States investment in Panama's future and expressed the hope that close relations between the two nations would continue. At this time President Chiari made a State visit to Washington as a result of the discussions of the Joint United States-Panama Commission. There he discussed the points of disagreement between the two countries and reached an accord concerning the flying of the Panamanian flag in the Canal Zone.

Relations between the nations seemed to be improving and Canal traffic soared to record heights. As the July 4th holiday approached the Americans in the Canal Zone contemplated the traditional Panamanian protests. True to expectations students demonstrated against United States policies, although banned from doing so by the Panamanian authorities. As a mob gathered and began to march on Shaler Triangle, it was intercepted by the *Guardia Nacional* which dispersed it, as it did another group gathering in front of the *Instituto Nacional* near the Canal Zone border. It appeared that another incident of Flag Riot proportions was about to begin. But the Panamanian authorities quelled the disturbance after only a ten-minute altercation led by Floyd Britton, the well known agitator. The *Guardia* was not reluctant, as it had been the previous January, to use tear gas and rifle butts to dissuade the demonstrators.

On August 7, 1964, Señor Manuel Moreno, Jr., who had served as ambassador to the United States since April 3, 1964, resigned his position. Ambassador Moreno was dissatisfied with his role in the negotiations with the United States and felt restrained by his President. This resignation was received pessimistically by Panamanians everywhere. The following day, August the 8th, *El Panamá America* stated: "It is fundamental that the people of this country know that construction of a sea level canal will mean the elimination of the 'Canal Zone' concept, which involves a basic fact of incalculable consequences, not only for the integrity of the nation and for the dignity of the country, but also for the economic independence and development possibilities of the human and natural resources which we possess."[24] The following few days in Panama were hectic as students continued to protest against everything from the resignation of Ambassador Moreno to the existence of poor educational facilities.

Fortunately no major eruptions took place between August 1964 and October 1, 1964, when President Marco A. Robles was inaugurated. It was hoped that Panama's thirty-third President could stabilize the dissension ridden nation. As the new President assumed his office, Panama still showed physical signs of the January 1964 riots. The ruins of the burned-out Pan-American Airways Building stood as a monument to the tumult of the times. The economy was faltering badly, the national deficit had reached twenty million dollars, and unemployment was approaching the twenty per cent

24. *El Panamá América,* August 8, 1964.

mark. Immediately the new Chief Executive began to work toward gaining or recouping the capital deposits that had been withdrawn from Panama after the riots. The government wondered whether or not United States aid would be forthcoming, as the tenor of feeling in Panama was anticipatory.

THE UNITED STATES RELENTS

The period of anticipation was short lived as, on December 18, 1964, President Lyndon B. Johnson made a startling announcement to the world. On the recommendation of Special Ambassador Robert Anderson, Secretary Mann, and Ambassador Vaughn, with the concurrence of former Presidents Truman and Eisenhower, President Johnson stated that he would propose to the government of Panama the negotiation of an entirely new treaty pertaining to the Canal and Canal Zone.[25] At the same time he announced that the United States was pressing forward negotiations with Panama and other interested nations, preparatory to the construction of a new sea level Canal. The President stated: "This government has completed an intensive review of policy toward the present and future of the Panama Canal."[26] The United States Congress authorized seventeen million dollars for studies of possible sites for the proposed sea level canal, and the government of Panama was informed that the United States would now meet her demands and begin negotiating a treaty to replace the one of 1903. The new treaty was to recognize the sovereignty of Panama and to provide for its own termination when a new sea level canal was in existence. Also,

25. "U.S. Plans New Sea Level Canal and New Treaty on Existing Canal," *Department of State Bulletin,* (January 4, 1965), p. 5.
26. *Ibid.*

the new treaty was to provide for hemispheric defense. Of course, the present treaties were to continue in effect until new accords could be reached.[27]

The willingness of the United States to accede to the demands of the Panamanians was not news to the Canal Company officers, but it caught the government of Panama off guard. So significant did Panama deem the news that Foreign Minister Fernando Eleta canceled an appearance before the United Nations in order to return home for consultations.[28] President Johnson's message was warmly received in Panama as a token of victory and for a few weeks the Panamanians were delighted. A serious blow to anti-United States propaganda had been delivered. Many of Panama's non-communist leftists and nationalists were chagrined, for they believed that this was a delaying tactic and that concessions from the United States would never be forthcoming. Then too, many of these persons were perplexed simply because they had devoted their efforts to agitating against the United States and now might have to find other outlets for their energies.

President Robles called the United States decision transcendental and proclaimed December 18 an historic day, favorable to Panama's demands. He hoped that it would terminate the odious policy of "perpetuity."[29] Despite the overt enthusiasm for President Johnson's announcement, Panamanians realized that the process of reaching agreement would not be easy. The simultaneous negotiation of two treaties would entail work, and considerable time would be consumed trying to reach an accord that would be mutually

27. *Ibid.*
28. Paul Kennedy, "Panama Ponders Policy on Canal," *New York Times,* December 21, 1964.
29. *New York Times,* December 18, 1964.

beneficial. Sixty-one years of internal friction and diplomatic discord could not be eradicated overnight.

RECENT EVENTS

Since resuming diplomatic relations with the United States, the government of Panama has been surprisingly cooperative. It is questionable whether the Panamanians have an alternative. The answer is not simple. The only viable alternative to cooperating with the United States would be to turn to the Communist Bloc. However, few Panamanians wish their nation to become another Cuba. At the time of this writing both the United States and Panama are laboring under an aura of amicable settlement. On the surface Panama is more tranquil than at any time since early 1963. Bomb attempts have subsided, and even though the United States personnel and their families still receive numerous threats, pressures seem to have eased.

The government of Panama has urged its citizens to desist from anti-United States action which might impede the progress of negotiations, and the *Guardia Nacional* under the command of Bolivar Villarino is valiantly endeavoring to preserve the peace. However, this internal police force has been spread thin, particularly in well populated Colón and the more remote areas of the nation. On January 9, 1965, the first anniversary of the Flag Riots, President Robles urged calm and posted national guardsmen in critical places to deter or surpress demonstrations. In observance of the 1964 riots, Panamanians maintained their flags at half mast for three days, but no violence occurred.

President Robles has turned out to be a good friend of the United States, but one who is under extreme pressure to secure concessions from the Yankees. Furthermore, the position of President Robles has been anything but secure. He has become increasingly more unpopular with the entrepreneur class who find his reforms reduce their profits, and there have been reports that members of the oligarchy would even deal with the communists to upset Robles. Nevertheless, the President of Panama has more popular support than his immediate predecessors. However, he may turn out to be primarily a "lip service" reformer, as changes in the system are difficult to achieve in light of debts owed to the political machine.

President Marco Robles is giving unknown, but qualified, individuals trials in government posts, thus causing insecurity among the old tested administrators. He has been appointing people to positions not exclusively by party, but by capabilities—a most difficult thing for Panamanians to comprehend. Many an old-time politician has begun to feel uneasy. A curious example of what President Robles has endeavored to accomplish took place during the summer of 1965. A young, thoroughly trained Panamanian economist was entrusted with the difficult task of collecting taxes for President Robles. For the first time in history the nation's largest companies had their books audited, and this they deeply resented. Ultimately the young man was dismissed from his position because he moved too far too rapidly and stepped on too many toes. Nevertheless, this was a beginning and is thrilling to those who have long awaited a much needed reform program in Panama.

As for the key members of the Robles administration, they should be judged as individuals and not merely as representatives of the regime. Some of Robles' advisors are genuinely interested in the welfare of their nation, but others are not so altruistic. Panama's current ambassador to the United States, ex-President Ricardo "Dicky" Arias is a suave and erudite American-trained physician who, although not warmly received during the Eisenhower administration, is well thought of in Washington social circles. The man in the street in Panama feels "Dicky" Arias is pro-United States and not sympathetic to the needs of his nation. One must not think of everyone as either for or against the United States but must allow for the individual who is primarily motivated by self-interest, which many believe Ambassador Arias to be.

The Foreign Service of a nation often reflects the attitudes and ideas of its ambassador and not necessarily the thinking of its people. Although Ambassador Arias is not particularly well liked by his own people, he has built rapport with the Americans. Perhaps that says little for the discernment of the Americans; nevertheless it is a fact of life. Ambassador Arias is realistic enough to know that Panama's economy is permanently linked to that of the United States. For example, in Philadelphia in April of 1965, while addressing the American Academy of Political and Social Science, Ambassador Arias made a plea for additional United States Alliance for Progress aid. The request of the sophisticated Arias was well received by Washington officialdom.

On April 20, 1965, President Johnson announced the appointment of Charles Wallace Adair, Jr., as United States Ambassador to Panama.[30] Ambassador Adair came to Panama City from a post as Deputy Chief of Mission in Buenos Aires. A fifty-one year old career Foreign Service Officer, Ambassador Adair had gained Latin American experience by serving in Mexico. Simultaneously President Johnson announced the appointment of John N. Irwin II of New York as Special Representative of the United States for inter-

30. "Servicio Información De Los Estados Unidos," *Boletín de Prensa y Radio Panamá*, República de Panamá, Communicado No. 330 (20 de abril de 1965).

oceanic canal negotiations. Mr. Irwin carried the personal rank of Ambassador and was to utilize his legal expertise to try to expedite talks with Panama.[31] Thus the United States was now represented in Panama by two new men in addition to Ambassador Anderson and by the Governor of the Canal Zone, whom many believe to be the real voice of America in Panama City. At the time of this writing it is too early to pass judgment upon these individuals who serve the United States in Panama. However, if stability is to be encouraged in Panama, then continuity of policy must be maintained by our diplomats in that nation. Specialists in Panamanian affairs must remain in their posts and not be promoted to positions in India or Africa where their experience on the Isthmus goes for naught.

Panamanian President Robles appointed Fernando Eleta as Foreign Minister, to whom fell the task of continuing to press for concessions without damaging relations between the nations. This diplomatic tack has been, and must continue to be, successful if Panama is to eventually have the Treaty of 1903 modified. When one realizes that the Treaty has never been modified, only amended twice, it is evident that Señor Eleta's job is formidable.

By summer of 1965 the government of Panama was striving to curtail incidents that might prove injurious to relations with the United States. Despite the concerted effort of the Robles administration, periodically the Panamanian press comes forth with headlines exclaiming such idiocies as *"Estados Unidos Compro La Zona Del Canal"* (United States bought the Canal Zone) which appeared in *La Prensa* on June 30, 1965.[32] This ludicrous statement was predicated upon an article published in *Christian Economics* spreading the idea

31. *Ibid.*
32. *La Prensa,* June 30, 1965.

that the United States had paid for the Canal Zone and thus it did not belong to Panama. The article categorized the Canal along with the Louisana and Alaska purchases and indicated that negotiations were absurd. Since the title to the Canal is supposedly vested in the United States and the United States feels that Panama is "well off" because of the Canal, negotiations are unnecessary. It is precisely this type of sensationalism that exacerbates nationalism and causes demonstrative anti-American sentiment to be unleashed. Yet President Robles has not endeavored to throttle the free press, but rather by the utilization of friendly persuasion has tried to illustrate the foolishness of upsetting the United States when progress toward desired goals is being made.

Panama is now strangely quiet. Incidents and demonstrations in 1965 and 1966 have been few and far between. In May of 1965 at the beginning of the academic year, a group of 6,000 students demonstrated. This harmless incident was the result of excess energy built up over the vacation period combined with the fact that a few students spent time in Castro's Cuba. Even during the crisis in the Dominican Republic in April of 1965 Panama did not react violently as might have been expected. While other Latin American nations protested against the United States intervention in Santo Domingo, officially Panama remained mute. Although anti-United States posters and leaflets abounded on the University campus and the United States was criticized for a return to "Big Stick" diplomacy of Theodore Roosevelt, the government realized that the communist situation, which supposedly fostered the United States invasion of the Dominican Republic, might be repeated on the Isthmus at some future date. Numerous Panamanians were of the opinion that President Johnson acted rapidly in the Dominican Republic because of the lesson learned in Panama in January of 1964.

Enlightened Panamanians with whom the writer discussed the Dominican crisis were of the opinion that some type of action was necessary to prevent another Cuba. However, they unanimously rejected United States unilateral action. The Panamanians felt the bypassing of the machinery of the Inter-American system to be a supreme insult. They believed that the Americans should have informed the nations of the hemisphere of their intention and offered them an opportunity to partake of a joint peace keeping venture in the Dominican Republic. But the Panamanians are realistic and know full well that the OAS is a weak organization, operating behind a façade of juridical equality and sovereignty for all states. When the United States subsequently turned over peace-keeping duties in the Dominican Republic to a combined OAS force, this confirmed the conviction that the hasty action of the United States irreparably destroyed the "non-interventionist" image that the Americans had labored to build since the 1930's.

In September of 1965 the United States House of Representatives passed by a 312–52 vote a bill authorizing intervention in Latin America or the hemisphere to prevent the spread of communism. Latin Americans were irate to think that, in light of the criticism of the intervention in the Dominican Republic, the United States could entertain such a proposal. Panamanians vehemently opposed the measure, which did not become law, but they offered no official protest.[33]

In both January of 1966 and 1967 as Panama observed the second and third anniversaries of the Flag Riots the nation was unusually restrained, as her diplomats endeavored to rectify the ills of the past and forge a better future.

33. It was not approved by the Senate. This abortive action gives rise to the ancient question of whether or not foreign policy can be legislated.

CHAPTER
EIGHT

Existing Problems

The people of Panama live in fear of awaking one morning to find that their precious Panama Canal has been closed. In this age of inter-continental ballistic missiles, the waterway, which has steadily diminished in military importance, is still the foremost feature of Panama's economy. How can the quest for a better life be attained as the significance of the Canal is reduced? The economy of the nation is already stagnating as the country's balance of payments shows a persistent deficit.[1]

Ever since Panama was an isolated and neglected Province of Colombia she has struggled for existence and sought independence and her own place in the hemisphere. Today the problems confronting Panama are numerous and diverse. Together with the sagging economy, tax reform is badly needed. The nation's population is overwhelmingly concentrated around the Canal, and migrations from rural areas increase daily. The nation's twenty-one main towns and cities outside of the Canal area are too small and lack the economic

1. According to the United Nations' *Comisión Económica para la América Latina,* Panama's GNP decreased 1.5% in 1964, while the rest of the nations of Latin America showed increases ranging from 1.1% to 10%.

potential to attract those seeking employment, while the major cities attract more persons than they can assimilate and employ. With this difficulty go the corresponding problems of a shortage in housing and expanding slums.[2]

As a result of the complexity of problems Panama is frustrated and vents its wrath upon the United States. In like manner, the United States is often used as a scapegoat by politicians who are to a great degree responsible for exploiting the people. To compound the difficulties, the people of Panama do not comprehend their own racial problems. For example, Jamaicans are resented by Panamanians who feel that they get the better jobs and vice versa. Frustrations in Panama are evident everywhere as the citizens are unusually surly, and it is at times impossible to get someone to perform a service gracefully.

As more concessions are made and United States influence is phased out, nationalism increases. So intense has this nationalism become that some Panamanians go to great lengths to annoy the United States, and have demonstrated their contempt by supporting such opponents of democracy as Algeria's deposed dictator Ben Bella and Cuba's Castro. *Nationalista* and *Hispanidad* parties, which are theoretically opposed to Communism, ally with it for the purpose of gathering anti-Yankee sentiment. The *Sinarquistas* who favor Spain's Franco and France's DeGaulle are also allied with the anti-American front. The preceding pages have offered many reasons for the anti-Yankee feelings in Panama, but the difference in the relative power of the respective nations has not been mentioned. This in itself engenders jealousy, a major cause of resentment.

Both Panama's external and internal problems require

2. Every first-time visitor to Panama City is asked his opinion of "Hollywood," a choice slum.

patience and understanding, and President Robles is attempting to do the impossible by creating harmony with the United States, while eleminating the causes of discord at home by enacting the necessary reforms which Panama's oligarchy has so long resisted. Repeatedly the oligarchy uses the Canal to divert attention from its own malpractices. A classic example of this type of manipulation was the 1960 Eisenhower nine-point program which was surpressed in the nation's press in order to prevent the easing of resentment toward the United States. Panama's ills cannot be cured overnight and unfortunately the Robles administration's ultimate success will be curtailed by the nation's Constitution which prohibits presidential succession. The absence of succession or even *continuismo* has always proved detrimental to the stability and continuity of policy and will have an adverse effect upon relations with the United States as President Robles will not have sufficient time to carry his policies through to fruition.

The foremost question in the minds of many is whether or not United States policy regarding the Panama Canal is obsolete. There can be no doubt that the Canal is on its way to obsolescence. By 1980 inter-oceanic traffic will exceed the capacity of the "Big Ditch." Panamanians are cognizant of the fact that United States Isthmian policy has not kept pace with the times and wonder if it will remain a vestige of the past. Then again, who would have thought in 1914 that within a half century fifty per cent of Japan's exports would pass through the Panama Canal, or that by 1965 approximately seventy-five United States vessels alone would be too large for the Canal.[3] In addition, there are approximately 125 to 130 ships in the world or under construction that are too large to enter the Canal's locks and almost six hundred

3. John W. Finney, "A Second Canal?," *The New Republic,* (March 28, 1964), p. 22.

ships which cannot pass through the locks fully laden.

Panama rises and falls on the prosperity of the Canal, a situation hardly conducive to stability. The Atlantic terminal city of Colón which prospered during World War II and the Korean conflict is now financially depressed, and aside from the Free Trade Zone business fluctuates according to Canal usage. Although Canal traffic has increased from thirty-six million tons annually to sixty-five million tons per year in the past ten years, other factors have decreased its efficiency and damaged Panama's economy. For instance, ships often wait for fifteen hours or more to pass through the Canal, and when they complete the passage they do not have time to dock at Panama City or Colón.

Panamanians contend that their ills would be cured if the United States were expelled from the Isthmus. But the real question that has to be answered is not whether the United States should control the Canal, but whether Panama could handle the job adequately. If Panama ran the Canal, would she benefit more or less than if it continues under United States jurisdiction? It is obvious that Panama does not have the technical personnel to run a gigantic operation like the Panama Canal. Not only are trained individuals required for the actual operation of the locks, but a vast number of supplementary personnel are necessary to maintain the sanitation and health of the Canal employees.

Perhaps the most pressing need, if Panama were to run the Canal, would be for pilots to guide world shipping safely through the intricate system of channels and locks. None of the 150 Canal pilots are Panamanians. This is a source of considerable criticism and nationalist propaganda, and the situation should be rectified. Currently to qualify as a Canal pilot it is mandatory that an individual have a Master's Certificate, command experience, and then undergo a period of apprenticeship. Under existing laws the required Master's Certificate is issued by the United States Coast Guard to United States citizens. The problem is not insurmountable and could be resolved by an act of Congress which would revise the law. The United States would be well advised to do so in light of Panama's constant and justified complaints about employment discrimination.

The United States is undergoing a period of inflationary costs in the operation of the Panama Canal. This is primarily attributable to wage increases which have come rapidly in the past few years for more than 14,000 Canal employees. The primary source of income for the Panama Canal Company is still tolls, which have risen little since 1914. At the same time the annuity paid by the United States to Panama has increased, and it is only through the increased Canal traffic that the Company has managed to remain solvent. Contrary to the common belief in Panama, the United States does not extract an excessive profit from the Canal and the total Canal investment has not been retired. Of the gross investment of $1.6 billion spent on the Canal enterprise over the years, the United States has recovered only $1.1 billion dollars. Nevertheless, Panama has continued to receive a yearly income not based upon the cost of operations adjustments.

The question is often asked whether Panama's primary quarrel is with United States foreign policy, Canal policy or Zone policy. A differentiation must be made in order to clarify the problem. Panamanians contend that the elimination of the American controlled Canal Zone would alleviate considerable tension on the Isthmus. The Panama Canal Zone is like a huge company town under the direction of the Panama Canal Company. The Canal Zone Governor controls civil affairs, health and sanitation, internal security, the Magistrate Courts as well as the social work in the area. Residents of the area, who are United States citizens, are treated and taxed as if they were living in the United States. The administration in the Canal Zone has not endeavored to make its thousands of American employees conscious of the fact that they live in a foreign land, nor do they acquire a comprehension of the culture and philosophy of their host nation.

Panama traditionally has painted an "Ugly American" picture of those privileged to work and reside in the Canal Zone. Panamanians contend that the Canal Zone is the epitome of colonialism, and that the United States fails to realize that the era of imperialism has passed. However, relinquishment of the Zone to the government of Panama is not a simple proposition. Canal Zone workers have militated against this move for years as they fear that many of their jobs would be lost. So strong has the lobbying by Canal employees and their unions been that the Zonian has come to feel secure in the belief that he will not see Panamian control of the Zone in his lifetime. It is interesting to note that while virtually all Panamanians would like to see their nation control the Zone, and all United States Zonians prefer the status quo, Americans who reside in Panama outside of the Zone generally concur with the Panamanians. Zonians contend that these American residents of Panama are jealous of privileges which do not extend to them. However, this is an unrealistic viewpoint, as the non-Zonian Americans are in a position to be more objective.

A major bone of contention between the United States and Panama in the Zone has been the "tropical differential," or elevated rate of pay given to United States employees. The justification for the twenty-five per cent higher wage was valid in 1903 when an American worker had to endure the hazards of malaria, dysentery, yellow fever, the lack of roads, running water and general sanitation. These hardships have now abated, yet the United States citizen still receives a 15 per cent "differential." Panamanians validly claim that this is unjustifiable discrimination. Traditionally there have been two kinds of workers in the Canal Zone, the United States or "gold rate" workers who hold choice positions, and the Panamanians or "silver rate" workers who hold inferior positions. The situation is not conducive to harmony, especially when there is a high standard of living in the Canal Zone and the opposite is true in Panama.

As of 1966 hourly wages in the Canal Zone ranged from 80 cents to $3.10, while for commensurate work in Panama workers received 20 cents to 45 cents per hour. In addition, privileges and fringe benefits in the Zone far exceed those in the Republic of Panama. Why should a United States citizen in the Canal Zone receive a higher wage than his Panamanian counterpart? Or even more important, why should he have a better life than a similar worker in the United States? Should the Zonian's life be filled with unnecessary luxuries if he is pursuing the occupation of his choice? Or is the Zonian there merely for the higher income available on the Isthmus?

Zone executives claim the "differential" compensates for the low salaries they receive as opposed to executives in private industry. On the other hand, most government executives in the United States are underpaid by corporate standards, but do not receive anything approximating the "differential." Why then is the worker in the Canal Zone singled out for special treatment? With the addition of the "differential," the majority of the Zonians engaged in menial tasks are overpaid and live better than their counterparts in the United States. The problem is at best difficult and can only be resolved to everybody's satisfaction by paying equal salaries to all.

The "differential" is not the only matter which perturbs the Panamanians with reference to the Canal Zone. Zonians purchase goods, at lower prices than available in Panama City, at the numerous commissaries run by the Panama Canal Company. Everything short of prostitution is for sale in the commissaries and Post Exchanges in the Canal Zone, and Panamanians feel this competition with their businesses should be eliminated. The ability to remain in the Zone for all of the comforts of life contributes to a Canal Zone snobbery. To the Panamanian, the Zonian appears to be a predatory, security conscious individual, who reaps the fruits of the welfare state. This attitude reflects envy, greed or competition and is a cause of considerable bitterness.

The Zonian lives at the will of the United States Congress which regulates his wages and his life. The resident of the Zone is disenfranchised, insofar as local government is concerned, although many Zonians vote in the United States by absentee ballot. Zonians contend that they incur many additional expenses which the average American does not. They cite the excessive cost of making the trips to the United States for family reunions and of sending children to colleges and universities in the United States. Zonians feel deprived because they cannot own property in the Canal Zone and must rent their homes.

In the final analysis, the grievances of the Zonians are superficial. Are not employees everywhere subject to the whims and caprices of their employers? Cannot the conscientious Zonian vote in national elections in absentia, and indirectly have a say in Canal Zone government? Is it not true that Zonians receive a free trip to the United States every two years? How many Americans living in areas removed from their loved ones have similar advantages? How many would reject the opportunity to occupy a spacious rented home in a tropical climate with the security of knowing that even the grass will be cut regularly by the government? Unfortunately the grass is always greener on the other side, and in this case the other side is thousands of miles away.

Panamanians constantly complain that discrimination is practiced in the Canal Zone. They resent the fact that natives who work in the Zone do not get the preferred positions and that the numerous military personnel there are really a class unto themselves. Despite the fact that many Zonians are married to Panamanians, who may be of mixed blood, segregation persists in the Canal Zone. This de facto segregation, a carryover from the days of Canal construction, is all-pervading and applies to schools and residential areas alike. Panamanians even discriminate against themselves in the Zone, as West Indians feel they receive only the most servile jobs, while *Latinos* fare better. Conversely, those of Latin extraction, who contemptuously call the West Indians *Chambos,* feel they are suffering because the United States does not dichotomize *Latinos* and Jamaicans, and those of indigenous extraction complain about unfair treatment meted out by all others.

English has traditionally been the official language of the Canal Zone, much to the dismay of the Panamanians. Few Zonians are conversant in Spanish and even signs in the Zone are in English. Spanish speaking workers in the area have been compelled to become acquainted with English or else be exposed to the hazards of being a stranger in a foreign land. On the other hand, the Zonians have never striven to acquire Spanish, which many of them deem superfluous. This is a prime insult to the natives, who feel that it is indicative of the low esteem in which they are held by the Yankees. At least an attempt at speaking Spanish would be appreciated by the people of Panama. This seems unusual in contrast to

Texas, where Spanish has been a requirement in the elementary schools for decades as part of the good neighbor policy directed toward Mexico. Recent attempts to teach Spanish in the Canal Zone schools have been farcical, as they have been introduced more for propaganda purposes than anything else. English speaking Americans tend to congregate together in the Canal Zone, and college age American students are rarely found on the campus of Panama's National University. For the most part, Zonians are reluctant to permit their offspring to be imbued with the Latin culture and prefer to send them to the United States for higher education and employment.

The Canal Zone presents a problem to Panama's Customs authorities. Zonians encourage smuggling, as huge quantities of liquor and cigarettes, in particular, are brought from the Canal Zone into the Republic of Panama. This problem stems from the fact that goods are cheaper in the Zone, and can only be rectified by making the Zonians purchase all of their wants in Panama, thus eliminating the need for contraband. Other problems of nuisance value to the authorities have arisen from time to time out of the existence of the Canal Zone. For example, for years Panamanians were required to have Zone driver's licenses prior to entering the area. The existence of dual postal services has long been confusing to Panamanians, and the government of Panama contends that it constitutes a deprivation of potential income. For decades unauthorized American personnel, such as tourists, could utilize Canal Zone facilities to the exclusion of the businesses of Panama. However since the 1964 riots, the Zone authorities have enforced the law more diligently, and the writer recently found it exceedingly difficult to make purchases in the commissaries without proper identification.

The source of this difficulty is the intense competition

between the Canal Zone Company enterprises and private businesses in Panama. Although it might be preferable to eliminate the competition altogether, if this is not feasible and business must be conducted in the Canal Zone, why not permit Panamanian businessmen to obtain concessions in the region? This would quell criticism of the "American monopoly" and enable Panama to retain many dollars which she claims are now unjustifiably lost.

DIPLOMATIC PROBLEMS

It was apparent by 1965 that President Lyndon B. Johnson desired to avoid being pressured into a commitment to negotiate differences with Panama. Internal dissensions had to be eased, and the United States Ambassador to Panama and the Canal Zone Governor, who often have major differences of opinion, had to agree upon the best course of action to pursue. Once the gap between the Pentagon and the Department of State had been bridged, then the United States could divert its attention to settlement of differences with Panama, provided there existed no preconditions and no pressures from the government of Panama.[4]

The United States could not accept Panama's offer to "negotiate" differences for fear that this would be interpreted as agreement to change the existing treaties. Also the United States did not wish to raise the hopes of Panama and all of Latin America by beginning negotiations rather than dis-

4. However, external pressures are impossible to eliminate. For example, both United States and Panamanian businessmen with interests in Panama were generally sympathetic to that nation, but often reluctant to speak out against Washington. Nevertheless, on February 24, 1964, the *San Francisco Chronicle* ran a full page advertisement sponsored by businessmen favoring renegotiation of the 1903 Treaty.

cussions. However the United States was prepared to discuss any issue with the government of Panama, as President Johnson was aware of the fact that the United States could not adhere to the rigid determination of sovereignty under the original treaty. He knew full well that the law had to be changed to fit the times.

In rejecting the authority of the United States with reference to the Canal and Canal Zone, Panamanians have repeatedly stressed the similarity between their situation and that in Suez. However they fail to realize that there is a fundamental difference between the Suez and Panama Canal situations. The Panama Canal had been governed by a bilateral treaty between the United States and Panama, whereas the Suez Canal was governed by an agreement between an international company and the Egyptian government. Thus only one government was involved in the Suez crisis in contrast to two in the Panama situation. Nevertheless, legal theoreticians believe that the 1903 Treaty was concluded in an atmosphere of ambiguity and thus is difficult to interpret.[5] Basic legal questions have to be solved, those being whether or not the Treaty of 1903 is valid and whether or not the United States violates that agreement. If the Canal were used exclusively for military purposes, then Panama would have no justifiable complaint. However, since civilians use it and occupy the Zone, the question of United States violating the Treaty of 1903 is implicit. In defense of Panama's contention, the 1903 Treaty, if judged by the standards of international law, is not a definitive legal treatise.[6]

Is it possible for two nations to share sovereignty over

5. Manuel Garcia-Mora, "The Panama Canal Controversy," *Vital Speeches* (April 15, 1964), p. 415.

6. For legal aspects see Richard R. Baxter, *The Law of International Waterways* (Cambridge: Harvard University Press, 1964).

the same area? Technically this problem was resolved by the Treaty of 1903 which provides for relations between the Canal Zone and the Republic of Panama. Since Panama does not accept the Treaty of 1903, the United States has after years of feuding decided to eliminate this primary source of consternation. When President Johnson made his historic announcement of December 18, 1964, he stated that the United States would retain its present holdings until a new waterway or canal was operational. Then the entire area covered by the 1903 Treaty would revert to Panama, provided the new waterway was not an extension of the existing one.[7]

Negotiations commenced in December, 1964, conducted by Robert Anderson assisted by Robert Newbegin for the United States and Ambassador Ricardo Arias, Dr. Roberto Aleman, Diogenes de la Rosa, Humberto Calamari and Guillermo Chapman for the Republic of Panama.[8] Canal Zone Governor Robert Fleming was not included in the conference between the nations, although he was kept informed of the proceedings. The United States wisely decided to confine the talks to the diplomatic level and keep the Canal Zone representatives, with their vested interests, out of the affair.

The talks with Panama have been conducted with an air of secrecy, with the press rarely reporting their progress. At the same time the United States has been involved in preparations necessary to enter into talks with Colombia, Nicaragua and Panama in reference to potential sites for a new interoceanic canal. These talks were designed to recognize the rights and sovereignty of Panama, or any other nation involved. The United States was not about to repeat the errors of the past. The United States would demand that the

7. *New York Times,* December 18, 1964.
8. *New York Times,* December 20, 1964.

new canal be open to all commercial traffic and that American military forces have the right of passage at all times, even if others do not.

The first step towards implementing President Johnson's new canal plans was taken in January of 1965, when Secretary of the Army Stephen Ailes and Secretary Mann began exploratory talks with Panama and visited potential new sites in Nicaragua, Panama, Costa Rica and Colombia. Throughout these preliminary discussions the United States realized that it bore the responsibility for the success or failure of the Robles regime in Panama.[9]

By July of 1965, a spokesman for the Inter-Oceanic Canal Commission stated that he hoped that an agreement with various nations would soon be reached in order that the actual survey for a new sea level canal could begin sometime that year.[10] The Commission requested that Congress immediately appropriate $7.5 million out of the total seventeen million dollars already allocated for the purpose of exploring new sea level canal possibilities. Under the watchful direction of Chairman Robert Anderson it was hoped that real progress could be made toward this end, while simultaneously solving disputes between the United States and Panama.

At this juncture one must ask whether or not a small nation such as Panama is in a position to embarrass a large one such as the United States to the point of dictating terms. In this era of Cold War, when rival blocs are vying for allies, the position of the smaller nation is strengthened.

Panama dislikes the possibility of a new canal being located outside her territory. Panama recognizes the fact that the present Canal is obsolete but is ambivalent about the con-

9. Failure to gain concessions from the United States could easily lead to political disaster.

10. *Latin American Times,* July 14, 1965.

struction of a new sea level waterway. If a new interoceanic waterway were to be constructed elsewhere, Panama would suffer severe consequences, as it would be difficult to rehabilitate or relocate the numerous workers who would be unemployed. It is estimated that a new lockless canal would require only one thousand workers, as opposed to the current 14,000 workers who are employed in the operation of the Panama Canal. Retention of the present Canal would be the only solution to the unemployment problem. Panama insists that wherever a new canal is to be built the United States has the moral and legal responsibility to continue the operation of the old Canal. Thus the economic viscissitudes of life are drastically opposed to Panama's desire for sovereignty. The answer must be pragmatic, even if it means the loss of face, as Panama is unable to maintain the present Canal.

An alternative might be to convert the present Canal into a sea level waterway. Governor Robert J. Fleming feels that to do this would add greatly to already existing problems.[11] Although it would be a complicated process, it would not be an impossible one. Currently, Zonians feel that talk of conversion to a sea level canal is merely political, designed to placate the Republic of Panama. What alternatives are left?

11. *Christian Science Monitor,* May 24, 1965. Canal Zone Governor Robert J. Fleming resigned from his post on Jan. 31, 1967 when he retired from the army. President Johnson, on Feb. 6, 1967, announced the appointment of Brig. Gen. Walter P. Leber as Fleming's successor. Gen. Leber has served as Lt. Gov. of the Canal Zone from 1961 to 1963. In announcing the new appointment the President noted that Gen. Fleming had served as Canal Zone Governor since Feb. 1, 1962—the longest term since that of Gen. George W. Goethals, the builder of the Panama Canal.

Since the scope of this book does not go beyond the term in office of Gov. Fleming, for the sake of clarity, references to him are in the present rather than the past tense.

The United States might take possession of and exercise sovereignty over the area in dispute as a foreign enclave. After all, was not this really the case during the period of suspended diplomatic relations in 1964? However, public opinion militates against this alternative. Certainly the administration of the existing international public waterway should only be changed in the presence of clear evidence that some other form of common administration would make the Canal a more efficient public utility and would insure the security of the Canal as well as the hemisphere. To date no such evidence has been presented by the Republic of Panama.

How then do the Panamanians view the numerous problems concerning the Panama Canal and the possibility of the construction of a rival sea level waterway? Even more important is the question of how the differences of opinion with the United States are to be resolved. In dealing with the United States, Panama's most effective weapon is public opinion, both domestic and hemispheric. The United States will endeavor to avoid antagonizing the rest of Latin America by her actions in Panama. Opinion in Panama is now severely divided. Nationalists, led by Jorge Illueca, desire complete abrogation of existing treaties with the United States and a return of all territory in dispute to the sovereignty of Panama.

Pragmatists such as Foreign Minister Fernando Eleta take a softer view with regard to the role of the United States on the Isthmus. Panama's politicians must be nationalistic in order to retain their popularity. Yet it is not always advisable to advocate a "Yankee go home," policy which might ultimately prove detrimental to the best interests of the nation. Many Panamanians denounce United States control over the Canal and advocate either nationalization or inter-nationalization because it is the thing to do, not because it is what they desire.

After President Johnson's speech of December, 1964, Panama presented a new list of demands to the United States. President Robles demanded the abrogation of the 1903 Treaty, the recognition of Panama's sovereignty in the Canal Zone, and the abolition of the "perpetuity clause." Panama then sought an unequivocal statement by the United States to the effect that Panama maintains exclusive sovereignty in the Canal Zone. One educated Panamanian, in an interview with the writer in July of 1965, expressed the demands of his nation with reference to the United States as analogous to the "rights of a landlord against a tenant."

On July 14, 1965, Panamanian representatives Roberto Aleman and Diogenes de la Rosa stated that talks with the United States had reached the critical stage. They indicated that the main points of discussion between the two nations were administration of the Panama Canal and environs, economic jurisdiction on the Isthmus, and mutual defense problems.[12] It might be added that Panama understands the military value of the Isthmus and has never really pressed for the demilitarization of the Canal Zone. However, Panama fears that the United States wants larger military bases on the Isthmus than are necessary for adequate Canal defense and perhaps even a NATO type of force. At this juncture Panamanians fear the awesome responsibility of operating the Canal; yet as a matter of pride and honor they would like it. Panama will agree to new proposals only if the United States can insure the economic security of the Republic.

12. *Latin American Times,* July 14, 1965.

CHAPTER NINE

Portents

Both the United States and Panama know that compromises must be made if their differences are to be resolved. If a new interoceanic canal is to be constructed it must be a diplomatic, political, economic and engineering triumph. Now that basic agreement has been reached on the need for a sea level waterway, the United States is able to meet some of Panama's demands. The difficulties arising out of the Canal Zone can be gradually eliminated along with a prime source of anti-Americanism.

A new treaty with Panama must be drawn and must stipulate the exact number of years it is to run, in order to preclude difficulties such as those caused by the "perpetuity clause." The new treaty should provide a permanent bi-national commission to preside over and adjudicate conflicts between the nations. The conclusion of such a treaty will not be easily accomplished. The communists will protract negotiations and make them unpleasant. In order to eliminate the plethora of communist and nationalist propaganda on the Isthmus, the new treaty will have to be explicit in all facets to prevent the United States from being criticized as imperialistic.

On April 18, 1965, the United States established a Canal

Commission. Robert Anderson was designated as President and the other members included Dr. Milton Eisenhower, President of Johns Hopkins University; Kenneth E. Fields, a private industrial consultant; and Robert G. Storey, President of the Legal Association of the Southwestern States. In order to reduce any possible conflicts of interest, the Commission and Special Ambassador Irwin are responsible only to the President of the United States. The Canal Commission has been given until June 30, 1968, to present a conclusive report as to the best site for and means of construction of a sea level waterway.

The negotiation process is exceedingly slow, and fortunately the Panamanian press has not urged acceleration. Panama has passed legislation prohibiting publicizing diplomatic negotiations in progress, and even the nation's National Assembly has no right to pry as does its counterpart in the United States. The negotiations will be beset with internal problems such as changes in personnel on both sides, which will cause months of new orientation.

On June 28, 1965, the newspaper *El Dia* announced that Panama was negotiating two treaties with the United States for the use, protection and maintenance of an interoceanic route.[1] The first treaty would eliminate the Hay-Bunau Varilla Pact of 1903 that precipitated the January 1964 riots, and the second deals directly with the Canal, eliminating the "perpetuity clause" and permitting increased Panamanian control.[2]

Under the existing treaties Panama did not grant land to the United States, only the right of use, occupation and control. Thus the rights of property are still vested in Panama.

1. *"Dos Tratados Se Negocian Con Los E.U.," El Dia,* June 28, 1965.

2. *Ibid.* This report was later corroborated by the State Department.

In international law there is no specific legal precedent befitting the circumstances as they exist with reference to the Panama Canal and Zone. However, a legal specialist, Dr. Garcia-Mora, points out that actually there is no lease or transfer of territory, and some legal minds refer to the situation in Panama as servitude, while others call it condominium.[3] The solution to the problems of negotiating for and constructing the projected new sea level canal, as well as revision of the 1903 Treaty with Panama, is in the formulative state. The United States is disposed to granting further concessions to Panama and to the relaxation of the frequently condemned "perpetuity clause." The new treaty must spell out the sovereignty of the Canal and Canal Zone and will in all probability give complete rights to Panama.

On June 22, 1965, President Lyndon Johnson requested that Congress appropriate 7.5 million dollars to finance a study concerning a place for a sea level canal to connect the Atlantic with the Pacific. The majority of the funds were earmarked for research information pertaining to the topography, geology and hydrology of possible sites for a new waterway. President Johnson requested five million dollars be appropriated to finance on-site surveys. It is estimated that the testing period necessary to ascertain the best possible site is four to six years, possibly extending the project to 1970. The tentative target date for the opening of a new sea level canal has been established as 1980. However, if preparations were to be launched immediately, with the ever-present delays it is doubtful that the canal would be completed by 1980, when it would be needed to keep pace with international naval traffic.

It is mandatory that the new canal be sea level, for such a

3. Garcia-Mora, Manuel R., "The Panama Canal Controversy," *Vital Speeches* (April 15, 1964), p. 414.

waterway would have decided economic and military advantages over the present lock variety of canal. Not only would it be cheaper to operate and maintain, but the defense burden would be considerably less than that existing now. A new sea level canal will take at least ten years to construct and will cost a considerable amount of money. Whether the new canal is carved by nuclear or conventional means, it has to be at least two to three times as wide as the present Canal, and at least two hundred feet deep. No matter what method of construction is utilized, the completion date cannot be accelerated, and the cost will undoubtedly rise.

Numerous problems will be encountered in the course of construction. There will be a need to institute flood control measures, build tunnels under the canal, construct new highways, develop power and utility sources, maintain sanitation, relocate displaced persons, increase housing, train security forces, assemble dry docks, clear airstrips out of jungle, and seek a viable water supply. Once these problems have been overcome, new problems arise as international usage agreements and controls have to be established, defense arrangements must be made, and trained administrators have to be furnished to keep the new waterway operational. Certainly the task is prodigious and requires a unique combination of engineering skill and diplomacy.

THE UNITED STATES POSITION

Canal Zone Governor Robert Fleming represents a "new look" in American thinking in Panama. Governor Fleming, a Major General in the United States Army, gives the impression of a somewhat colorless but nonetheless competent politician. In June of 1965, Governor Fleming stated that crises were not solely confined to Panama, but were world wide. He realized the need for change all over and the corresponding need for flexibility.[4] It was obvious to Governor Fleming that a great deal of United States difficulties in Panama are attributable to American obdurateness. He ascribed the chaos of 1964 directly to the United States unwillingness to keep pace with the times.[5] The Governor opined that the United States has to face the inevitability of change in relations with Panama, and if it is done gracefully it can enhance the position of the Americans.[6]

This attitude is inimical to the thinking of the majority of the Zonians who prefer the status quo to change. The more Governor Fleming has endeavored to create equality among the peoples on the Isthmus, the more unpopular he has become with the American Zonians. He has reduced the privileges of the Zonians, although too late, since it should have been done years ago. Yet under his aegis the Canal Zone has by no means become a hardship area, nor has Governor Fleming moved too rapidly in preparing more natives for duties in the Canal. On the other hand, any progress is too much for those whose thinking reflects the nineteenth century.

In regard to the existing treaties between the United States and Panama, Governor Fleming believes them to be antiquated. He realizes that no nation can remain static and that treaties of this nature need frequent revision. In June of 1965, the Governor averred: "There is general realization that something has to give."[7] Obviously this statement was made in reference to President Johnson's announcement of December 18, 1964. Governor Fleming knows that the history of

4. Don Bohning, "Winds for Change Blowing Harder in Canal Zone," *The Evening Bulletin*, (Philadelphia), June 15, 1965. A comprehensive interview with the Governor.
5. *Ibid.*
6. *Ibid.*
7. *Ibid.*

our past actions in Panama is dim insofar as Panamanians are concerned. The joint flying of flags in the Canal Zone is hardly sufficient to diminish the years of frustration and anxiety caused the people of Panama by the United States.

The Governor has by no means sold out to the opposition. He is cognizant of his first line of duty and expressed this when he said: "In any changes here which affect the American employees of the Canal Zone the United States has an obligation to those people. Our success now depends upon sophistication and the ease with which we can bring about certain things which can be changed."[8]

Governor Robert J. Fleming, who is also President of the Panama Canal Company, feels that it will be years before a new sea level canal can be opened to traffic, consequently, the existing Canal must be made to handle the increasing flow of traffic.[9] It is mandatory that the Panama Canal continue to operate at peak efficiency until it can be ultimately phased out by a new waterway. Governor Fleming contends that the basic problem now is to maintain this peak of efficiency without excessive spending.[10] One of the most pressing difficulties is a shortage of water necessary to handle the ever increasing flow of Canal traffic. This problem could possibly be solved by the construction of the new Trinidad Dam in Gatun Lake. It is questionable whether this is a worthwhile project if conducted on a short term basis. Is the expenditure warranted considering the insecure future of the Panama Canal? Certainly such a project is worthwhile if the Panama Canal is to remain the primary interoceanic waterway for at least the next twenty years. Governor Fleming predicts that we are twenty to twenty-five years away from a sea level canal and

8. *Ibid.*
9. *Christian Science Monitor,* May 24, 1965.
10. *Ibid.*

hopefully would like to see it operational by the end of the twentieth century.[11]

In the case of a new sea level waterway being built in Panama, the United States would not demand absolute sovereignty and would probably go along with international control, inter-American control, or even Panamanian control. The United States under no circumstances desires to infringe upon the sovereignty of any nation through which a new canal is constructed. However the United States will insist that the sovereign power has no right to restrict access to the canal constructed on its territory.

Certainly the United States will take no steps toward amelioration of difficulties over the Panama Canal, or the construction of a sea level canal in the Republic of Panama until that nation is relatively tranquil. Future eruptions of violence will force the United States Congress not to appropriate funds for another canal in any nation where the government cannot control the populace. At present, the United States has not formally indicated a preference for any of the suggested new canal routes, but a Panamanian route has the inside track.

Proceeding on the assumption that United States aid and know-how are necessary to the construction of another canal in the hemisphere, many other conundrums arise. In the event that the United States chooses a site for a sea level canal outside of Panama, is there a moral obligation under the 1903 Treaty not to jeopardize that nation? To build a canal elsewhere would be injurious to Panama. How far does one go in quest of progress? Surely in the past many a nation has disregarded her neighbor in order to advance. From a purely economic viewpoint, Panama has cost the United

11. *Ibid.*

States a fortune. Yet the Americans are not to blame for Panama's impoverishment, for without the United States, Panama would be even poorer. The United States is not to blame for the misuse of its foreign aid funds by Panama's oligarchy. Most assuredly, if the United States had maintained a tight rein over aid dispatched to Panama, it would have received even more criticism as an intervener. In light of past expenditures, the cost of a new canal should be the least of the United States' concerns.

The United States is going to be accused of playing one nation of Latin America against another in regard to extracting concessions for the construction of a new canal. The Johnson administration hoped to conclude formal pacts concerning a new canal route by the end of 1966. However that is most unlikely, for as late as July 30, 1965, Congressman Daniel Flood, a Pennsylvania Democrat, stated that the House of Representatives was not receiving background material pertinent to the studies on a new canal.[12] It might be added that this long-time critic of Panama also laid the blame for the delays on the executive agencies of the United States government, which controlled the studies, and he believed the same ones were responsible for long failures in the past. So vast are the difficulties entailed in trying to secure a potential site for a new interoceanic water that the best way out would be to have the United States make an outright purchase of a route.[13]

In a more realistic vein, the United States is willing to share the bulk of the initial cost of construction of a new waterway across the terrain of some Latin American nation. But financial participation on the part of Western Europe and Japan

12. *Latin American Times,* July 30, 1965.

13. Of course this suggestion is absurd, as no nation would agree to transfer its territory to the U.S.

should be encouraged, insofar as they would derive considerable benefit from the project. The United States would be foolish to undertake a project in an area where there could be fifty more years of conflict. At this point a partnership between the United States and Panama would be the best bet for a new canal. This is feasible, even more so in view of the fact that we have already been through every conceivable type of problem with Panama and know what to expect. Definitely, the security aspect of a new canal in Panama would be made easier by the existence of United States installations on the Isthmus. It would not be very difficult to lease these sites from the government of Panama in order to insure the safety of the hemisphere. The merits of the route across Panama are as impressive today as in the era of Theodore Roosevelt and certainly exceed the merits of most other possible routes. From economic, military and political standpoints the United States would stand to profit by retaining Panama as the home of a new sea level Canal. All of these factors are well known to the government of Panama.

As soon as a new canal is assured it will be feasible for the United States to relinquish some or all of its interests in the Panama Canal and all interests in the Canal Zone. This holds true even in the event that the present Canal would be converted into a sea level waterway. Since the United States has ostensibly recovered its initial investment it would have no qualms about selling the Panama Canal to the Republic of Panama if another canal were going to be constructed. Until such a time it might be wise for the United States to maintain her annuity to Panama and simultaneously give the Republic a percentage of incoming revenue in order to quell the cries of inequities. If the day comes when the United States relinquishes control over the Panama Canal, and it appears imminent, Alliance for Progress funds might be used to help prepare Panama for control.

On September 25, 1965, President Johnson announced that eventually Panama would become a partner in the Panama Canal and her sovereignty would be recognized in the area. He implied that there was a good possibility that Panama would be the site for a new sea level waterway. In this speech, given to inform the public of the progress of the negotiations between the nations, President Johnson indicated that the 1903 Treaty would be abrogated.[14] To Washington observers it was a sign that the Johnson administration was desirous of bringing about complete harmony with Panama. The United States was now willing to conclude a new treaty with Panama abrogating the one of 1903 and was willing to rectify inequities sooner than anyone had anticipated. The new treaty was to govern the Canal and the Canal Zone until such time as a sea level canal could be constructed.

The statement regarding the negotiations came at a most propitious time. It helped to allay charges of a reversion to "Big Stick Diplomacy" evolving out of the 1965 crisis in the Dominican Republic and the fact that the House of Representatives passed a bill permitting United States intervention in the hemisphere. Although the announcement pertaining to Panama stifled some of the adverse criticism emanating from Latin America, it evoked some negative response in the United States. Mrs. Leonor Sullivan, a Democratic Congresswoman from Missouri, called President Johnson's speech terrible. She asserted that it was one-sided and its benefits would ultimately accrue to the upper classes in Panama to the exclusion of the masses.[15]

On the same day that President Johnson made his head-

14. *Latin American Times,* September 27, 1965.
15. *Ibid.*

line announcement, the Senate confirmed a bill approving wages for the members of a special canal route study group which was to begin on-site surveys in January, 1966. Two days later Representative William H. Harsha echoed a minority opinion when he stated: "The United States Government has completely capitulated to the demands of Panama concerning the Canal and we have come home from the so called negotiations like a whipped pup with its tail between its legs."[16] The significance of this crude assessment is not relative to Panama directly, but to the rest of Latin America. One begins to wonder which Latin American nation will be the next to make demands upon the United States, and how far the Americans will go with these concessions.

On October 12, 1965, Jack Hood Vaughn, then Assistant Secretary of State for Inter-American Affairs, commented: "It was our judgment and continues to be our judgment that many of the provisions of the 1903 Treaty are out of date and no longer reflect the kind of relationship that equal partners should have."[17] He stated that there was a definite need to "redress this series of anachronistic agreements and arrangements."[18] At long last the aspirations of Panama had been recognized. In conclusion, one might bear in mind that, despite the apparent capitulation to Panama, as long as the United States is in the position to choose the site of the new canal, Panama cannot dictate terms.

PANAMA'S POSITION

Panama expects full reimbursement for any economic dislocation it might experience if the United States constructs a sea level canal. However, uppermost in the minds of Pana-

16. *Latin American Times,* September 28, 1965.
17. *Latin American Times,* October 13, 1965.
18. *Ibid.*

manians is the possibility that the new waterway will be built across the Isthmus of Panama, preferably on the site of the present Canal. The Panamanians do not believe that their situation is hopeless or that they are at the mercy of the United States. If this were the case, then they would definitely stop trying. The fact that they continue to engage in demonstrations, designed to propagate the idea of a new canal being built in Panama, indicates that they feel that there is a chance that the United States will live up to what they believe to be its moral obligation and at the same time be sympathetic to Panamanian aspirations. Although Panama cannot risk violence, she must fight for the enlargement of the existing canal or the construction of a new one nearby, or suffer severe financial consequences. The thought of Panama City and Colón becoming ghost towns is frightening to Panamanians.

Panama has no assurances where a new sea level canal will be built, but she wants it only if she can be sovereign. As much as Panama would like to see the new canal in her Capitol area, under no circumstances would she consent to it under terms similar to those which govern the existing Canal. Panama is unrelenting in her demand for full sovereignty over the Canal Zone and is not likely to yield in the event that she is asked to do so in return for guarantees that a new canal would be located in her territory.

While canal plans are in a state of transition, Panama has suspended progress in many areas that might ultimately be affected by the creation of a new waterway. For example, the Institute of Housing and Urbanization has halted planning in light of the fact that the Canal Zone will probably be turned over to Panama.[19] Unfortunately, the economy of Panama will be retarded to some extent until a decision concerning the new canal is made, as businessmen are reluctant to invest in uncertainties.

19. *Latin American Times,* July 30, 1965.

Former President de la Guardia has remarked that "It is simpler to deal with one nation over Canal affairs than twenty,"[20] indicating that some in Panama feel that their nation has the inside track on the new waterway. Panamanians feel they can, after extensive training, operate the Canal without the United States. Even now, as talk about phasing out the Panama Canal increases, it has become more difficult to recruit American personnel, and more Panamanians have been given the training necessary to handle Canal duties.

The idea of a partnership between the United States and Panama, with regard to the Canal, has not been well received in Panama City. Although this measure would not satisfy many in Panama, one must not lose sight of the fact that without United States tourists and capital, Panama stands to lose considerable revenue. In addition, international maritime interests would feel insecure if the Canal were exclusively in the hands of Panama. Thus shipping and the concomitant revenues would undoubtedly be reduced if the United States were to be entirely excluded from the operation of the Canal.

In August of 1965, publisher-politician, Jorge Illueca attacked his government for not giving the interests of the people of Panama sufficient consideration in the negotiations for the new canal. Señor Illueca, who was relieved of his position as negotiator in December of 1964, stated that the United States was bi-partisan in her dealings with Panama, but that Panama's administration ignored the feelings of its political opposition.[21] Señor Illueca further stated that the United States should be prohibited from making land studies rele-

20. Mercer D. Tate, "The Panama Canal and Political Partnership," *Journal of Politics* (February, 1963), p. 135.
21. *Latin American Times*, August 8, 1965.

vant to a new canal until Panama's demands concerning the existing treaty are satisfied.[22]

In Panama politics often supercedes the national interest, and the opposition *Panameñista* Party led by Arnulfo Arias, who was defeated at the polls by Marco Robles in the last presidential election, continues to militate against the realistic action of the incumbents. Overtly Panama gives the impression of being bereft of unity, but little credence can be ascribed to the outcries of the political opposition. In actuality, if the *Panameñistas* under Señor Arias, were in the driver's seat, they would take the same course of action pursued by President Robles. Nevertheless, political considerations are bound to obstruct negotiations with the United States. Conversely, little of this type of politicking has been observed in the United States.

President Robles feels that the September, 1965, speech of President Johnson is fully compatible with the aspirations of his nation. Although surprised by the American's willingness to agree to his demands, Robles believed the five points referred to by President Johnson to be advantageous.[23] The Administration of President Marco A. Robles has the full support of Colonel Bolivar Villarino, Commandant of Panama's *Guardia Nacional,* a most valuable ally when dealing with political opposition.

On the pessimistic side, President Johnson's announcement was regarded by many as a move to bolster the unpopular Robles administration and thereby make the negotiation task less difficult. Members of the *Panameñista* Party, which contends that President Robles was elected fraudulently, have been skeptical of the joint statement, as was the Christian Democratic Party which opposes and fears the use of nuclear

22. *Ibid.*
23. *Latin American Times*, September 30, 1965.

explosives in canal construction projects. Together with other nationalists, these factions, in late 1965, created a United Front to oppose Robles' new treaties with the United States.

Diogenes de la Rosa, Panama's negotiatior, made public his nation's demands in a report to the National Assembly in October of 1965.[24] Panama requested that the existing United States regime in the Canal Zone be abolished and that the administration of justice and legislation for the area be placed under Panama's control, except for special matters dealing directly with the Canal. Panama suggested that all services in the Canal Zone be placed under her authority, except for services to ships which it prefers under joint United States-Panamanian authority. The Panamanians also requested that the Canal Zone Postal System be required to use Panamanian postage and that Spanish be declared the official language of the Zone. Panama also demands an increase in Canal tolls from two to three times their present rate, for the nation is in desperate need of additional funds to finance development programs, and, unless increased income is derived from tolls, huge sums will have to be borrowed by 1970. These demands reveal that although Panama insists upon sovereignty in the Canal Zone, she is not ready to assume full control over the Canal and its shipping functions.

SEA LEVEL CANAL ROUTES

The race has begun to see which nation will be chosen as the site for the proposed sea level canal to link the Atlantic and Pacific Oceans. What factors will determine this choice? The answer is complex and requires considerable investigation and introspection. Ultimately the site will be determined

24. These demands were presented to the United States on January 25, 1965.

by diplomatic, political, economic, geographic and geological factors. Funds have been allocated to enable the Atlantic-Pacific Interoceanic Canal Commission, designated by President Johnson, to begin surveys by January 1, 1966. It will be 1968 or later before the new sea level surveys are completed and a decision is made as to a site for the new canal.

Preliminary accords must be reached with the various nations concerned, prior to continuing work on the surveys to determine the best possible canal routes. Then problems of earth formation, geological and climactic factors, and engineering skill must be carefully evaluated, along with hundreds of rock borings to test the feasibility of potential sites. Once the numerous tests prove conclusive, agreement will have to be reached with the nation or nations through whose territory the proposed canal will be constructed.

No nation involved in the surveys for a new canal would consider yielding such rights as exist in the 1903 Treaty between the United States and Panama. Obviously the United States does not expect terms which would lead to similar problems as encountered in Panama. Any nation permitting the construction of a new canal through its terrain must realize that it would take forty to fifty years to amortize mortgages necessary to the completion of the project. During this time the nation would derive little revenue in terms of tolls. However, the port cities that are sure to rise at either end of the canal would profit handsomely. Naturally, employment will gain momentum in the nation selected for the new canal, and economic prospects will be enhanced.

Over the past century more than twenty sites have been studied for a new sea level canal. From the days of the *Conquistadores* there has been talk about the construction of a canal across the narrows of Tehuantepec. In fact, Hernán Cortés recommended this course of action, which most

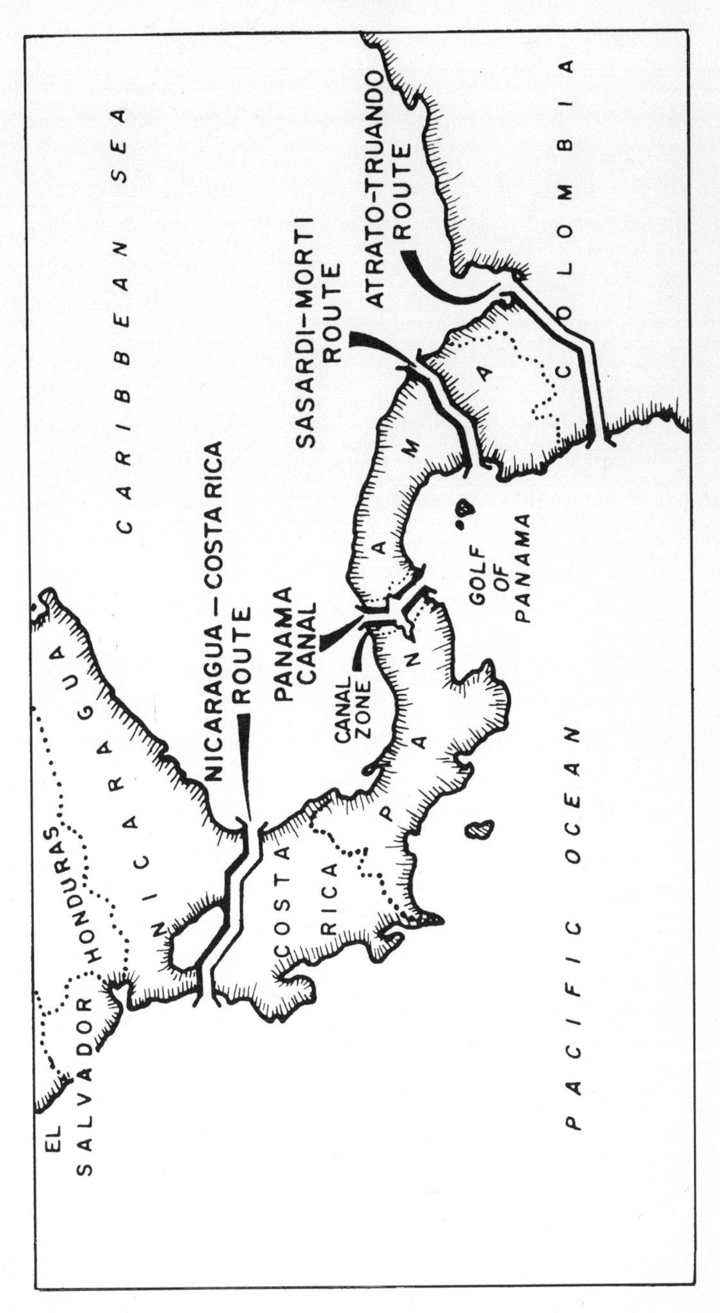

CARIBBEAN SEA
PACIFIC OCEAN
EL SALVADOR
HONDURAS
NICARAGUA
COSTA RICA
NICARAGUA — COSTA RICA ROUTE
PANAMA CANAL
CANAL ZONE
PANAMA
GOLF OF PANAMA
SASARDI-MORTI ROUTE
ATRATO-TRUANDO ROUTE
COLOMBIA

recently has been reiterated by Senator Mike Mansfield, Democrat of Montana.[25] *Petroles Mexicanos* made an intensive study of the possibilities of a canal across the Tehuantepec region and estimated that it would cost four hundred eighty million dollars to build a canal with locks.[26] A canal of this type is not viable by today's standards, and it is highly unrealistic to give serious consideration to the construction of a substandard canal across this twelve-mile route.

Former Mexican Foreign Minister Manuel Tello emphasized that if a canal were ever to be constructed in Mexico, the government would demand full sovereignty. Under no circumstances would Mexico consider sharing canal authority with the United States, and there is little likelihood that Mexico would change this position. Yet the project would be too costly for Mexico to undertake alone. The primary advantage of building a canal in Mexico is the political stability which other nations with whom the United States might deal do not possess.

The Central American Nations would also insist upon complete sovereignty if a canal were to be constructed across their territory. Recently the Central American nations have avoided direct reference to the possibility of sharing or yielding authority over a new canal to the United States. These states would prefer not to encourage a situation approximating that existing in Panama. They have remained mute for fear that statements contrary to the desires of the United States might have an adverse affect upon United States foreign aid or Alliance for Progress funds which they so desperately need.

In April of 1964, the United States and Colombia launched on the scene studies of a proposed canal route in the South

25. *Excelsior,* January 25, 1964.
26. *Ibid.*

American nation. Six different sites across Colombia have been suggested for the prospective waterway. One, the Atrato-Truando strip, is far superior to the others. This uninhabited swampland is approximately 102 miles long and could be made into a sea level canal for a sum slightly in excess of one billion dollars. If this canal route were to be used, about 55 miles of the channel could be cut through the low lying plains on the Atlantic, by conventional means, to provide a channel 60 feet deep by 600 feet wide. The remaining 40 miles, passing through the Continental Divide, could be excavated by nuclear blasting to create a channel 60 feet deep by 1,000 feet wide.

The Colombian route because of its lack of population would be ideal for the use of nuclear devices which consulting engineers have recommended, but as of yet a bill paving the way for a nuclear project has not passed the Colombian Congress.

From time immemorial persons have suggested an interoceanic canal through Nicaragua. More recently Senator Wayne Morse, Democrat of Oregon and Chairman of the Senate Subcommittee on American Republics Affairs, has reiterated this proposal. Although this route would be longer than many of the other possibilities, it would be closer to both coasts of the United States and economically and militarily advantageous.

President René Shick Gutiérrez of Nicaragua has stated that a new canal across his nation would not be possible until the United States agreed to a revision of the Bryan-Chamorro Treaty, which granted the United States the right, in perpetuity, to build a canal across Nicaragua.[27] There would be additional problems in the construction of a new canal across Nicaragua. These problems would involve the Gulf of Fon-

27. *New York Times,* January 10, 1965.

seca, which is claimed by El Salvador and owned jointly by Nicaragua and Honduras. Nicaragua disagrees with the ownership claims of her neighbors and the construction of a canal in the area would necessitate United States involvement in an ugly dispute. El Salvador is critical of the Nicaraguan route, as well as the Bryan-Chamorro Treaty which grants to the United States the right to build a naval base on the shores of the Gulf of Fonseca. Under international law El Salvador claims that the Gulf is an inland sea, jointly owned by herself, Nicaragua and Honduras. In order to pursue canal construction in this area intricate diplomatic dealings with El Salvador and Honduras would be necessary and would prolong the overall operation.

Of the seven possible routes involving Nicaragua, only one would be well suited for a sea level canal. This would entail making a 168 mile slice through Nicaragua and Costa Rica, would cost approximately two billion dollars, and is the longest of all of the proposed routes. The possibility of reaching agreement with Nicaragua over a proposed route is remote. As recently as the middle of 1964, Nicaragua's Congress repudiated the Bryan-Chamorro Treaty,[28] and the situation with reference to that nation and the United States is similar to that existing between the United States and Panama. It would be ludicrous for the United States to become involved in this type of imbroglio in Nicaragua.

From the geological standpoint the best sites for a new canal remain in Panama, where the Isthmus narrows to as little as 30 miles. Across the San Blas region of Panama is the shortest of the various prospective sites. This 37 mile strip is close to a population center of 1.2 million people, and the use of atomic devices for blasting here is not feasible.

28. James H. Stratton, "Sea Level Canal: How And Where," *Foreign Affairs* (April, 1965), p. 517.

Currently the two best routes in Panama appear to be either a sea level canal near the Colombian border or an expansion of the existing Canal. The year ending June 30, 1965, saw 11,834 vessels pass through the Panama Canal,[29] and many more would have taken the route had expanded facilities been present. The United States is willing to meet this need by spending up to two billion dollars on a new canal facility in Panama.

Various routes across Panama are now being evaluated on their geographic, geological, economic and political merits. A 46 mile route through southern Darien's wilds—the Sasardi-Morti route—is the cheapest, costing about seven hundred seventy million dollars, and could be cut by nuclear explosives of diverse yields which would affect only a small number of people.[30] It would cross the Isthmus at a point where the Continental Divide reaches an altitude of 1,100 feet, and its channel would have a minimum width of 1,000 feet and be 60 feet deep, thus accommodating even the largest vessels afloat and on the drawing boards.

If a new canal were to be constructed elsewhere, the best that Panama could hope for would be to turn the present Canal into a hydroelectric project. Even this move would not prevent the nation from regressing from her position as the hub of the hemisphere's transportation, and one of the world's commercial centers. In this event Panama would certainly demand millions in compensation for her losses. Numerous problems might be avoided by the retention of the existing Canal as a site for a sea level waterway. Even that would not be a panacea, for a sea level canal along the present route would still give rise to unemployment and criticism.

29. *Latin American Times,* September 27, 1965.

30. Lawrence Galton, "A New Canal Dug by Atom Bombs," *New York Times Magazine* (September 20, 1964), p. 72.

The House Committee on Merchant Marine and Fisheries studied the problem and recommended that a third set of locks, at a cost of seven hundred million dollars, be built to insure the efficiency of the existing Canal until the year 2000. Nevertheless, a sea level canal would be far superior and not much more expensive. In order to enlarge the present Canal it would be necessary to construct by-passing locks and to widen the Gallard Cut by conventional methods. This operation might cost two billion dollars, but it could be accomplished rather swiftly. It is conceivable, but highly unlikely, that such a process would only necessitate closing the Canal for twelve days.

In the final analysis, a sea level canal is the only answer. Numerous stop-gap measures might be instituted, but ultimately they would be obsolete and new measures would be needed. The conversion of the present waterway into a sea level canal would provide the best solution to a multitude of problems. The terms of the 1903 Treaty do not prohibit the unilateral conversion of the present Canal into a sea level waterway. In light of the severe criticism that unilateral United States action is bound to evoke in Latin America and the communist propaganda that would evolve, a bilateral or multi-lateral course might best be pursued.

Proceeding on the above premise, the enlargement of the existing Canal would require new treaty negotiations with Panama, and in light of recent developments such negotiations are feasible. Converting the Panama Canal to sea level operation would cost anywhere from $1.25 billion to $2.6 billion, a sum not so great as the estimated cost of routes in other areas. To accomplish the enlargement the present 51-mile wide Canal would have to be widened and the locks eliminated, a task which could best be accomplished by the utilization of nuclear blasting devices. Contrary to the propaganda being spread by the Zonians, atomic methods could be used and would cause relatively little permanent damage. Naturally, some citizens would have to be temporarily relocated, hardly an exorbitant price to pay for such an achievement.

From the standpoint of the Johnson Administration, the conversion of the present Canal into a sea level waterway would simplify matters. It would prevent the further deterioration of relations with Panama and would preclude similar diplomatic difficulties with other nations which have canal route potential. It would alleviate the intolerable situation with regard to the Canal Zone, which would be placed under the jurisdiction of Panama. Currently from the economic, sociological, political, diplomatic and military standpoints the existing Panama Canal route is preferable to any alternatives.

THE NUCLEAR DILEMMA

The most frequently asked question with regard to the digging of a new sea level canal is whether or not the use of nuclear devices is feasible. Engineers agree that when possible the utilization of nuclear explosives is preferable to conventional blasting. The old blasting process entails digging out ground by the use of chemical explosives and then removing the remaining earth and rock, piece by piece, with mechanical equipment. The ease of using nuclear blasting devices is amazing in comparison to the difficulties involved in conventional methods. When a thermonuclear device is detonated underground, earth and rock are broken and ejected forming a crater. By controlling the size of the crater one simultaneously determines the size of the ditch.[31] If nuclear charges are placed in a line or strip and exploded simultaneously the

31. *Ibid.*

matter that is ejected will line only the sides of craters, not the ends, and thus would leave ideal openings for canal entrances and exits.

Nuclear explosives are faster than dynamite, performing similar tasks in one-fifth the time. Also, nuclear devices reduce the cost of blasting operations by as much as ninety per cent. Even the workers removed during the blasting could return to their areas in a matter of a few weeks. There can be no doubt that the utilization of nuclear devices would accelerate and simplify a sea level canal building operation.

It would take approximately four to five years of intensive experimentation to develop the proper type of nuclear blasting necessary to dig a new interoceanic waterway and at the same time insure a proper reduction in radioactivity.[32] Engineers estimate that about twenty-five atomic blasts along the proposed route would be necessary to clear a new interoceanic passageway. But this project is far from operational, as there is a need to study the effects of nuclear blasting on life, other than human, in the Central America and Panama region, as all biological risks must be minimized.

The Atomic Energy Commission has indicated that a sea level canal can be accomplished safely with radioactive fallout being held to a minimum, if the project is not hurried and necessary precautions are taken. In conjunction with widespread fears of radioactivity leading to atmospheric contamination, it is encouraging to note that in a thermonuclear detonation of the type that would be utilized in the construction of a new sea level canal, ninety per cent of the debris is trapped permanently under molten rock, and there is little chance of radiation damage.

32. In a hearing before the Joint Congressional Committee on Atomic Energy, Dr. Glenn Seaborg estimated that it would take at least five years to develop devices safe for this type of nuclear blasting.

The idea of using nuclear blasting devices originated in 1956, during the Suez crisis, when the United States contemplated the construction of a new canal through Israel. The idea was carried further by Dr. Edward Teller's "Project Plowshare." In July of 1962, "Project Plowshare" proved the feasibility of a nuclear blasting program in the "Sedan Test" in Nevada which successfully controlled the size of a crater dug by a nuclear explosion.

There is one major stumbling block to the use of nuclear blasting in the construction of a new sea level canal, the Nuclear Test Ban Treaty. This pact, to which the United States is a signatory, might well be invoked by the Soviet Union to preclude the use of nuclear devices for canal blasting. The Atomic Energy Commission is of the belief that the pact has to be modified, since it bans explosions that blast radioactive debris across international boundaries. If the pact is to be modified, the Russians must give their approval.

There is by no means a consensus as to the validity of the Test Ban Treaty as it pertains to the use of nuclear devices for canal construction. The United States Arms Control and Disarmament Agency, in contrast to the beliefs of the Atomic Energy Commission, has stated that the Treaty will not prevent development of devices for use in peaceful projects such as "Project Plowshare."[33] There can be little doubt that the construction of an interoceanic waterway, accessible to nations of the world, is anything but a peaceful endeavor. Of course, the communists might contend that placing the new canal under the hegemony of the United States automatically gives the West a military and strategic advantage and takes nuclear construction out of the realm of peaceful usage.

It would be realistic to assume that the Soviet Union

33. *The Panama Canal—Its Past and Future* (Washington: American Enterprise Institute For Public Policy Research, 1964), p. 51.

might agree upon the merits of a new sea level canal being dug by nuclear devices, as the Russians purport to espouse world freedom. As far back as 1949, Soviet Foreign Minister Andrei Vishinsky hinted that his nation advocated the peaceful housing of nuclear power. But the Chinese Communists have indicated opposition to nuclear blasting and the Sino-Soviet split might well alter the Russian position.

Even if the United States could persuade the Soviet Bloc of her peaceful intentions and requested an amendment to the Test Ban Treaty permitting peaceful usage of nuclear devices, there would be objection from the world's anti-contaminationists. Not only would the "ban the bombers" object vociferously to nuclear blasting, but so would the residents of the Canal Zone if the new sea level waterway were to be constructed near or on the present Canal site. Zonians with whom the author has spoken believed nuclear blasting to be inimical to their interests and would exert pressure to preclude such action.

The Atomic Energy Commission has been asked to conduct research on the effects of nuclear explosives and the concurrent radioactive fallout. Until such time as these tests prove conclusive, the use of nuclear blasting will remain an enigma. The solution to this problem and the previously mentioned diplomatic conundrum might best be delayed until the site for the sea level canal is selected. To do otherwise would cause unnecessary delays as well as excessive research and expenditures.

OWNERSHIP AND CONTROL OF THE PANAMA CANAL

In light of recent agitation against United States unilateral control over the Panama Canal, would it be feasible to multi-

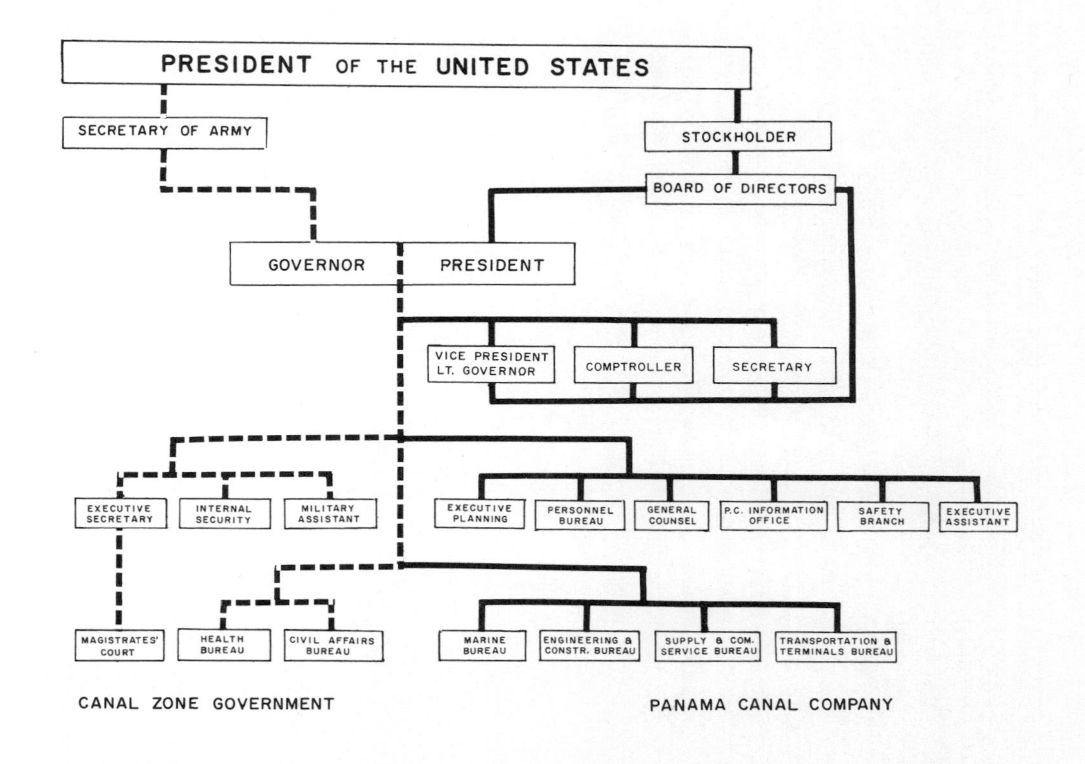
PRESIDENT OF THE UNITED STATES
SECRETARY OF ARMY
STOCKHOLDER
BOARD OF DIRECTORS
GOVERNOR
PRESIDENT
VICE PRESIDENT
LT. GOVERNOR
COMPTROLLER
SECRETARY
EXECUTIVE SECRETARY
INTERNAL SECURITY
MILITARY ASSISTANT
EXECUTIVE PLANNING
PERSONNEL BUREAU
GENERAL COUNSEL
P.C. INFORMATION OFFICE
SAFETY BRANCH
EXECUTIVE ASSISTANT
MAGISTRATES' COURT
HEALTH BUREAU
CIVIL AFFAIRS BUREAU
MARINE BUREAU
ENGINEERING & CONSTR. BUREAU
SUPPLY & COM. SERVICE BUREAU
TRANSPORTATION & TERMINALS BUREAU
CANAL ZONE GOVERNMENT
PANAMA CANAL COMPANY

lateralize the Canal? Whether the Panama Canal is to remain as is, or be converted to a sea level waterway, it need not be owned and operated exclusively by the United States. When deciding upon control of the Panama Canal or a new canal, the interests of all of the American nations must be considered.

Since the nationalization of the Suez Canal by Egypt, the Latin American left, led by the Christian Democratic parties, has agitated for control of the Panama Canal by Panama, and recently the Department of State has indicated that this is a distinct possibility. Opinion is divided as to the merits of this action; certainly the Department of State is correct in its belief that a Canal under Panama's direction would curtail Yankeephobia on the Isthmus as well as temporarily squelch some internal dissensions. However, Professor J. F. Rippy is also correct in assessing the nationalization of the Panama Canal as a serious loss to Panama as well as to the United States and the world.[34] The question is, is the presence of the United States on the Isthmus necessary to the proper operation of the Canal, hemispheric security and the overall economy of Panama?

As long ago as 1924, Víctor Raúl Haya de la Torre, the Peruvian theoretician, included in the five basic points of his *Aprista* doctrine the internationalization of the Panama Canal. Subsequently this idea was incorporated into the thinking of numerous *Latinos* as well as Anglos. At one time or another, Vice-President Hubert Humphrey and the late Adlai Stevenson, Ambassador to the U.N., advocated placing the Panama Canal under international control. Perhaps the greatest exponents of this plan have been Professors Martin B. Travis and James T. Watkins, who in April of 1960 forecast a

34. J. Fred Rippy, "The U.S. and Panama: Endless Appeasement," *Modern Age* (Summer, 1964), p. 283.

revolution in Panama that subsequently took place.[35]

In December of 1959, Northwestern University proposed to the Eisenhower administration that the Panama Canal be internationalized. The proposal was rejected by the Department of State. In February, 1960, Senator George Aiken, Republican of Vermont, a member of the Senate Foreign Relations Committee specializing in Latin American affairs, indicated that internationalization of the Panama Canal would be superior to OAS control of the Canal, since most of the world's shipping came from outside of the boundaries of the hemisphere.[36]

One of the more unique Canal control plans that has been proposed is the *Primer Plan Colombiano* promoted by a private Panamanian-Colombian group. Under this plan an international company would be formed through the world-wide subscription of stock, but the company would be presided over by the host nation. This might assure the success of a projected sea level canal and prove to be a profitable venture.

A somewhat similar approach to the matter was taken by Professor Robert Potash of the University of Massachusetts, who in January of 1964 criticized the internationalization of the Panama Canal under the United Nations and also the transfer of the waterway to Panama's control. His imaginative solution approximated the system under which the New York Port Authority operates. Professor Potash would create a Panama Canal Authority, with membership limited to American nations fronting on the two oceans and for whom the Canal assists domestic communications.[37] Under the "Potash"

35. Martin B. Travis and James T. Watkins, "Time Bomb in Panama," *The Nation* (April 30, 1960), p. 381.
36. *New York Times,* February 2, 1960.
37. Robert A. Potash, "Letters to the Editor," *New York Times,* January 24, 1964.

proposal the United States, Canada, Mexico, Colombia, Guatemala, Nicaragua, Costa Rica, and Panama would all be involved. However the diplomatic complexities of this plan might create problems that would prove insurmountable.

Professor James L. Busey of the University of Colorado has proposed that the United States purchase the entire Central American half of the Republic of Panama, from the present Canal Zone to the Costa Rican frontier, presumably in order to have a freer hand in Canal control.[38] Panama would never concede to such a preposterous plan, which should be placed in the same category with suggestions advocating the elimination of Panama and the turning over of its territory to neighboring Costa Rica and Colombia.

Many oppose internationalization of the Panama Canal on the grounds that such a move would place some modicum of control in the hands of the Soviets. It is interesting to note that the internationalization of the Panama and Suez Canals was mentioned at the Potsdam Conference in July, 1945. Had that course of action been followed, Arab nationalism may have been thwarted and Nasser's take-over of the Suez Canal possibly averted. Of course there is little likelihood that Panama could ever take drastic measures as did the Egyptians.

On the other hand, internationalization of the Panama Canal under the jurisdiction of the United Nations would enhance the security of the waterway, as the Soviets too would be responsible for its ownership. United Nations control would not solve all of the problems of Panamanian nationalism but would be more acceptable to Panama than United States domination of the Canal. At least under United Nations jurisdiction such problems as discrimination and partiality would, hopefully, abate.

38. James L. Busey, "Conflict in Panama," *The New Leader* (February 15, 1960), p. 19.

In 1960 the House Subcommittee on Inter-American Affairs conducted extensive research into the possibility of the Panama Canal being controlled by the United Nations. The Committee decided that such a move would be unwise as it would facilitate communist efforts to disrupt the political and economic stability of the Republic of Panama and Latin America. The Committee indicated that it would be ludicrous to afford the Communist Bloc nations a part in the administration of a waterway in the Western Hemisphere. In light of diminishing world respect for the stability and effectiveness of the United Nations, a proposal to place the Panama Canal under its jurisdiction would meet with overpowering resistance.

Latin Americans prefer to handle their own problems when possible. The majority of the nations of the hemisphere would rather utilize the machinery of the Organization of American States than the United Nations, where the alternative exists. The placing of the Panama Canal under the aegis of the OAS has been frequently proposed. But Latin American nations have been reluctant to go along with such a plan, predicating their stand on the doctrine of non-intervention under which this would be an encroachment upon the sovereignty of the Republic of Panama. *Latinos* have overwhelmingly rejected OAS control over the Panama Canal in favor of Panamanian ownership.

In April of 1959, Dr. José Figueres, the ex-President of Costa Rica, suggested that the Canal Zone be governed by the OAS, while the United States be permitted to retain military responsibility for the Canal. In theory, what President Figueres proposed was a multilateral approach to the problem. The soundness of his proposal is suspect, for in essence it would amount to a repetition of the existing facade of multilateralism. This gives rise to the question of whether or not it is sensible to go through the motions and added expense of multi-lateralism, just to satisfy the egos of Latin Americans who demand juridical equality with the United States.

Whether the Panama Canal is controlled by the United States, the United Nations, or the Organization of American States, the Panamanians will not be entirely satisfied. Nor will they fare better economically or politically. Nevertheless, the existing system, dominated by the United States, is untenable. Panamanians fear United Nations control would play into the hands of Cold War enemies, and the Organization of American States does not possess sufficient resources to manage Canal operations. Complete control by Panama has already been examined and found to be a poor answer. Thus the only viable solution is some type of partnership arrangement whereby Panama would participate with those nations or nation that possess the financial resources and technological knowledge necessary to the proper operation of an inter-oceanic waterway.

CHAPTER TEN

Reflections

Down through the years there has been an overabundance of tension in United States—Panamanian relations. Numerous members of the *Guardia Nacional* are seen in Panama City, and Americans walk the city's streets during the day but dare not venture downtown after dark. Despite the precautions, Panama is outwardly calm, and a hopeful air of eager anticipation pervades the atmosphere as negotiations with the United States proceed.

Unfortunately the current Panamanian situation is frequently distorted by the press in the United States. Headlines depicting riots, demonstrations and violence make good copy and sell newspapers. For example, while the writer was seated in Canal Zone Headquarters during the summer of 1965 he was shown a newsclipping which had appeared in the previous day's papers in Miami, Florida, and San Juan, Puerto Rico. The reports indicated that all civilian personnel had been evacuated from Panama because of the existing anti-American violence. These journalistic allegations were entirely fallacious; nothing resembling a demonstration had taken place for many weeks, and no personnel evacuations were contemplated. It is a pity that some members of the press corps imbibe their knowledge at the bar in the Panama

Hilton, a most commodious lounge, but a difficult place to conduct accurate research.[1] An erroneous impression of Panama is often conveyed to the American public, and one can only hope that the United States government is more discerning than some reporters.

There is considerable apprehension in Panama as to its future. No Panamanian viewpoint, per se, exists; opinion is divided. In some circles a colonialist mentality exists, one approximating that found in Algeria prior to its independence. One senses escapism in the people of the nation who believe in the inevitability of a new sea level canal and feel that no matter where it is located the results will cause some distress. Panamanians are not closemouthed about their plight and are quite ebullient and willing to talk about their future prospects. Except for the oligarchy and bureaucrats, most Panamanians are reconciled to a future requiring some subordination and deprivation. But all see better days ahead.

Enlightened Panamanians do not categorize the United States as imperialistic, yet they do not expect the Americans to take an altruistic approach to relations with their nation. They realize that the first allegiance of the United States is to itself, but they hope and believe that the Americans will assist Panama on the road to democracy. The majority of the enlightened people in Panama are not against or indifferent to the United States, but rather they are staunch supporters of their powerful northern ally. After close association with educated Panamanians one derives the impression that many would prefer even closer ties to the United States if sovereignty could be retained. More than one Panamanian has mentioned that an arrangement approximating the one be-

1. These remarks in no way refer to Ralph Skinner, who for years has reported accurately and intelligently for the *Christian Science Monitor*.

tween the United States and Puerto Rico would be desirable. Certainly few Panamanians are genuinely united by a feeling of deprivation at the hands of the United States.

The underlying resentment of the United States, which does exist, is predicated upon fear of the unknown, rather than the knowledge of exploitation. In reality the very Panamanians who complain about low wages in the Canal Zone are the ones who underpay their workers. The nationalists who speak the loudest are the same individuals who forget that the United States helped create their nation by support of their revolution and construction of the Panama Canal. The exorbitant cost to the United States is never alluded to by the malcontents, and the fact that many of their businesses are prospering because of the Yankee dollar is sloughed off as inconsequential. The fact that the Zonians alone spend more money in Panama than the entire annual national budget must be emphasized. With a scarcity of domestic capital for industrial expansion, it appears as if Panama will have to continue to rely heavily upon the Canal and the United States.

Rarely is the possibility of converse exploitation in Panama explored. Professor J. Fred Rippy is of the opinion that the United States retention of options or zones in Panama has been used by that nation as a lever against the United States Treasury in time of crisis.[2] For example, during World War II Panama received more than a million dollars for use of bases and lands outside of the Canal Zone and reaped a handsome profit for a short term loan. Too often this polite form of extortion has tapped the United States reserves and exploited the American's good nature.

Many of Panama's problems are of the home grown vari-

2. J. Fred Rippy, *Globe and Hemisphere* (Chicago: Henry Regnery Co., 1958), p. 109.

ety. Speak with a Panamanian malcontent, especially one in the United States, and he will decry the poor treatment his nation has received at the hands of the Yankees. Or he might go out of his way to illustrate the deplorable social and economic conditions caused by the presence of the United States in his native land. Ask him what his contribution to the rectification of these ills has been, and he may well be at a loss for words. Something deeper than indifference is reflected in this attitude. Many bright and energetic Panamanians are sent abroad to be educated, in order that they might eventually return home to lead the struggle for progress. Too many scholarship students remain in the United States or other comfortable places rather than return home to fight what they consider a losing battle. Panamanians are contributing greatly to their own defeat. Those who return to Panama after having reaped the benefits of higher education abroad find Panama a confused and disorganized place in which to live, and often prefer to enter private business or return to brighter situations, rather than involve themselves in the nation's bureaucratic tangle. This lack of organization among the disillusioned educated has generally led to a few meaningless outbursts followed by periods of lassitude and reconcilliation to one's lot in life.

Panama's political future is uncertain. While President Marco A. Robles is an advocate of orderliness and has managed to keep the nationalists and communists in line, it is impossible to determine how long this peace will last. To the outsider, Panama's political structure conveys the impression of instability and vulnerability to subversion. But, by Latin American standards, Panama is relatively stable. Excessive violence did not occur in the nation until the 1960's, and this has been exaggerated in the minds of the peoples of other nations. Presidents may topple, but Panama's political structure remains intact. Bureaucrats may change positions, but Panama's oligarchy manages to retain control of the nation, and blame the United States for their governing inadequacies. Certainly the politicians and people of Panama are at times as guilty of abusing the generosity of the United States as the United States is guilty of abusing their sovereignty.

In light of other Latin American experiences, it is possible to question whether Panamanian democracy offers too many liberties. For example, is the issuance of scholarships for rising young liberals a direct attempt to sidetrack these potential social revolutionaries by preparing them for overseas appointments which will keep them in a political Siberia? Just how much hope is there for the Young Turks in Panama's Liberal Party? Can this group of educated and inexperienced individuals stand up to the oligarchy in order to bring the reforms that the nation so desperately needs? These and numerous other questions now confront us, but some solace and hope can be derived from the fact that this Young Turk group is growing.

Crises of the Dominican Republic 1965 type are feasible in Panama but extremely unlikely, in view of the close watch there by the governments of Panama and the United States. The danger of communism taking over the country is not imminent but serves to make the people cognizant of the presence of social inequities and inequalities. The communists and the *Fidelistas* have made, and will continue to make, the most out of the unrest evolving from the presence of the United States in the Canal Zone, and clear and present dangers will have to be recognized and separated from mere propaganda. The communists have made no genuine headway in Panama, and even though there is a reluctance to admit it, Panamanians favor the United States with whom they have had close ties for many years. Nevertheless, Panama will continue to use communism and the Cold War as a lever to extract more concessions from the United States. How far down this path the United States will travel is a question even the Department of State has difficulty answering. At this point the road appears endless.

The United States is so oriented to world trouble spots that only when a crisis comes to a head in a previously insignificant area does it take it seriously . . . then it is often too late. There can be little doubt that the United States was not entirely surprised when the lid blew off in Panama in January of 1964, only unprepared. As the United States is learning in Panama, putting out the fire is exceedingly more intricate than its prevention. No easy solutions are presently in sight, and the United States must proceed cautiously in her negotiations with Panama. Presently negotiations conducted by the Johnson and Robles administrations are moving in the right direction, but before the results can be positive mutual mistrust and fear of recrimination must be eliminated.

There has been a need from the immediate post-World War II years until now to correct inequalities in Panama, in order to avert communist gains. Now that the United States is aware of this fact, it would be wise to set as its objective the political, economic, and social integration of Panama, especially in relation to the Canal Zone. This brings another question to mind; to what extent does the United States use the concept of communist infiltration in Panama as a means of maintaining its place in the nation? The answer is obvious, to a great extent! One wonders whether or not this is necessary, for in the long run Panama depends upon the United States defensively and thus must pursue an anti-communist and anti-Castro policy, even if it hurts to do so. The defenses of Panama are not unique with respect to the rest of Latin America, and in the event of ultimate global conflict the

United States is committed to defend the entire hemisphere. How does one reconcile this with the fact that the United States has not made a concerted effort to gain similar influence in most other Latin American nations?

One cannot expect an economic curtain around Cuba and the Alliance for Progress to overshadow years of deep resentment and suspicion of the United States. With this in mind, it was indeed fortunate that Panama had no charismatic Fidel-like leader during the violent January, 1964 episode. What did occur in Panama has been effective in bringing about a long needed re-evaluation of United States relations with that nation. The United States must recognize what exists in the minds of Panamanians regardless of whether or not it corresponds to American sentiments.

On the other hand, the Panamanians must be understanding, as well, and realize that the United States flag is not a symbol of exclusive sovereignty on the Isthmus. Panamanians must understand that the United States legally, in law or equity, owes nothing to Panama as a result of 1903, even though some contend that a moral obligation exists. How long must the American people be responsible for the acts of their ancestors?

The United States continues to assist Panama economically, socially and militarily, and continues to be suspect on the Isthmus. The Canal Zone problem must be solved immediately if Panama is to avert economic disaster. At the same time, Panama must consider that the United States constructed the Canal, and that it is still dominated by North American shipping. It is impossible to calculate all of the benefits, psychological, economic, and intangible which Panama derived from alliances with the United States. No one can expect the United States to walk away and leave millions of dollars in military, naval and air force installations in the

Canal Zone. Even if the United States were to relinquish the Canal Zone, Panama would lose its annuity. But the real loss would not be the annuity, which in actuality amounts to only about one quarter of the sum paid annually to Panama by the United Fruit Company alone, for taxes on local operations. The overall enormity of the loss Panama would sustain if the United States pulled out is incomprehensible.

It is true that continued appeasement by the United States will only whet the appetite of Panama. But then again imperialistic gestures are still food for communist propaganda, and the advantages of one must be carefully weighed against the other.

On June 26, 1967, both Presidents Johnson and Robles announced that an agreement had been reached on "the form and content" of three treaties. Under the terms of the new treaties, the 1903 treaty was to be abrogated and Panama's sovereignty was to be recognized in the Canal Zone. The Panama Canal Company was to be supplanted by a United States-Panamanian partnership governing the defense, neutrality, and operation of the existing Canal, and other new sea level canals constructed in Panama.

With the publication of the terms of the three new treaties, a heated political debate was touched off in Panama by the demands of the Nationalists for more concessions from the United States. This, coupled with the opposition aroused in the United States, threatens to protract the renegotiation period.

The *muy simpatico* policy of Kennedy has been obtrusively replaced by the "Johnson Doctrine," but bona fide progress in relations between the United States and Panama has been, and must continue to be, made.

SELECTED BIBLIOGRAPHY

PRIMARY SOURCES

American and Panamanian general claims arbitration under the convention between U.S. and Panama of July 28, 1926 and Dec. 17, 1932. *Report of Bert L. Hunt, Agent for the U.S.* Washington: Government Printing Office, 1934.

Arosemena, G. & Diogenes. A., *Documentary diplomatic history of the Panama Canal.* Panama: 1961.

Colombia. Congreso. Senado. Comisión de Relaciones Exteriores. *Informe de la comisión de relaciones exteriores del senado sobre el proyecto de ley "que apruba las modificaciones introducidas por el senado norte-americano al tratado de 6 de abril de 1914" entre Colombia y los Estados Unidos de América.* Bogotá, 1921.

Department of State Bulletin

"Implementation of Treaty With Panama" (September 16, 1957), p. 477.

"O.A.S. Council Moves to Assist in Solving U.S.—Panama Dispute" (February 24, 1964), pp. 300–4.

"Panamanian Economic Mission Concludes Talks at Washington" (October 30, 1961), pp. 728–30.

"President Chiari of Panama Holds Talks With President Kennedy" (July 9, 1962), pp. 81–2.

"President Kennedy Replies to Letter From President Chiari of Panama" (December 4, 1961), pp. 932–3.

"President of Panama Proclaims Point Four Week" (March 31, 1958), pp. 572–3.

"President Restates U.S. Position on Panama and Canal Zone" (February 10, 1964), pp. 195–6.

"Secretary Rusk Interviewed on Voice of America" (March 2, 1964), pp. 330–6.

"The Situation in Panama" (February 3, 1964), pp. 152–7.

"Transfer of Property to Panama" (November 18, 1957), p. 804.

"United States and Panama Reestablish Diplomatic Relations" (April 27, 1964), pp. 655–6.

"United States and Panama Sign Atomic Energy Agreement" (July 13, 1959), p. 45.

"U.S. and Panama Announce Results of Canal Zone Talks" (August 17, 1963), pp. 246–7.

"U.S. and Panama Exchange Notes on Anti-American Demonstrations" (November 23, 1959), pp. 759–60.

"U.S. Plans New Sea Level Canal And New Treaty On Existing Canal" (January 4, 1965), pp. 5–6.

Wright, Almon R. "Defense Site Negotiations Between the United States and Panama, 1936–1948" (August 11, 1952), pp. 212–20.

Foreign Relations of The United States. Washington: Government Printing Office, Vols. 1900–1943.

Inter-American Development Bank. *Social Progress Trust Fund Third Annual Report.* Washington: Inter-American Development Bank, 1964.

Inter-American Development Bank. *Social Progress Trust Fund Fourth Annual Report.* Washington: Inter-American Development Bank, 1965.

International Commission of Jurists. *Investigating Committee Report on events in Panama January 9–12, 1964.* Geneva, 1964.

Ministerio de Relaciones Exteriores. *Documentos relacionados con los Estados Unidos, 1903–1965.*

Servicio Información De Los Estados Unidos. *Boletín de Prensa y Radio Panamá.* Republica de Panamá, comunicado No. 330 (20 de abril de 1965).

The Panama Canal. *Treaties and Acts of Congress Relating to the Isthmian Canal.* Washington: Government Printing Office, 1914.

United Nations. Security Council. Official Records. *Minutes of the emergency session of January 10–11, 1964 on Panama* (S—Pw1086).

USAID. *Program Budget Report* FY–64.

U.S. Congress, 86th Session. House of Representatives Committee on Foreign Affairs. *United States Relations with Panama, hearings before Subcommittee on Inter-American Affairs,* January 15, 1960.

U.S. Department of State. *Diplomatic History of the Panama Canal.* Correspondence relating to the negotiation and application of certain treaties on the subject of the construction of an interoceanic canal, and accompanying papers. Washington: Government Printing Office, 1914.

GENERAL AND MONOGRAPHIC WORKS

Alexander, Robert. *Communism in Latin America.* New Brunswick: Rutgers University Press, 1957.

Alfaro, Ricardo J. *Los canales internacionales Panamá.* Panamá: Escuela de Temporado Universidad de Panamá, 1957.

———. *Medio diglo de relaciones entre Panamá y los Estados Unidos.* Panamá: Impr. Nacional, 1953.

American University. Special Operations Research Office. Foreign Area Studies. *Special Warfare Area Handbook For Panama.* Washington: Government Printing Office, 1962.

Arias, Harmodio. *El canal de Panamá, un estudio en derecho internacional y diplomacia.* Panama: Editora Panamá América, 1957.

Ballesteros, Marto. (ed.) *Fiscal Survey of Panama.* Baltimore: The Johns Hopkins Press, 1964.

Batista Ballesteros, Isias. *El drama de Panamá y América, neustras relaciones con los E.E.U.U.* Panama: Impr. Panamá, 1961.

Baxter, R.R. *The Law of International Waterways.* Cambridge: Harvard University Press, 1964.

Bemis, Samuel F. *The Latin American Policy of the United States.* New York: Harcourt Brace & World Inc., 1943.

Berle, Adolf A. *Latin America Diplomacy And Reality.* New York: Council on Foreign Relations, 1962.

Biesanz, John and Mavis. *The People of Panama.* New York: Columbia University Press, 1955.

Bunau-Varilla, Philippe. *Historia auténtica de la escandalosa negociación del tratado del canal de Panamá escrita por el propio autor de esa convención*. Panamá: Talleres Imp., 1964.

Castillo Pimentel, Ernesto. *Panamá y los Estados Unidos*. Panama, 1953.

———. *Política exterior de Panamá los objetivos de neustra política exterior, los instrumentos o medios para lograrlos y las bases generales del nuevo tratado que debe la República de Panamá negociar con los Estados Unidos de América*. Panama: Impr. Panamá, 1961.

Donovan, John. *Red Machete: Communist Infiltration in the Americas*. Indianapolis: Bobbs Merrill Co. Inc., 1962.

Dreier, John C. *The Organization of American States*. New York: Council on Foreign Relations, 1962.

Dubois, Jules. *Danger Over Panama*. Indianapolis: Bobbs Merrill Co. Inc., 1964.

Du Val, Miles Percy. *Cadiz to Cathay . . . the story of the long diplomatic struggle for the Panama Canal*. Stanford: Stanford University Press, 1947.

Ealy, Lawrence O. *The Republic of Panama In World Affairs 1903–1950*. Philadelphia: University of Pennsylvania Press, 1951.

Fraga Iribaine, Manuel. *El canal de Panamá geopolítica diplomacia y derecho internacional*. Madrid: Consejo Superior de Investigaciones Científicas, Instituto Francisco de Vitoria, Sección de Derecho Marítimo, 1953.

Gerassi, John. *The Great Fear*. New York: Macmillan Co., 1963.

Goldrich, Daniel. *Political Systems of Latin America*, Martin Needler, editor. Princeton: D. Van Nostrand Co., Inc., 1964.

Guerrant, Edward O. *Roosevelt's Good Neighbor Policy*. Albuquerque: University of New Mexico Press, 1950.

Howard, Harry. *Military Government in the Panama Canal Zone*. Norman: University of Oklahoma Press, 1931.

King, Thelma. *El problema de la soberanía en las relaciones entre Panamá y los Estados Unidos de América*. Panama: Ministerio de Educación, 1961.

Lieuwen, Edwin. *Arms and Politics in Latin America.* New York: Frederick A. Praeger, 1961.

McCain, William D. *The United States and The Republic of Panama.* Durham: Duke University Press, 1937.

Mecham, J. Lloyd. *The United States And Inter-American Security 1889–1960.* Austin: University of Texas Press, 1962.

Padelford, Norman J. *The Panama Canal In Peace And War.* New York: Macmillan Co., 1942.

Parks, E. Taylor. *Colombia And The United States 1765–1934.* Durham: Duke University Press, 1934.

Perkins, Dexter. *A History Of The Monroe Doctrine.* Boston: Little, Brown & Co., 1963.

Poppino, Rollie. *International Communism in Latin America.* New York: The Free Press of Glencoe, 1964.

Quimbaza, Anteo. *Problemas historicas de actualidad, por qué el canal de Panamá debe ser y será de los panameños?* Bogotá: Ediciones Suramérica, 1964.

Radler, Don H. *El Gringo.* Philadelphia: Chilton Co., 1962.

Ray, Philip A. *South Wind Red.* Chicago: Henry Regnery Co., 1962.

Rippy, J. Fred. *Globe and Hemisphere.* Chicago: Henry Regnery Co., 1958.

Schmitt, Karl and David Burks. *Evolution or Chaos.* New York: Frederick A. Praeger, 1964.

Sociedad Panameñia de Acción Internacional. *Panama-United States relations. A situation that must be changed for the welfare of Panama and the honor of the United States. True history of the Panama Canal Treaty, born from fraud, perfidy, inequity, dishonor, coercion, chicanery, menace, disloyalty, and injustice.* Panama, 1934.

Stuart, Graham H. *Latin America And The United States.* New York: Appleton-Century Crofts, Inc., 1955.

Szulc, Tad. *The Winds of Revolution. Latin America Today and Tomorrow.* New York: Frederick A. Praeger, 1963.

The American Enterprise Institute For Public Policy Research. *The Panama Canal—Its Past And Future.* Washington, 1964.

Tondel, Lyman H. (ed.) *The Panama Canal.* Dobbs Ferry: Oceana Publications, Inc., 1965.

Urquidi, Victor L. *The Challenge of Development in Latin America.* New York: Frederick A. Praeger, 1964.

Westerman, George W. *Blocking Them At The Canal.* Panama, 1952.

———. *Fifty years* (1903–1953) *of treaty negotiations between the United States and the Republic of Panama.* Panama: Panama's Newspaper Guild, 1953.

PERIODICAL WORKS

Allan, Donald A., and Sherman, George. "Panama: Distrust and Delay," *The Reporter,* XXX (February 27, 1965), pp. 28–29.

Ameringer, Charles D. "Philippe Bunau-Varilla: New Light on the Panama Canal Treaty," *Hispanic American Historical Review,* February, 1966, pp. 28–52.

Aragon, Leopoldo. "Has The Panama Canal a Future?," *The New Republic,* July 30, 1962, pp. 16–17.

Baldwin, Hanson W. "Panama Canal's Value," *New York Times* Jan. 16, 1964, p. 14.

Bohning, Don. "Winds for Change Blowing Harder in Canal Zone" (Interview with Governor Fleming) *The Evening Bulletin,* June 15, 1965, p. 31.

Busey, James L. "Conflict in Panama," *The New Leader,* February 15, 1960, p. 19.

Ewing, Ann. "Dig With Nuclear Energy," *Science News Letter,* January 2, 1965, p. 3.

Fenwick, C. G. "Legal Aspects of the Panama Case," *American Journal of International Law*, April, 1964, pp. 436–41.

Finney, John W. "A Second Canal?" *The New Republic,* March 28, 1964, pp. 21–24.

Galton, Lawrence, "A New Canal Dug by Atom Bombs," *New York Times Magazine,* September 20, 1964, p. 254.

Garcia-Mora, Manuel R. "The Panama Canal Controversy," *Vital Speeches,* April 15, 1964, pp. 412–16.

Geyelin, Philip. "The Irksome Panama Wrangle," *The Reporter,* XXX (April 9, 1965), pp. 14–17.

Goldrich, Daniel, "Panamanian Students' Orientations Toward Government and Democracy," *Journal of Inter-American Studies, Vol. V* (July 1963), p. 397.

Goldrich, Daniel, "Requisites For Political Legitimacy in Panama," *Public Opinion Quarterly,* Winter, 1962, pp. 664–68.

Hispanic American Report 1948–1964. Sections designated "Panama."

Kempton, Murray. "The Orange Is Squeezed," *The New Republic,* January 25, 1964, pp. 15–18.

Kennedy, Paul P. "Panama Ponders Policy on Canal," *New York Times,* December 21, 1946, p. 14.

Latin American Times. (A daily published briefly in 1965.)

Matthews, Herbert L. "Communist Party in Panama is Deemed Potential Threat," *New York Times*, March 3, 1952, p. 5.

Niebuhr, Reinhold. "The Panama Crisis," *The New Republic,* February 1, 1964, pp. 5–6.

"Panama," *United Nations Review,* February, 1964, p. 6–8.

Poor, Peggy. "A View From The Canal," *The New Republic,* February 22, 1964, pp. 13–14.

Rippy, J. Fred, "The United States and Panama: The High Cost of Appeasement," *Inter-American Economic Affairs,* Spring, 1964, 87–94.

———. "The U.S. and Panama: Endless Appeasement," *Modern Age,* Summer, 1964, p. 277.

de la Rosa, Diógenes. "Panama—An American Problem," *Politica,* March, 1960.

Stratton, James H. "Sea Level Canal: How and Where," *Foreign Affairs,* April, 1965, pp. 513–18.

Tate, Mercer D. "The Panama Canal And Political Partnership," *The Journal of Politics, February*, 1963, pp. 119–38.

"The Panama Crisis," *Political Affairs,* March 1964, p. 3.

Thomas, J. Parnell. "Reds In the Panama Canal Zone," *Liberty,* May, 1948, pp. 14–15—.

Travis, Martin and James Watkins. "Control Of The Panama Canal: An Obsolete Shibboleth?," *Foreign Affairs,* April, 1959, pp. 407–18.

Travis, Martin and James Watkins. "Time Bomb in Panama," *The Nation,* April 30, 1960, pp. 378–81.

Tufty, Barbara. "Canal Route Problems," *Science News Letter,* February 1, 1964, p. 75.

"Up a Gum Tree in Darien," *The Economist,* January 18, 1964, pp. 201–2.

Whelan, James. "Calming the Storms Spawned By Violence in Panama Canal Zone," *The Latin American Times,* July 6, 1965, p. 2.

Excerpts

THE "HAY-HERRÁN" TREATY

Between the United States and Colombia,
Signed at Washington, January 22, 1903

THE UNITED STATES of America and the Republic of Colombia, being desirous to assure the construction of a ship canal to connect the Atlantic and Pacific Oceans and the Congress of the United States of America having passed an Act approved June 28, 1902, in furtherance of that object, a copy of which is hereunto annexed, the high contracting parties have resolved, for that purpose, to conclude a Convention and have accordingly appointed as their plenipotentiaries,

The President of the United States of America, John Hay, Secretary of State, and

The President of the Republic of Colombia, Thomas Herrán, Chargé d'Affaires, thereunto specially empowered by said governnment, who, after communicating to each other their respective full powers, found in good and due form, have agreed upon and concluded the following Articles:

ARTICLE 1

The Government of Colombia authorizes the New Panama Canal Company to sell and transfer to the United States its rights, privileges, properties, and concessions, as well as the Panama Railroad and all the shares or part of the shares of that company; but the public lands situated outside of the zone hereinafter specified, now corresponding to the concessions of both said enterprises shall revert to the Republic of Colombia, except any property now owned by or in the possession of the said companies within Panama or Colon, or the ports and terminals thereof.

But it is understood that Colombia reserves all its rights to the special shares in the capital of the New Panama Canal Company to which reference is made in Article 4 of the contract of December 10, 1890, which shares shall be paid their full nominal value at least; but as such right of Colombia exists solely in its character of stockholder in said Company, no obligation under this provision is imposed upon or assumed by the United States.

The Railroad Company (and the United States as owner of the enterprise) shall be free from the obligations imposed by the railroad concession, excepting as to the payment at maturity by the Railroad Company of the outstanding bonds issued by said Railroad Company.

ARTICLE 2

The United States shall have the exclusive right for the term of one hundred years, renewable at the sole and absolute option of the United States, for periods of similar duration so long as the United States may desire, to excavate, construct, maintain, operate, control, and protect the Maritime Canal with or without locks from the Atlantic to the Pacific Ocean, to and across the territory of Colombia, such canal to be of sufficient depth and capacity for vessels of the largest tonnage and greatest draft now engaged in commerce, and such as may be reasonably anticipated, and also the same rights for the construction, maintenance, operation, control, and protection of the Panama Railroad and of railway, telegraph and telephone lines, canals, dikes, dams and reservoirs, and such other auxiliary works as may be necessary and convenient for the construction, maintenance, protection and operation of the canal and railroads.

ARTICLE 3

To enable the United States to exercise the rights and privileges granted by this Treaty the Republic of Colombia grants to that Government the use and control for the term of one hundred years, renewable at the sole and absolute option of the United States, for periods of similar duration so long as the United States may desire, of a zone of territory along the route of the canal to be constructed five kilometers in width on either side thereof measured from its center line including therein the necessary auxiliary canals not exceeding in any case fifteen miles from the main canal and other works, together with ten fathoms of water in the Bay of Limon in extension of the canal, and at least three marine miles from mean low water mark from each terminus of the canal into the Caribbean Sea and the Pacific Ocean respectively. So far as necessary for the construction, maintenance and operation of the canal, the United States shall have the use and occupation of the group of small islands in the Bay of Panama named Perico, Naos, Culebra and Flamenco, but the same shall not be construed as being within the zone herein defined or governed by the special provisions applicable to the same.

This grant shall in no manner invalidate the titles or rights of private land holders in the said zone of territory, nor shall it interfere with the rights of way over the public roads of the Department; provided, however, that nothing herein contained shall operate to diminish, impair or restrict the rights elsewhere herein granted to the United States.

This grant shall not include the cities of Panama and Colon, except so far as lands and other property therein are now owned by or in possession of the said Canal Company or the said Railroad Company; but all the stipulations contained in Article 35 of the Treaty of 1846–48 between the contracting parties shall continue and apply in full force to the cities of Panama and Colon and to the accessory community lands and other property within the said zone, and the territory thereon shall be neutral territory, and the United States shall continue to guarantee the neutrality thereof and the sovereignty of Colombia thereover, in conformity with the above mentioned Article 35 of said Treaty.

In furtherance of this last provision there shall be created a Joint Commission by the Governments of Colombia and the United States that shall establish and enforce sanitary and police regulations.

ARTICLE 4

The rights and privileges granted to the United States by the terms of this convention shall not affect the sovereignty of the Republic of Colombia over the territory within whose boundaries such rights and privileges are to be exercised.

The United States freely acknowledges and recognizes this sovereignty and disavows any intention to impair it in any way whatever or to increase its territory at the expense of Colombia or of any of the sister republics in Central or South America, but on the contrary, it desires to strengthen the power of the republics on this continent, and to promote, develop and maintain their prosperity and independence.

ARTICLE 5

The Republic of Colombia authorizes the United States to construct and maintain at each entrance and terminus of the proposed canal a port of vessels using the same, with suitable light houses and other aids to navigation, and the United States is authorized to use and occupy within the limits of the zone fixed by this convention, such parts of the coast line and of the lands and islands adjacent thereto as are necessary for this purpose, including the construction and maintenance of breakwaters, dikes, jetties, embankments, coaling stations, docks and other appropriate works, and the United States undertakes the construction and maintenance of such works and will bear all the expense thereof. The ports when established are declared free, and their demarcations shall be clearly and definitely defined.

To give effect to this Article, the United States will give special attention and care to the maintenance of works for drainage, sanitary and healthful purposes along the line of the canal, and its dependencies, in order to prevent the invasion of epidemics or of securing their prompt suppression should they appear. With this end in view the United States will organize hospitals along the line of the canal, and will suitably supply or cause to be supplied the towns of Panama and Colon with the necessary aqueducts and drainage works, in order to prevent their becoming centers of infection on account of their proximity to the canal.

The Government of Colombia will secure for the United States or its nominees the lands and rights that may be required in the towns of Panama and Colon to effect the improvements above referred to, and the Government of the United States or its nominees shall be authorized to impose and collect equitable water rates, during fifty years for the service rendered; but on the expiration of said term the use of the water shall be free for the inhabitants of Panama and Colon, except to the extent that may be necessary for the operation and maintenance of said water system, including reservoirs, aqueducts, hydrants, supply service, drainage and other works.

ARTICLE 6

The Republic of Colombia agrees that it will not cede or lease to any foreign Government any of its islands or harbors within or adjacent to the Bay of Panama, nor on the Atlantic Coast of Colombia, between the Atrato River and the western boundary of the Department of Panama, for the purpose of establishing fortifications, naval or coaling stations, military posts, docks or other works that might interfere with the construction, maintenance, operation, protection, safety, and free use of the canal and auxiliary works. In order to enable Colombia to comply with this stipulation, the Government of the

United States agrees to give Colombia the material support that may be required in order to prevent the occupation of said islands and ports, guaranteeing there the sovereignty, independence and integrity of Colombia.

ARTICLE 7

The Republic of Colombia includes in the foregoing grant the right without obstacle, cost, or impediment, to such control, consumption and general utilization in any manner found necessary by the United States to the exercise by it of the grants to, and rights conferred upon it by this Treaty, the waters of the Chagres River and other streams, lakes and lagoons, of all non-navigable waters, natural and artificial, and also to navigate all rivers, streams, lakes and other navigable water-ways, within the jurisdiction and under the domain of the Republic of Colombia, in the Department of Panama, within or without said zone, as may be necessary or desirable for the construction, maintenance and operation of the canal and its auxiliary canals and other works, and without tolls or charges of any kind; and to raise and lower the levels of the waters, and to deflect them, and to impound any such waters, and to overflow any lands necessary for the due exercise of such grants and rights to the United States; and to rectify, construct and improve the navigation of any such rivers, streams, lakes and lagoons at the sole cost of the United States; but any such water-ways so made by the United States may be used by citizens of Colombia free of tolls or other charges. And the United States shall have the right to use without cost, any water, stone, clay, earth or other minerals belonging to Colombia on the public domain that may be needed by it.

All damages caused to private land owners by inundation or by the deviation of water courses, or in other ways, arising out of the construction or operation of the canal, shall in each case be appraised and settled by a joint commission appointed by the Governments of the United States and Colombia, but the cost of the indemnities so agreed upon shall be borne solely by the United States.

ARTICLE 8

The Government of Colombia declares free for all time the ports at either entrance of the Canal, including Panama and

Colon and the waters thereof in such manner that there shall not be collected by the Government of Colombia custom house tolls, tonnage, anchorage, light-house, wharf, pilot, or quarantine dues, nor any other charges or taxes of any kind shall be levied or imposed by the Government of Colombia upon any vessel using or passing through the Canal or belonging to or employed by the United States, directly or indirectly, in connection with the construction, maintenance and operation of the main work or its auxiliaries, or upon the cargo, officers, crew, or passengers of any such vessels; it being the intent of this convention that all vessels and their cargoes, crews, and passengers, shall be permitted to use and pass through the Canal and the ports leading thereto, subject to no other demands or impositions than such tolls and charges as may be imposed by the United States for the use of the Canal and other works. It being understood that such tolls and charges shall be governed by the provisions of Article 16.

The ports leading to the Canal, including Panama and Colon, also shall be free to the commerce of the world, and no duties or taxes shall be imposed, except upon merchandise destined to be introduced for the consumption of the rest of the Republic of Colombia, or the Department of Panama, and upon vessels touching at the ports of Colon and Panama and which do not cross the Canal.

Though said ports shall be free and open to all, the Government of Colombia may establish in them such custom houses and guards as Colombia may deem necessary to collect duties on importations destined to other portions of Colombia and to prevent contraband trade. The United States shall have the right to make use of the ports at the two extremities of the Canal including Panama and Colon as places of anchorage, in order to make repairs for loading, unloading, depositing, or transshipping cargoes either in transit or destined for the service of the Canal and other works.

Any concessions or privileges granted by Colombia for the operation of light houses at Colon and Panama shall be subject to expropriation, indemnification and payment in the same manner as is provided by Article 14 to the property therein mentioned; but Colombia shall make no additional grant of any such privilege nor change the status of any existing concession.

ARTICLE 9

There shall not be imposed any taxes, national, municipal, departmental, or of any other class, upon the canal, the vessels that may use it, tugs and other vessels employed in the service of the canal, the railways and auxiliary works, store houses, work shops, offices, quarters for laborers, factories of all kinds, warehouses, wharves, machinery and other works, property, and effects appertaining to the canal or railroad or that may be necessary for the service of the canal or railroad and their dependencies, whether situated within the cities of Panama and Colon, or any other place authorized by the provisions of this convention.

Nor shall there be imposed contributions or charges of a personal character of whatever species upon officers, employees, laborers, and other individuals in the service of the canal and its dependencies.

ARTICLE 10

It is agreed that telegraph and telephone lines, when established for canal purposes, may also, under suitable regulations, be used for public and private business in connection with the systems of Colombia and the other American Republics and with the lines of cable companies authorized to enter the ports and territories of these Republics; but the official dispatches of the Government of Colombia and the authorities of the Department of Panama shall not pay for such service higher tolls than those required from the officials in the service of the United States.

ARTICLE 11

The Government of Colombia shall permit the immigration and free access to the lands and workshops of the canal and its dependencies of all employees and workmen of whatever nationality under contract to work upon or seeking employment or in any wise connected with the said canal and its dependencies, with their respective families, and all such persons shall be free and exempt from the military service of the Republic of Colombia.

ARTICLE 12

The United States may import at any time into the said zone, free of customs duties, imposts, taxes, or other charges, and without any restriction, any and all vessels, dredges, engines, cars, machinery, tools, explosives, materials, supplies, and other articles necessary and convenient in the construction, maintenance and operation of the canal and auxiliary works, also all provisions, medicines, clothing, supplies and other things necessary and convenient for the officers, employees, workmen and laborers in the service and employ of the United States and for their families. If any such articles are disposed of for use without the zone excepting Panama and Colon and within the territory of the Republic, they shall be subject to the same import or other duties as like articles under the laws of Colombia or the ordinances of the Department of Panama.

ARTICLE 13

The United States shall have authority to protect and make secure the canal, as well as railways and other auxiliary works and dependencies, and to preserve order and discipline among the laborers and other persons who may congregate in that region, and to make and enforce such police and sanitary regulations as it may deem necessary to preserve order and public health thereon, and to protect navigation and commerce through and over said canal, railways and other works and dependencies from interruption or damage.

I. The Republic of Colombia may establish judicial tribunals within said zone, for the determination, according to its laws and judicial procedure, of certain controversies hereinafter mentioned.

Such judicial tribunal or tribunals so established by the Republic of Colombia shall have exclusive jurisdiction in said zone of all controversies between citizens of the Republic of Colombia, or between citizens of the Republic of Colombia and citizens of any foreign nation other than the United States.

II. Subject to the general sovereignty of Colombia over said zone, the United States may establish judicial tribunals thereon, which shall have jurisdiction of certain controversies hereinafter mentioned to be determined according to the laws and judicial procedure of the United States.

Such judicial tribunal or tribunals so established by the United States shall have exclusive jurisdiction in said zone of all controversies between citizens of the United States, and between citizens of the United States and citizens of any foreign nation other than the Republic of Colombia; and of all controversies in any wise growing out of or relating to the construction, maintenance or operation of the canal, railway and other properties and works.

III. The United States and Colombia engage jointly to establish and maintain upon said zone, judicial tribunals having civil, criminal and admiralty jurisdiction, and to be composed of jurists appointed by the Governments of the United States and Colombia in a manner hereafter to be agreed upon between said Governments, and which tribunals shall have jurisdiction of certain controversies hereinafter mentioned, and of all crimes, felonies and misdemeanors committed within said zone, and of all cases arising in admiralty, according to such laws and procedure as shall be hereafter agreed upon and declared by the two Governments.

Such joint judicial tribunal shall have exclusive jurisdiction in said zone of all controversies between citizens of the United States and citizens of Colombia, and between citizens of nations other than Colombia or the United States; and also of all crimes, felonies and misdemeanors committed within said zone, and of all questions of admiralty arising therein.

IV. The two Governments hereafter, and from time to time as occasion arises, shall agree upon and establish the laws and procedures which shall govern such joint judicial tribunal and which shall be applicable to the persons and cases over which such tribunal shall have jurisdiction, and also shall likewise create the requisite officers and employees of such court and establish their powers and duties; and further shall make adequate provision by like agreement for the pursuit, capture, imprisonment, detention and delivery within said zone of persons charged with the commitment of crimes, felonies or misdemeanors without said zone; and for the pursuit, capture, imprisonment, detention and delivery without said zone of persons charged with the commitment of crimes, felonies and misdemeanors within said zone.

ARTICLE 14

The works of the canal, the railways and their auxiliaries are declared of public utility, and in consequence all areas of land and water necessary for the construction, maintenance, and operation of the canal and other specified works may be expropriated in conformity with the laws of Colombia, except that the indemnity shall be conclusively determined without appeal, by a joint commission appointed by the Governments of Colombia and the United States.

The indemnities awarded by the Commission for such expropriation shall be borne by the United States, but the appraisal of said lands and the assessment of damages shall be based upon their value before the commencement of the work upon the canal.

ARTICLE 15

The Republic of Colombia grants to the United States the use of all the ports of the Republic open to commerce as places of refuge for any vessels employed in the canal enterprise, and for all vessels in distress having the right to pass through the canal and wishing to anchor in said ports. Such vessels shall be exempt from anchorage and tonnage dues on the part of Colombia.

ARTICLE 16

The canal, when constructed, and the entrance thereto shall be neutral in perpetuity, and shall be opened upon the terms provided for by Section I of Article three of, and in conformity with all the stipulations of, the treaty entered into by the Government of the United States and Great Britain on November 18, 1901.

ARTICLE 17

The Government of Colombia shall have the right to transport over the canal its vessels, troops, and munitions of war at all times without paying charges of any kind. This exemption is to be extended to the auxiliary railway for the transportation of persons in the service of the Republic of Colombia or of the Department of Panama, or of the police force charged with the preservation of public order outside of said zone, as well as to their baggage, munitions of war and supplies.

ARTICLE 18

The United States shall have full power and authority to establish and enforce regulations for the use of the canal, railways, and the entering ports and auxiliary works, and to fix rates of tolls and charges thereof, subject to the limitations stated in Article 16.

ARTICLE 19

The rights and privileges granted to the United States by this convention shall not affect the sovereignty of the Republic of Colombia over the real estate that may be acquired by the United States by reason of the transfer of the rights of the New Panama Canal Company and the Panama Railroad Company lying outside of the said canal zone.

ARTICLE 20

If by virtue of any existing treaty between the Republic of Colombia and any third power, there may be any privilege or concession relative to an interoceanic means of communication which especially favors such third power, and which in any of its terms may be incompatible with the terms of the present convention, the Republic of Colombia agrees to cancel or modify such treaty in due form, for which purpose it shall give to the said third power the requisite notification within the term of four months from the date of the present convention, and in case the existing treaty contains no clause permitting its modification or annulment, the Republic of Colombia agrees to procure its modification or annulment in such form that there shall not exist any conflict with the stipulations of the present convention.

ARTICLE 21

The rights and privileges granted by the Republic of Colombia to the United States in the preceding Articles are understood to be free of all anterior concessions or privileges to other Governments, corporations, syndicates or individuals, and consequently, if there should arise any claims on account of the present concessions and privileges or otherwise, the claimants shall resort to the Government of Colombia and not to the United States for any indemnity or compromise which may be required.

ARTICLE 22

The Republic of Colombia renounces and grants to the United States the participation to which it might be entitled in the future earnings of the canal under Article 15 of the concessionary contract with Lucien N. B. Wyse now owned by the New Panama Canal Company and any and all other rights or claims of a pecuniary nature arising under or relating to said concession, or arising under or relating to the concessions to the Panama Railroad Company or any extension or modification thereof; and it likewise renounces, confirms and grants to the United States, now and hereafter, all the rights and property reserved in the said concessions which otherwise would belong to Colombia at or before the expiration of the terms of ninety-nine years of the concessions granted to or held by the above mentioned party and companies, and all right, title and interest which it now has or may hereafter have, in and to the lands, canal, works, property and rights held by the said companies under said concessions or otherwise, and acquired or to be acquired by the United States from or through the New Panama Canal Company, including any property and rights which might or may in the future either by lapse of time, forfeiture or otherwise, revert to the Republic of Colombia under any contracts of concessions, with said Wyse, the Universal Panama Canal Company, the Panama Railroad Company and the New Panama Canal Company.

The aforesaid rights and property shall be and are free and released from any present or reversionary interest in or claims of Colombia and the title of the United States thereto upon consummation of the contemplated purchase by the United States from the New Panama Canal Company, shall be absolute, so far as concerns the Republic of Colombia, excepting always the rights of Colombia specifically secured under this treaty.

ARTICLE 23

If it should become necessary at any time to employ armed forces for the safety or protection of the canal, or of the ships that make use of the same, or the railways and other works, the Republic of Colombia agrees to provide the forces necessary for such purpose, according to the circumstances of the case, but if the Government of Colombia cannot effectively comply with this obligation, then, with the consent of or at the request of Colombia, or of her Minister at Washington, or of the local authorities, civil or military, the United States shall employ such force as may be necessary for that sole purpose; and as soon as the necessity shall have ceased will withdraw the forces so employed. Under exceptional circumstances, however, on account of unforeseen or imminent danger to said canal, railways and other works, or to the lives and property of the persons employed upon the canal, railways, and other works, the Government of the United States is authorized to act in the interest of their protection, without the necessity of obtaining the consent beforehand of the Government of Colombia; and it shall give immediate advice of the measures adopted for the purpose stated; and as soon as sufficient Colombian forces shall arrive to attend to the indicated purpose, those of the United States shall retire.

ARTICLE 24

The Government of the United States agrees to complete the construction of the preliminary works necessary, together with all the auxiliary works, in the shortest time possible; and within two years from the date of the exchange of ratification of this convention the main works of the canal proper shall be commenced, and it shall be opened to the traffic between the two oceans within twelve years after such period of two years. In case, however, that any difficulties or obstacles should arise in the construction of the canal which are at present impossible to foresee, in consideration of the good faith which the Government of the United States shall have proceeded, and the large amount of money expended so far on the works and the nature of the difficulties which may have arisen, the Government of Colombia will prolong the terms stipulated in this Article up to twelve years more for the completion of the work of the canal.

But in case the United States should, at any time, determine to make such canal practically a sea level canal, then such period shall be extended for ten years further.

ARTICLE 25

As the price or compensation for the right to use the zone granted in this convention by Colombia to the United States for the construction of a canal, together with the proprietary right over the Panama Railroad, and for the annuity of two hundred and fifty thousand dollars gold, which Colombia ceases to receive from the said railroad, as well as in compensation for other rights, privileges and exemptions granted to the United States, and in consideration of the increase in the administrative expenses of the Department of Panama consequent upon the construction of the said canal, the Government of the United States binds itself to pay Colombia the sum of ten million dollars in gold coin of the United States on the exchange of the ratification of this convention after its approval according to the laws of the respective countries, and also an annual payment during the life of this convention of two hundred and fifty thousand dollars in like gold coin, beginning nine years after the date aforesaid.

The provisions of this Article shall be in addition to all other benefits assured to Colombia under this convention.

But no delay nor difference of opinion under this Article shall affect nor interrupt the full operation and effect of this convention in all other respects:

ARTICLE 26

No change either in the Government or in the laws and treaties of Colombia, shall, without the consent of the United States, affect any right of the United States under the present convention, or under any treaty stipulation between the two countries (that now exist or may hereafter exist) touching the subject matter of this convention.

If Colombia shall hereafter enter as a constituent into any other Government or into any union or confederation of States so as to merge her sovereignty or independence in such Government, union, or confederation, the rights of the United States under this convention, shall not be in any respect lessened or impaired.

ARTICLE 27

The joint commission referred to in Articles 3, 7, and 14 shall be established as follows:

The President of the United States shall nominate two persons and the President of Colombia shall nominate two persons and they shall proceed to a decision; but in case of disagreement of the Commission (by reason of their being equally divided in conclusion) an umpire shall be appointed by the two Governments, who shall render the decision. In the event of death, absence or incapacity of any Commissioner or umpire, or of his omitting, declining or ceasing to act, his place shall be filled by the appointment of another person in the manner above indicated. All decisions by a majority of the Commission or by the umpire shall be final.

ARTICLE 28

This convention when signed by the contracting parties, shall be ratified according to the laws of the respective countries and shall be exchanged at Washington within a term of eight months from this date, or earlier if possible.

In faith whereof, the respective plenipotentiaries have signed the present convention in duplicate and have hereunto affixed their respective seals.

Done at the City of Washington, the 22nd day of January in the year of our Lord nineteen hundred and three.

(Signed) JOHN HAY SEAL

(Signed) TOMÁS HERRÁN SEAL

"HAY-BUNAU-VARILLA" CONVENTION

Between the United States and Panama,
Signed at Washington, November 18, 1903

The Treaty was ratified by the President of the United States, February 25, 1904, and ratifications exchanged February 26, 1904

ISTHMIAN CANAL CONVENTION

THE UNITED STATES of America and the Republic of Panama being desirous to insure the construction of a ship canal across the Isthmus of Panama to connect the Atlantic and Pacific oceans, and the Congress of the United States of America having passed an act approved June 28, 1902, in furtherance of that object, by which the President of the United States is authorized to acquire within a reasonable time the control of the necessary territory of the Republic of Colombia, and the sovereignty of such territory being actually vested in the Republic of Panama, the high contracting parties have resolved for that purpose to conclude a convention and have accordingly appointed as their plenipotentiaries,—

The President of the United States of America, JOHN HAY, Secretary of State, and

The Government of the Republic of Panama, PHILIPPE BUNAU-Varilla, Envoy Extraordinary and Minister Plenipotentiary of the Republic of Panama, thereunto specially empowered by said government, who after communicating with each other their respective full powers, found to be in good and due form, have agreed upon and concluded the following articles:

ARTICLE 1

The United States guarantees and will maintain the independence of the Republic of Panama.

ARTICLE 2

The Republic of Panama grants to the United States in perpetuity the use, occupation and control of a zone of land and land under water for the construction, maintenance, operation, sanitation and protection of said Canal of the width of ten miles extending to the distance of five miles on each side of the center line of the route of the Canal to be constructed; the said zone beginning in the Caribbean Sea three marine miles from mean low water mark and extending to and across the Isthmus of Panama into the Pacific ocean to a distance of three marine miles from mean low water mark with the proviso that the cities of Panama and Colon and the harbors adjacent to said cities, which are included within the boundaries of the zone above described, shall not be included within this grant. The Republic of Panama further grants to the United States in perpetuity the use, occupation and control of any other lands and waters outside of the zone above described which may be necessary and convenient for the construction, maintenance, operation, sanitation and protection of the said Canal or of any auxiliary canals or other works necessary and convenient for the construction, maintenance, operation, sanitation and protection of the said enterprise.

The Republic of Panama further grants in like manner to the United States in perpetuity all islands within the limits of the zone above described and in addition thereto the group of small islands in the Bay of Panama, named Perico, Naos, Culebra and Flamenco.

ARTICLE 3

The Republic of Panama grants to the United States all the rights, power and authority within the zone mentioned and described in Article 2 of this agreement and within the limits of all auxiliary lands and waters mentioned and described in said Article 2 which the United States would possess and exercise if it were the sovereign of the territory within which said lands and waters are located to the entire exclusion of the exercise by the Republic of Panama of any such sovereign rights, power or authority.

ARTICLE 4

As rights subsidiary to the above grants the Republic of Panama grants in perpetuity to the United States the right to use the rivers, streams, lakes and other bodies of water within its limits for navigation, the supply of water or water-power or other purposes, so far as the use of said rivers, streams, lakes and bodies of water and the waters thereof may be necessary and convenient for the construction, maintenance, operation, sanitation and protection of the said Canal.

ARTICLE 5

The Republic of Panama grants to the United States in perpetuity a monopoly for the construction, maintenance and operation of any system of communication by means of canal or railroad across its territory between the Caribbean Sea and the Pacific ocean.

ARTICLE 6

The grants herein contained shall in no manner invalidate the titles or rights of private land holders or owners of private property in the said zone or in or to any of the lands or waters granted to the United States by the provisions of any Article of this treaty, nor shall they interfere with the rights of way over the public roads passing through the said zone or over any of the said lands or waters unless said rights of way or private rights shall conflict with rights herein granted to the United States in which case the rights of the United States shall be superior. All damages caused to the owners of private lands or private property of any kind by reason of the grants contained in this treaty or by reason of the operations of the United States, its agents or employees, or by reason of the construction, maintenance, operation, sanitation and protection of the said Canal or of the works of sanitation and protection herein provided for, shall be appraised and settled by a joint Commission appointed by the Governments of the United States and the Republic of Panama, whose decisions as to such damages shall be final and whose awards as to such damages shall be paid solely by the United States. No part of the work on said Canal or the Panama railroad or on any auxiliary works relating thereto and authorized by the terms of this treaty shall be prevented, delayed or impeded by or pending such proceedings to ascertain such damages. The appraisal of said private lands and private property and the assessment of damages to them shall be based upon their value before the date of this convention.

ARTICLE 7

The Republic of Panama grants to the United States within the limits of the cities of Panama and Colon and their adjacent harbors and within the territory adjacent thereto the right to acquire by purchase or by the exercise of the right of eminent domain, any lands, buildings, water rights or other properties necessary and convenient for the construction, maintenance, operation and protection of the Canal and of any works of sanitation, such as the collection and disposition of sewage and the distribution of water in the said cities of Panama and Colon, which, in the discretion of the United States may be necessary and convenient for the construction, maintenance, operation, sanitation and protection of the said Canal and railroad. All such works of sanitation, collection and disposition of sewage and distribution of water in the cities of Panama and Colon shall be made at the expense of the United States, and the Government of the United States, its agents or nominees shall be authorized to impose and collect water rates and sewerage rates which shall be sufficient to provide for the payment of interest and the amortization of the principal of the cost of said works within a period of fifty years and upon the expiration of said term of fifty years the system of sewers and water works shall revert to and become the properties of the cities of Panama and Colon respectively, and the use of the water shall be free to the inhabitants of Panama and Colon, except to the extent that water rates may be necessary for the operation and maintenance of said system of sewers and water.

The Republic of Panama agrees that the cities of Panama and Colon shall comply in perpetuity with the sanitary ordinances whether of a preventive or curative character prescribed by the United States and in case the Government of Panama is unable or fails in its duty to enforce this compliance by the cities of Panama and Colon with the sanitary ordinances of the United States the Republic of Panama grants to the United States the right and authority to enforce the same.

The same right and authority are granted to the United States for the maintenance of public order in the cities of Panama and Colon and the territories and harbors adjacent thereto in case the Republic of Panama should not be, in the judgment of the United States, able to maintain such order.

ARTICLE 8

The Republic of Panama grants to the United States all rights which it now has or hereafter may acquire to the property of the New Panama Canal Company and the Panama Railroad

Company as a result of the transfer of sovereignty from the Republic of Colombia to the Republic of Panama over the Isthmus of Panama and authorizes the New Panama Canal Company to sell and transfer to the United States its rights, privileges, properties and concessions as well as the Panama Railroad and all the shares or part of the shares of that company; but the public lands situated outside of the zone described in Article 2 of this treaty now included in the concessions to both said enterprises and not required in the construction or operation of the Canal shall revert to the Republic of Panama except any property now owned by or in the possession of said companies within Panama or Colon or the ports or terminals thereof.

ARTICLE 9

The United States agrees that the ports at either entrance of the Canal and the waters thereof, and the Republic of Panama agrees that the towns of Panama and Colon shall be free for all time so that there shall not be imposed or collected custom house tolls, tonnage, anchorage, lighthouse, wharf, pilot, or quarantine dues or any other charges or taxes of any kind upon any vessel using or passing through the Canal or belonging to or employed by the United States, directly or indirectly, in connection with the construction, maintenance, operation, sanitation and protection of the main Canal, or auxiliary works, or upon the cargo, officers, crew, or passengers of any such vessels, except such tolls and charges as may be imposed by the United States for the use of the Canal and other works, and except tolls and charges imposed by the Republic of Panama upon merchandise destined to be introduced for the consumption of the rest of the Republic of Panama, and upon vessels touching at the ports of Colon and Panama and which do not cross the Canal.

The Government of the Republic of Panama shall have the right to establish in such ports and in the towns of Panama and Colon such houses and guards as it may deem necessary to collect duties on importations destined to other portions of Panama and to prevent contraband trade. The United States shall have the right to make use of the towns and harbors of Panama and Colon as places of anchorage, and for making repairs, for loading, unloading, depositing, or trans-shipping cargoes either in transit or destined for the service of the Canal and for other works pertaining to the Canal.

ARTICLE 10

The Republic of Panama agrees that there shall not be imposed any taxes, national, municipal, departmental, or of any other class, upon the Canal, the railways and auxiliary works, tugs and other vessels employed in the service of the Canal, store houses, work shops, offices, quarters for laborers, factories of all kinds, warehouses, wharves, machinery and other works, property, and effects appertaining to the Canal or railroad and auxiliary works, or their officers or employees, situated within the cities of Panama and Colon, and that there shall not be imposed contributions or charges of a personal character of any kind upon officers, employees, laborers, and other individuals in the service of the Canal and railroad and auxiliary works.

ARTICLE 11

The United States agrees that the official dispatches of the Government of the Republic of Panama shall be transmitted over any telegraph and telephone lines established for canal purposes and used for public and private business at rates not higher than those required from officials in the service of the United States.

ARTICLE 12

The Government of the Republic of Panama shall permit the immigration and free access to the lands and workshops of the Canal and its auxiliary works of all employees and workmen of whatever nationality under contract to work upon or seeking employment upon or in any wise connected with the said Canal and its auxiliary works, with their respective families, and all such persons shall be free and exempt from the military service of the Republic of Panama.

ARTICLE 13

The United States may import at any time into the said zone and auxiliary lands, free of custom duties, imposts, taxes, or other charges, and without any restrictions, any and all vessels, dredges, engines, cars, machinery, tools, explosives, materials, supplies, and other articles necessary and convenient in the construction, maintenance, operation, sanitation and protection of the Canal and auxiliary works, and all provisions, medicines, clothing, supplies and other things necessary and convenient for the officers, employees, workmen and laborers in the service and employ of the United States and for their families. If any such articles are disposed of for use outside of the zone and auxiliary lands granted to the United States and within the territory of the Republic, they shall be subject to the same import or other duties as like articles imported under the laws of the Republic of Panama.

ARTICLE 14

As the price or compensation for the rights, powers and privileges granted in this convention by the Republic of Panama to the United States, the Government of the United States agrees to pay to the Republic of Panama the sum of ten million dollars ($10,000,000) in gold coin of the United States on the exchange of the ratification of this convention and also an annual payment during the life of this convention of two hundred and fifty thousand dollars ($250,000) in like gold coin, beginning nine years after the date aforesaid.

The provisions of this Article shall be in addition to all other benefits assured to the Republic of Panama under this convention.

But no delay or difference of opinion under this Article or any other provisions of this treaty shall affect or interrupt the full operation and effect of this convention in all other respects.

ARTICLE 15

The joint commission referred to in Article 6 shall be established as follows:

The President of the United States shall nominate two persons and the President of the Republic of Panama shall nominate two persons and they shall proceed to a decision; but in case of disagreement of the Commission (by reason of their being equally divided in conclusion) an umpire shall be appointed by the two Governments who shall render the decision. In the event of the death, absence, or incapacity of a Commissioner or umpire, or of his omitting, declining or ceasing to act, his place shall be filled by the appointment of another person in the manner above indicated. All decisions by a majority of the Commission or by the umpire shall be final.

ARTICLE 16

The two governments shall make adequate provision by future agreement for the pursuit, capture, imprisonment, detention and delivery within said zone and auxiliary lands to the authorities of the Republic of Panama of persons charged with the commitment of crimes, felonies or misdemeanors without said zone and for the pursuit, capture, imprisonment, detention and delivery without said zone to the authorities of the United States of persons charged with the commitment of crimes, felonies and misdemeanors within said zone and auxiliary lands.

ARTICLE 17

The Republic of Panama grants to the United States the use of all the ports of the Republic open to commerce as places of refuge for any vessels employed in the Canal enterprise, and for all vessels passing or bound to pass through the Canal which may be in distress and be driven to seek refuge in said ports. Such vessels shall be exempt from anchorage and tonnage dues on the part of the Republic of Panama.

ARTICLE 18

The Canal, when constructed, and the entrances thereto shall be neutral in perpetuity, and shall be opened upon the terms provided for by Section I of Article three of, and in conformity with all the stipulations of, the treaty entered into by the Governments of the United States and Great Britain on November 18, 1901.

ARTICLE 19

The Government of the Republic of Panama shall have the right to transport over the Canal its vessels and its troops and munitions of war in such vessels at all times without paying charges of any kind. The exemption is to be extended to the auxiliary railway for the transportation of persons in the service of the Republic of Panama, or of the police force charged with the preservation of public order outside of said zone, as well as to their baggage, munitions of war and supplies.

ARTICLE 20

If by virtue of any existing treaty in relation to the territory of the Isthmus of Panama, whereof the obligations shall descend or be assumed by the Republic of Panama, there may be any privilege or concession in favor of the Government or the citizens and subjects of a third power relative to an interoceanic means of communication which in any of its terms may be incompatible with the terms of the present convention, the Republic of Panama agrees to cancel or modify such treaty in due form, for which purpose it shall give to the said third power the requisite notification within the term of four months from the date of the present convention, and in case the existing treaty contains no clause permitting its modifications or annulment, the Republic of Panama agrees to procure its modification or annulment in such form that there shall not exist any conflict with the stipulations of the present convention.

ARTICLE 21

The rights and privileges granted by the Republic of Panama to the United States in the preceding Articles are understood to be free of all anterior debts, liens, trusts, or liabilities, or concessions or privileges to other Governments, corporations, syndicates or individuals, and consequently, if there should arise any claims on account of the present concessions and privileges or otherwise, the claimants shall resort to the Government of the Republic of Panama and not to the United States for any indemnity or compromise which may be required.

ARTICLE 22

The Republic of Panama renounces and grants to the United States the participation to which it might be entitled in the future earnings of the Canal under Article 15 of the concessionary contract with Lucien N. B. Wyse now owned by the New Panama Canal Company and any and all other rights or claims of a pecuniary nature arising under or relating to said concession, or arising under or relating to the concessions to the Panama Railroad Company or any extension or modification thereof; and it likewise renounces, confirms and grants to the United States, now and hereafter, all the rights and property reserved in the said concessions which otherwise would belong to Panama at or before the expiration of the terms of ninety-nine years of the concessions granted to or held by the above mentioned party and companies, and all right, title and interest which it now has or may hereafter have, in and to the lands, canal, works, property and rights held by the said companies under said concessions or otherwise, and acquired or to be acquired by the United States from or through the New Panama Canal Company, including any property and rights which might or may in the future either by lapse of time, forfeiture or otherwise, revert to the Republic of Panama under any contracts or concessions, with said Wyse, the Universal Panama Canal Company, the Panama Railroad Company and the New Panama Canal Company.

The aforesaid rights and property shall be and are free and released from any present or reversionary interest in or claims of Panama and the title of the United States thereto upon consummation of the contemplated purchase by the United States from the New Panama Canal Company, shall be absolute, so far as concerns the Republic of Panama, excepting always the rights of the Republic specifically secured under this treaty.

ARTICLE 23

If it should become necessary at any time to employ armed forces for the safety or protection of the Canal, or of the ships that make use of the same, or the railways and auxiliary works, the United States shall have the right, at all times and in its discretion, to use its police and its land and naval forces or to establish fortifications for these purposes.

ARTICLE 24

No change either in the Government or in the laws and treaties of the Republic of Panama shall, without the consent of the United States, affect any right of the United States under the present convention, or under any treaty stipulation between the two countries that now exists or may hereafter exist touching the subject matter of this convention.

If the Republic of Panama shall hereafter enter as a constituent into any other Government or into any union or confederation of states, so as to merge her sovereignty or independence in such Government, union or confederation, the rights of the

United States under this convention shall not be in any respect lessened or impaired.

ARTICLE 25

For the better performance of the engagements of this convention and to the end of the efficient protection of the Canal and the preservation of its neutrality, the Government of the Republic of Panama will sell or lease to the United States lands adequate and necessary for naval or coaling stations on the Pacific coast and on the western Caribbean coast of the Republic at certain points to be agreed upon with the President of the United States.

ARTICLE 26

This convention when signed by the Plenipotentiaries of the Contracting Parties shall be ratified by the respective Governments and the ratifications shall be exchanged at Washington at the earliest date possible.

In faith whereof the respective Plenipotentiaries have signed the present convention in duplicate and have hereunto affixed their respective seals.

Done at the City of Washington the 18th day of November in the year of our Lord nineteen hundred and three.

JOHN HAY SEAL

P. BUNAU VARILLA SEAL

"ROOT-CORTES-AROSEMENA" TREATIES

TREATY WITH PANAMA

The United States of America and the Republic of Panama, mutually desiring to facilitate the construction, maintenance and operation of the interoceanic canal across the Isthmus of Panama and to promote a good understanding between the nations most closely and directly concerned in this highway of the world's commerce, and thereby to further its construction and protection, deem it well to amend and in certain respects supplement the treaty concluded between the United States of America and the Republic of Panama on the 18th of November, 1903, and to that end have appointed their respective Plenipotentiaries, to wit:

The President of the United States of America, Elihu Root, Secretary of State of the United States;

The President of the Republic of Panama, Carlos Constantino Arosemena, Envoy Extraordinary and Minister Plenipotentiary of the Republic of Panama,

Who, after exchange of their full powers, found to be in good and due form, have agreed upon the following articles:

ARTICLE I.

It is mutually agreed between the High Contracting Parties that Article XIV of the treaty concluded between them on the 18th day of November, 1903, be and the same is hereby amended by substituting therein the words "four years" for the words "nine years," and accordingly the United States of America agrees to make the annual payments therein provided for beginning four years from the exchange of said treaty instead of nine years from that date.

The United States of America consents that the Republic of Panama may assign and transfer, in advance, to the Republic of Colombia, and to its assigns or nominees, the first ten annual installments of Two Hundred and Fifty Thousand Dollars each, so falling due under said treaty as thus amended, on the 26th days of February in the years 1908 to 1917, both inclusive, and its right and title thereto, and, upon the direction and acquittance therefor of the Republic of Panama, will pay said ten installments as they respectfully fall due directly to the Republic of Colombia, its assigns or nominees, for account of the

Republic of Panama. Such installments as may have matured when the ratifications of this treaty shall be exchanged pursuant to its terms shall be payable on the ninetieth day after the date of such exchange.

ARTICLE II.

Final delimitation of the cities of Panama and Colon and of the harbors adjacent thereto, under and to effectuate the provisions of Article II of said treaty of November 18th, 1903, shall be made by agreement between the Executive Departments of the two Governments, immediately upon the exchange of ratifications of this treaty.

It is further agreed that the Republic of Panama shall have the right, upon one year's previous notice, at any time within the period of fifty years mentioned in Article VII of said treaty of November 18th, 1903, to purchase and take over from the United States of America so much of the water mains and distributing system of the water works mentioned in said article, for the supply of the City of Panama, and of the appliances and appurtenances thereof, as may lie outside the Canal Zone, and terminate the provisions of said treaty for the ultimate acquisition by the Republic of Panama of said water works, upon payment of such sum in cash as may be agreed upon as just by the Presidents of the two High Contracting Parties, who are hereby fully empowered so to agree; if there shall arise any dispute or difference between the High Contracting Parties with respect to such delimitation, or if their Presidents shall not be able to agree as to the sum so to be paid, then upon the request of either party, any such difference shall be submitted to the Tribunal of Arbitration, hereinafter provided for.

ARTICLE III.

It is further agreed that all differences which may arise relating to the interpretation or application of the treaty between the United States of America and the Republic of Panama concluded on the 18th day of November, 1903, which it may not have been possible to settle by diplomacy, shall be referred on the request of either party, to a Tribunal of Arbitration to consist of three members, of whom the United States shall nominate one member, the Republic of Panama shall nominate one member, and the two members thus nominated shall jointly nominate a third member, or, in the event of their failure to agree within three months after appointment, upon the nomination of the third member, such member shall be appointed by the President of Peru. Said Tribunal shall decide by a majority vote all questions respecting its procedure and action, as well as all questions concerning the matters submitted to it. The Tribunal shall deliver duplicate copies of its decisions upon any of the matters submitted to it, as hereinafter specified, to the United States and to the Republic of Panama, and any such decision signed by a majority of the members of the Tribunal shall be conclusively deemed the decision of the Tribunal. Any vacancy in the membership of the Tribunal caused by the death, incapacity, or withdrawal of any member shall be filled in the manner provided for the original appointment of the member whose office shall thus become vacant. The determinations of said Tribunal shall be final, conclusive and binding upon the High Contracting Parties hereto, who bind themselves to abide by and conform to the same.

The temporary working arrangement or modus vivendi contained in the Executive Orders of December 3rd, 6th, 16th, and 28th, 1904, and January 5, 1905, made at Panama by the Secretary of War of the United States, and by the President of Panama, on December 6, 1904, which was entered into for the purpose of the practical operation of the aforesaid Treaty of November 18, 1903, shall be submitted to revision by the Executive Departments of the two Governments with the view to making the same and the practice thereunder conform (if in any respect they shall be found not to conform) to the true intent and meaning of the said treaty and to the preservation and protection of the rights of the two Governments and of the citizens of both parties thereunder; and any question as to such conformity arising upon such revision which shall remain in dispute shall be submitted to said Tribunal of Arbitration.

It is now agreed, however, that the rate of duty to be levied by the Republic of Panama and fixed at 10 per cent *ad valorem* by the first proviso to said Executive Order of December 3rd, 1904, may be increased to any rate not exceeding twenty per cent *ad valorem,* at the pleasure of said Republic.

ARTICLE IV.

There shall be a full, entire and reciprocal liberty of commerce and navigation between the citizens of the two High Contracting Parties, who shall have reciprocally the right, on conforming to the laws of the country, to enter, travel, and reside in all parts of the respective territories, saving always the right of expulsion of undesirable persons which right each Government reserves to itself, and they shall enjoy in this respect, for the protection of their persons and their property, the same treatment and the same rights as the citizens or subjects of the most favored nation; it being understood and agreed that citizens of either of the two Republics thus residing in the territory of the other shall be exempt from military service imposed upon the citizens of such Republic.

And the United States of America further agrees that the Republic of Panama and the citizens thereof shall and shall be accorded on equal terms all such privileges, rights, and advantages in respect to the construction, operation, and use of the Canal, railroad, telegraph and other facilities of the United States within the Canal Zone, and in respect of all other matters relating thereto, operating within or affecting the Canal Zone or property and persons therein, as may at any time be granted by the United States of America in accord with said treaty of November 18th, 1903, directly or indirectly, to any other nation or the citizens or subjects thereof, it being the intention of the Parties that the Republic of Panama and the citizens thereof shall be with respect thereto placed at least on an equal footing with the most favored nation and the citizens or subjects thereof.

ARTICLE V.

It is expressly understood and agreed that this treaty shall not become operative nor its provisions obligatory upon either of the High Contracting Parties, until and unless the treaties of even date between the Republic of Colombia and the Republic of Panama and between the Republic of Colombia and the United States of America are both duly ratified and the ratifications thereof are exchanged simultaneously with the exchange of ratifications of the present treaty.

ARTICLE VI.

This treaty shall be ratified and the ratifications thereof shall be exchanged at Washington as soon as possible.

In witness whereof, we the respective Plenipotentiaries have signed the present treaty, in duplicate, in the English and Spanish languages and have hereunto affixed our respective seals.

Done at Washington the 9th day of January, in the year of our Lord one thousand nine hundred and nine.

(Signed) ELIHU ROOT SEAL

(Signed) C. C. AROSEMENA SEAL

TREATY WITH COLOMBIA

The United States of America and the Republic of Colombia, being equally animated by the desire to remove all obstacles to a good understanding between them and to facilitate the settlement of the questions heretofore pending between Colombia and Panama by adjusting at the same time the relations of Colombia to the canal which the United States is now constructing across the Isthmus of Panama, have resolved to conclude a Treaty and to that end have appointed as their Plenipotentiaries:

The President of the United States of America, Elihu Root, Secretary of State of the United States;

The President of the Republic of Colombia, Senor don Enrique Cortes, Envoy Extraordinary and Minister Plenipotentiary of the Republic of Colombia at Washington;

Who, after communicating to each other their respective full powers, which were found to be in due and proper form, have agreed upon the following articles:

ARTICLE I.

There shall be mutual and inviolable peace and sincere friendship between the Governments and peoples of the two High Contracting Parties without exception of persons or places under their respective dominion.

ARTICLE II.

In consideration of the provisions and stipulations hereinafter contained it is agreed as follows:

The Republic of Colombia shall have liberty at all times to

convey through the ship canal now in course of construction by the United States across the Isthmus of Panama the troops, materials for war and ships of war of the Republic of Colombia, without paying any duty to the United States; even in the case of an international war between Colombia and another country.

While the said interoceanic canal is in course of construction the troops and materials for war of the Republic of Colombia, even in the case of an international war between Colombia and any other country, shall be transported on the railway between Ancon and Cristobal, or on any other railway substituted therefor, upon the same conditions on which similar service is rendered to the United States.

The officers, agents and employees of the Government of Colombia shall, during the same period, be entitled to free passage upon the said railway across the Isthmus of Panama upon due notification to the railway officials and the production of evidence of their official character.

The foregoing provisions of this article shall not, however, apply in case of war between Colombia and Panama.

ARTICLE III.

The products of the soil and industry of the Republic of Colombia, such as provisions, cattle, etc., shall be admitted to entry in the Canal Zone subject only to such duty as would be payable on similar products of the United States of America under similar conditions, so far as the United States of America has any right or authority to fix the conditions of such importations.

Colombian laborers employed in the Canal Zone during the construction of the canal, who may desire that their own families supply them with provisions for their personal use, shall be entitled to have such provisions admitted to the Canal Zone for delivery to them free of any duty, provided that declaration thereof shall first have been made before the commissary officers of the Isthmian Canal Commission, in order to obtain the previous permit for such entry, and subject to such reasonable regulations as shall be prescribed by the Commission for ensuring the *bona fides* of the transaction.

ARTICLE IV.

Colombian mails shall have free passage through the Canal Zone and through the post-offices of Ancon and Cristobal in the

Canal Zone, paying only such duties or charges as are paid by the mails of the United States.

During the construction of the canal Colombian products passing over the Isthmian Railway from and to Colombia ports shall be transported at the lowest rates which are charged for similar products of the United States passing over said railway to and from the ports of the United States; and sea salt, exclusively produced in Colombia, passing from the Atlantic coast of Colombia to any Colombian port on the Pacific coast, shall be transported over said railway free of any charge except the actual cost of handling and transportation, not exceeding one-half of the ordinary freight charges.

ARTICLE V.

The United States recognizes and accepts notice of the assignment by the Republic of Panama to the Republic of Colombia of the right to receive from the United States payment of $250,000 in American gold in each year from the year 1908 to the year 1917, both inclusive, such assignment having been made in manner and form as contained in the treaty between the Republic of Colombia and the Republic of Panama bearing even date herewith, whereby the independence of the Republic of Panama recognized by the Republic of Colombia and the Republic of Panama is released from obligation for the payment of any part of the external and internal debt of the Republic of Colombia.

ARTICLE VI.

The Republic of Colombia grants to the United States the use of all the ports of the Republic open to commerce as places of refuge for any vessels employed in the canal enterprise, and for all vessels in distress passing or bound to pass through the canal and seeking shelter or anchorage in said ports, subject in time of war to the rules of neutrality properly applicable thereto. Such vessels shall be exempt from anchorage or tonnage dues on the part of the Republic of Colombia.

The Republic of Colombia renounces all rights and interests in connection with any contract or concession made between it and any corporation or person relating to the construction or operation of a canal or railway across the Isthmus of Panama.

ARTICLE VII.

As soon as practicable after the exchange of ratifications of this treaty and the contemporaneous treaties of even date herewith between the United States of America and the Republic of Panama, and between the Republic of Colombia and the Republic of Panama, the United States of America and the Republic of Colombia will enter into negotiations for the revision of the Treaty of Peace, Amity, Navigation, and Commerce between the United States of America and the Republic of New Granada, concluded on the 12th day of December, 1846, with a view to making the provisions therein contained conform to existing conditions, and to including therein provision for a general treaty of arbitration.

ARTICLE VIII.

This treaty, duly signed by the High Contracting Parties, shall be ratified by each according to its respective laws, and the ratifications thereof shall be exchanged at Washington as soon as possible.

But it is understood that such ratifications are not to be exchanged nor the provisions of this treaty made obligatory upon either party, until and unless the aforesaid treaties between the Republic of Colombia and the Republic of Panama, and between the United States of America and the Republic of Panama, bearing even date herewith, are both duly ratified, and the ratifications thereof are exchanged simultaneously with the exchange of ratifications of this treaty.

In witness whereof, We, the respective Plenipotentiaries, have signed the present treaty in duplicate, in the English and Spanish languages, and have hereunto affixed our respective seals.

Done at the City of Washington, the 9th day of January, in the year of our Lord nineteen hundred and nine.

(Signed) ELIHU ROOT SEAL

(Signed) ENRIQUE CORTES SEAL

TREATY BETWEEN THE REPUBLICS OF PANAMA AND COLOMBIA

The Republic of Colombia and the Republic of Panama, equally animated by the desire to remove all obstacles to their good understanding to adjust their pecuniary and other relations to each other and to secure mutually the benefits of amity and accord, have determined to conclude a convention for these purposes and, therefore, have appointed as their respective Plenipotentiaries, that is to say:

The President of the Republic of Colombia, Enrique Cortes, Envoy Extraordinary and Minister Plenipotentiary of the Republic of Colombia, in Washington, and

The President of the Republic of Panama, Carlos Constantino Arosemena, Envoy Extraordinary and Minister Plenipotentiary of the Republic of Panama, in Washington.

Who, after having communicated to each other their respective full powers, found in good and due form, have agreed upon and concluded the following articles:

ARTICLE I.

The Republic of Colombia recognizes the Independence of the Republic of Panama and acknowledges it to be a free, sovereign, and independent nation.

ARTICLE II.

There shall be a mutual and inviolable peace and friendship between the Government of the Republic of Colombia and its citizens on the one part and the Government of the Republic of Panama and its citizens on the other part, without exception of persons or places under their respective dominion.

ARTICLE III.

The Republic of Panama assigns and transfers to the Republic of Colombia, and its assigns and nominees, in lawful and due form, the first ten annual installments of two hundred and fifty thousand dollars gold coin each becoming due to it, the Republic of Panama, from the United States of America, on the 25th days of February in the years 1908 to 1917, both inclusive, under and pursuant to the provisions of Article XIV of the treaty between the United States of America and the Republic of Panama concluded November 18, 1903, and under and pursuant to the amendment thereof, embodied in a treaty of even date between said nations, whereby said Article XIV is amended by substituting the words "four years" for the words "nine years," so that the first annual payment of which that article treats shall begin four years from the exchange of ratifications of said treaty on February 26th, 1904, instead of nine years from said date, in such manner that the said installments shall be paid by the United States of America directly to the Republic of Colombia or its assigns and nominees for account of the Republic of Panama, in lawful and due form, beginning the 26th day of February, 1908. Such installments as may have matured when the ratifications of this treaty shall be exchanged pursuant to its terms, shall be payable on the ninetieth day after the date of such exchange.

In consideration of the payments and releases which the Republic of Panama makes to the Republic of Colombia, the latter recognizes and agrees that the Republic of Panama has no liability upon and no obligations to the holders of the external and internal debt of the Republic of Colombia, nor to the Republic of Colombia, by reason of any such indebtedness or claims relating thereto. The Republic of Colombia recognizes and agrees that it is itself solely obligated for such external and internal debt; assumes the obligation to pay and discharge the same by itself alone; and agrees to indemnify and hold harmless the Republic of Panama, should occasion arise, from any liability in respect of such external and internal indebtedness, and from any expense which may result from failure or delay in respect of such payment and discharge.

ARTICLE IV.

Each of the contracting Republics releases and discharges the other from all pecuniary claims and obligations of any nature whatever, including the external and internal debt of the Republic of Colombia, which either had against the other on the 3rd day of November, 1903, it being understood that this reciprocal exoneration relates only to the national debts and claims of one against the other, and that it does not relate to individual rights and claims of the citizens of either Republic. Neither party shall be bound to allow or satisfy any of such individual claims arising from transactions or occurrences prior to November 3, 1903, unless the same would be valid according to the laws of the country against which the claim is made, as such laws existed on November 3rd, 1903.

ARTICLE V.

The Republic of Panama recognizes that it has no title or ownership of any sort to the fifty thousand shares of the capital stock of the New Panama Canal Company, standing in the name of the Republic of Colombia on the books of said company at Paris, and the Republic of Panama confirms the abandonment of all right and title, which, with respect to said shares, it made in the Courts of Justice of France.

ARTICLE VI.

The citizens of each Republic, residing in the territory of the other, shall enjoy the same civil rights which are or shall hereafter be accorded by the laws of the country of residence to the citizens of the most favored nation. It being understood, however, that the citizens of either of the two Republics residing in the other shall be exempt from military service imposed upon the citizens of such Republic.

All persons born within the territory now of the Republic of Panama, prior to the 3rd day of November, 1903, who were, on that day, residents of the territory now of the Republic of Colombia, may elect to be citizens of the Republic of Colombia or of the Republic of Panama; and all persons born within the territory now of the Republic of Colombia who were, on said 3rd day of November, 1903, residents of the territory now of the Republic of Panama, may elect to be citizens of the Republic of Panama or of the Republic of Colombia, by making declaration of their election in the manner hereinafter provided, within one year from the date of the proclamation of the exchange of the ratifications of this treaty, or, in case of any persons who shall not on that day be of full age, within one year from their attainment of their majority according to the laws of the country of their residence.

Such election may be made by filing in the office of the Minister or Secretary of Foreign Affairs of the country of residence a declaration of such election. Such declaration may be made before any officer authorized to administer oaths and may be transmitted by mail to such Minister or Secretary of Foreign Affairs, whose duty it shall be to file and register the same, and no other formality except the transmission thereof shall be required and no fees shall be imposed for making of filing thereof. It shall be the duty of the respective Departments of Foreign Affairs of the High Contracting Parties to communicate promptly to each other the names, occupations, and addresses of the persons so exercising such election.

All persons entitled to make such declarations who shall not have made the same within the period hereinbefore limited shall be deemed to have elected to become citizens of the country within whose present territory they were born. But no further declaration shall be required from any such person who has already by formal declaration before a public official of either country, and in accordance with its laws, made election of the nationality of that country.

The natives of the countries of either of the two contracting Republics who have heretofore or shall hereafter become citizens by naturalization, or otherwise as herein provided for, in the other Republic, shall not be punished, molested, or discriminated against by reason of their acts of adhesion to the country whose citizenship they have adopted.

ARTICLE VII.

Both Republics agree, each for itself, that neither of them shall admit to form any part of its nationality any part of the territory of the other which separates from it by force.

ARTICLE VIII.

As soon as this treaty and the contemporaneous treaties of even date between the United States of America and the Republic of Colombia and between the United States of America and the Republic of Panama shall be ratified and exchanged, negotiations shall be entered upon between the Republics of Colombia and Panama for the conclusion of additional treaty or treaties, covering questions of commerce, postal, telegraph, copyright, consular relations, extradition of criminals, arbitration and the like.

ARTICLE IX.

It is agreed between the High Contracting Parties and is declared, that the dividing line between the Republic of Colombia and the Republic of Panama shall be as follows, to wit:

From Cape Tiburon on the Atlantic to the headwaters of the Rio de la Miel, and following the range by the Cerro de Gandi to the Sierra de Chugargun and that of Mali, going down by the Cerros of Nique to the heights of Aspave, and from there to the Pacific at such point and by such line as shall be determined by the Tribunal of Arbitration hereinafter provided for, and the determination of said line shall conform to the decision of such Tribunal of Arbitration as next provided.

As to the territory submitted to arbitration (the region of Jurado) the boundaries and attribution of which to either the Republic of Colombia or the Republic of Panama will be fixed by the determination of the line aforesaid by said Tribunal of Arbitration, the title thereto and the precise limits thereof, and the right to the sovereignty thereof as between the High Contracting Parties, shall be conclusively determined by arbitration in the following manner:

A Tribunal of Arbitration shall be created to investigate and determine all questions of fact and law concerning the rights of the High Contracting Parties to or in all the territory in the above mentioned region of Jurado. The Tribunal shall consist of three members; the Republic of Colombia shall nominate one member, the Republic of Panama shall nominate one member, both of whom shall be nominated within three months after the exchange of ratifications of this treaty, and the two members of the Tribunal thus nominated shall jointly nominate a third member, or, in the event of their failure to agree within three months next after the appointment of the last of them, and on request of the President of either of the High Contracting Parties, the third member of the Tribunal shall be appointed by the President of the Republic of Cuba.

The Tribunal shall hold its sessions at such place as the Tribunal shall determine.

The case on behalf of each party, with the papers and documents, shall be communicated to the other party within three months after the appointment of the third Member of the Tribunal.

The counter-cases shall be similarly communicated with the

papers and documents within three months after communication of the cases respectively.

And within two months after communication of the counter-case the other party may communicate its reply.

The proceedings of the Tribunal shall be governed by the provisions, so far as applicable, of the Convention for the Pacific Settlement of International Disputes signed at The Hague by the representatives of both the parties hereto on the 18th day of October, 1907.

The Tribunal shall take into consideration all relevant laws and treaties and all facts proved of occupancy, possession and political or administrative control in respect of the territory in dispute.

ARTICLE X.

This treaty shall not be binding upon either of the High Contracting Parties, nor have any force until and unless the treaties signed on this same date between the Republic of Colombia and the United States of America and between the Republic of Panama and the United States of America are both duly ratified and ratifications thereof are exchanged simultaneously with the exchange of the ratifications of this treaty.

ARTICLE XI.

The present treaty shall be submitted for ratification to the respective Governments, and ratifications hereof exchanged at Washington as soon as possible.

In Witness Whereof, We, the respective Plenipotentiaries, have signed the present treaty in duplicate in the Spanish and English languages, and have hereunto affixed our respective seals.

Done at the City of Washington, the 9th day of January, in the year of our Lord one thousand nine hundred and nine.

(Signed) ENRIQUE CORTES SEAL

(Signed) C. C. AROSEMENA SEAL

TREATY

Between the United States and Colombia,
Signed at Bogotá, April 6, 1914

TREATY between the United States of America and the Republic of Colombia for the settlement of their differences arising out of the events which took place on the Isthmus of Panama in November 1903.

The United States of America and the Republic of Colombia, being desirous to remove all the misunderstandings growing out of the political events in Panama in November 1903; to restore the cordial friendship that formerly characterized the relations between the two countries, and also to define and regulate their rights and interests in respect of the interoceanic canal which the Government of the United States has constructed across the Isthmus of Panama, have resolved for this purpose to conclude a Treaty and have accordingly appointed as their Plenipotentiaries:

His Excellency the President of the United States of America, Thaddeus Austin Thomson, Envoy Extraordinary and Minister Plenipotentiary of the United States of America to the Government of the Republic of Colombia; and

His Excellency the President of the Republic of Colombia, Francisco José Urrutia, Minister for Foreign Affairs; Marco Fidel Suárez, First Designate to exercise the Executive Power; Nicolás Esguerra, Ex-Minister of State; José María González Valencia, Senator; Rafael Uribe Uribe, Senator; and Antonio José Uribe, President of the House of Representatives;

Who, after communicating to each other their respective full powers, which were found to be in due and proper form, have agreed upon the following:

ARTICLE 1

The Republic of Colombia shall enjoy the following rights in respect to the interoceanic Canal and the Panama Railway, the title to which is now vested entirely and absolutely in the United States of America, without any incumbrances or indemnities whatever.

1. The Republic of Colombia shall be at liberty at all times to transport through the interoceanic Canal its troops, materials of war and ships of war, without paying any charges to the United States.

2. The products of the soil and industry of Colombia passing through the Canal, as well as the Colombian mails, shall be exempt from any charge or duty other than those to which the products and mails of the United States may be subject. The products of the soil and industry of Colombia, such as cattle, salt and provisions, shall be admitted to entry in the Canal Zone, and likewise in the islands and mainland occupied or which may be occupied by the United States as auxiliary and accessory thereto, without paying other duties or charges than those payable by similar products of the United States.

3. Colombian citizens crossing the Canal Zone shall, upon production of proper proof of their nationality, be exempt from every toll, tax or duty to which citizens of the United States are not subject.

4. Whenever traffic by the Canal is interrupted or whenever it shall be necessary for any other reason to use the Railway, the troops, materials of war, products and mails of the Republic of Colombia, as above mentioned, shall be transported on the Railway between Ancon and Cristobal or on any other Railway substituted therefor, paying only the same charges and duties as are imposed upon the troops, materials of war, products and mails of the United States. The officers, agents and employees of the Government of Colombia shall, upon production of proper proof of their official character or their employment, also be entitled to passage on the said Railway on the same terms as officers, agents and employees of the Government of the United States.

5. Coal, petroleum and sea salt, being the products of Colombia, for Colombian consumption passing from the Atlantic coast of Colombia to any Colombian port on the Pacific coast, and vice-versa, shall, whenever traffic by the Canal is interrupted, be transported over the aforesaid Railway free of any charge except the actual cost of handling and transportation, which shall not in any case exceed one half of the ordinary freight charges levied upon similar products of the United States passing over Railway and in transit from one port to another of the United States.

ARTICLE 2

The Government of the United States of America agrees to pay at the City of Washington to the Republic of Colombia the sum of twenty-five million dollars, gold, United States money, as follows: The sum of five million dollars shall be paid within six months after the exchange of ratifications of the present treaty, and reckoning from the date of that payment, the remaining twenty million dollars shall be paid in four annual installments of five million dollars each.

ARTICLE 3

The Republic of Colombia recognizes Panama as an independent nation and taking as a basis the Colombian Law June 9, 1855, agrees that the boundary shall be the following: From Cape Tiburón to the headwaters of the Rio de la Miel and following the mountain chain by the ridge of Gandi to the Sierra de Chugargun and that of Mali going down by the ridges of Nigue to the heights of Aspave and from thence to a point on the Pacific halfway between Cocalito and La Ardita.

In consideration of this recognition, the Government of the United States will, immediately after the exchange of the ratifications of the present Treaty, take the necessary steps in order to obtain from the Government of Panama the despatch of a duly accredited agent to negotiate and conclude with the Government of Colombia a Treaty of Peace and Friendship, with a view to bring about both the establishment of regular diplomatic relations between Colombia and Panama and the adjustment of all questions of pecuniary liability as between the two countries, in accordance with recognized principles of law and precedents.

ARTICLE 4

The present Treaty shall be approved and ratified by the High Contracting Parties in conformity with their respective laws, and the ratifications thereof shall be exchanged in the city of Bogotá, as soon as may be possible.

In faith whereof, the said Plenipotentiaries have signed the present Treaty in duplicate and have hereunto affixed their respective seals.

Done at the city of Bogotá, the sixth day of April in the year of our Lord nineteen hundred and fourteen.

Signatures.

PANAMA-UNITED STATES GENERAL TREATY OF FRIENDSHIP AND COÖPERATION

Signed at Washington, March 2, 1936;
Ratifications Exchanged July 27, 1939

The United States of America and the Republic of Panama, animated by the desire to strengthen further the bonds of friendship and coöperation between the two countries and to regulate on a stable and mutually satisfactory basis certain questions which have arisen as a result of the construction of the interoceanic canal across the Isthmus of Panama, have decided to conclude a treaty, and have designated for this purpose as their plenipotentiaries:

The President of the United States of America:

Mr. Cordell Hull, Secretary of State of the United States of America, and Mr. Sumner Welles, Assistant Secretary of State of the United States of America; and

The President of the Republic of Panama:

The Honorable Doctor Ricardo J. Alfaro, Envoy Extraordinary and Minister Plenipotentiary of Panama to the United States of America, and The Honorable Doctor Narciso Garay, Envoy Extraordinary and Minister Plenipotentiary of Panama on special mission;

Who, having communicated their respective full powers to each other, which have been found to be in good and due form, have agreed upon the following:

ARTICLE I

Article I of the Convention of November 18, 1903, is hereby superseded.

There shall be a perfect, firm and inviolable peace and sincere friendship between the United States of America and the Republic of Panama and between their citizens.

In view of the official and formal opening of the Panama Canal on July 12, 1920, the United States of America and the Republic of Panama declare that the provisions of the Convention of November 18, 1903, contemplate the use, occupation and control by the United States of America of the Canal Zone and of the additional lands and waters under the jurisdiction of the United States of America for the purposes of the efficient maintenance, operation, sanitation and protection of the Canal and of its auxiliary works.

The United States of America will continue the maintenance of the Panama Canal for the encouragement and use of interoceanic commerce, and the two Governments declare their willingness to coöperate, as far as it is feasible for them to do so, for the purpose of insuring the full and perpetual enjoyment of the benefits of all kinds which the Canal should afford the two nations that made possible its construction as well as all nations interested in world trade.

ARTICLE II

The United States of America declares that the Republic of Panama has loyally and satisfactorily complied with the obligations which it entered into under Article II of the Convention of November 18, 1903, by which it granted in perpetuity to the United States the use, occupation and control of the zone of land and land under water as described in the said article, of the islands within the limits of said zone, of the group of small islands in the Bay of Panama, named Perico, Naos, Culebra and Flamenco, and of any other lands and waters outside of said zone necessary and convenient for the construction, maintenance, operation, sanitation and protection of the Panama Canal or of any auxiliary canals or other works, and in recognition thereof the United States of America hereby renounces the grant made to it in perpetuity by the Republic of Panama of the use, occupation and control of lands and waters, in addition to those now under the jurisdiction of the United States of America outside of the zone as described in Article II of the aforesaid convention, which may be necessary and convenient for the construction, maintenance, operation, sanitation and protection of the Panama Canal or of any auxiliary canals or other works necessary and convenient for the construction, maintenance, operation, sanitation and protection of the said enterprise.

While both Governments agree that the requirement of further lands and waters for the enlargement of the existing facilities of the Canal appears to be improbable, they nevertheless recognize, subject to the provisions of Articles I and X of this treaty, their joint obligation to insure the effective and continuous operation of the Canal and the preservation of its neutrality, and consequently, if, in the event of some now unforeseen contingency, the utilization of lands or waters additional to those already employed should be in fact necessary for the maintenance, sanitation or efficient operation of the Canal, or for its effective protection, the Governments of the United States of America and the Republic of Panama will agree upon such measures as it may be necessary to take in order to insure the maintenance, sanitation, efficient operation and effective protection of the Canal, in which the two countries are jointly and vitally interested.

ARTICLE III

In order to enable the Republic of Panama to take advantage of the commercial opportunities inherent in its geographical situation, the United States of America agrees as follows:

1) The sale to individuals of goods imported into the Canal Zone or purchased, produced or manufactured therein by the Government of the United States of America shall be limited by it to the persons included in classes (a) and (b) of Section 2 of this article; and with regard to the persons included in classes (c), (d) and (e) of the said section and members of their families, the sales above mentioned shall be made only when such persons actually reside in the Canal Zone.

2) No person who is not comprised within the following classes shall be entitled to reside within the Canal Zone:

(a) Officers, employees, workmen or laborers in the service or employ of the United States of America, the Panama Canal or the Panama Railroad Company, and members of their families actually residing with them;

(b) Members of the armed forces of the United States of America and members of their families actually residing with them;

(c) Contractors operating in the Canal Zone and their employees, workmen and laborers during the performance of contracts;

(d) Officers, employees or workmen of companies entitled under Section 5 of this article to conduct operations in the Canal Zone;

(e) Persons engaged in religious, welfare, charitable, educational, recreational and scientific work exclusively in the Canal Zone;

(f) Domestic servants of all the beforementioned persons and members of the families of the persons in classes (c), (d) and (e) actually residing with them.

3) No dwellings belonging to the Government of the United States of America or to the Panama Railroad Company and situated within the Canal Zone shall be rented, leased or sublet except to persons within classes (a) to (e), inclusive of Section 2 hereinabove.

4) The Government of the United States of America will continue to coöperate in all proper ways with the Government of the Republic of Panama to prevent violations of the immigration and customs laws of the Republic of Panama, including the smuggling into territory under the jurisdiction of the Republic of goods imported into the Canal Zone or purchased, produced or manufactured therein by the Government of the United States of America.

5) With the exception of concerns having a direct relation to the operation, maintenance, sanitation or protection of the Canal, such as those engaged in the operation of cables, shipping, or dealing in oil or fuel, the Government of the United States of America will not permit the establishment in the Canal Zone of private business enterprises than those existing therein at the time of the signature of this treaty.

6) In view of the proximity of the port of Balboa to the city of Panamá and of the port of Cristobal to the City of Colón, the United States of America will continue to permit, under suitable regulations and upon the payment of proper charges, vessels entering at or clearing from the ports of the Canal Zone to use and enjoy the dockage and other facilities of the said ports for the purpose of loading and unloading cargoes and receiving or disembarking passengers to or from the territory under the jurisdiction of the Republic of Panama.

The Republic of Panama will permit vessels entering at or clearing from the ports of Panamá or Colón, in case of emergency and also under suitable regulations and upon the payment of proper charges, to use and enjoy the dockage and other facilities of said ports for the purpose of receiving or disembarking passengers to or from the territory of the Republic of Panama under the jurisdiction of the United States of America, and of loading and unloading cargoes either in transit or destined for the service of the Canal or of works pertaining to the Canal.

7) The Government of the United States of America will extend to private merchants residing in the Republic of Panama full opportunity for making sales to vessels arriving at terminal ports of the Canal or transiting the Canal, subject always to appropriate administrative regulations of the Canal Zone.

ARTICLE IV

The Government of the Republic of Panama shall not impose import duties or taxes of any kind on goods destined for or consigned to the agencies of the Government of the United States of America in the Republic of Panama when the goods are intended for the official use of such agencies, or upon goods destined for or consigned to persons included in classes (a) and (b) in Section 2 of Article III of this treaty, who reside or sojourn in territory under the jurisdiction of the Republic of Panama during the performance of their service with the United States of America, the Panama Canal or the Panama Railroad Company, when the goods are intended for their own use and benefit.

The United States of America shall not impose import duties or taxes of any kind on goods, wares and merchandise passing from territory under the jurisdiction of the Republic of Panama into the Canal Zone.

No charges of any kind shall be imposed by the authorities of the United States of America upon persons residing in territory under the jurisdiction of the Republic of Panama passing from the said territory into the Canal Zone, and no charges of any kind shall be imposed by the authorities of the Republic of Panama upon persons in the service of the United States of America or residing in the Canal Zone passing from the Canal Zone into territory under the jurisdiction of the Republic of Panama, all other persons passing from the Canal Zone into territory under the jurisdiction of the Republic of Panama being subject to the full effects of the immigration laws of the Republic.

In view of the fact that the Canal Zone divides the territory under the jurisdiction of the Republic of Panama, the United States of America agrees that, subject to such police regulations as circumstances may require, Panamanian citizens who may occasionally be deported from the Canal Zone shall be assured transit through the said Zone, in order to pass from one part to another of the territory under the jurisdiction of the Republic of Panama.

ARTICLE V

Article IX of the Convention of November 18, 1903, is hereby superseded.

The Republic of Panama has the right to impose upon merchandise destined to be introduced for use or consumption in territory under the jurisdiction of the Republic of Panama, and upon vessels touching at Panamanian ports and upon the officers, crew or passengers of such vessels, the taxes or charges provided by the laws of the Republic of Panama; it being understood that the Republic of Panama will continue directly and exclusively to exercise its jurisdiction over the ports of Panamá and Colón and to operate exclusively with Panamanian personnel such facilities as are or may be established therein by the Republic or by its authority. However, the Republic of Panama shall not impose or collect any charges or taxes upon any vessel using or passing through the Canal which does not touch at a port under Panamanian jurisdiction or upon the officers, crew or passengers of such vessels, unless they enter the Republic; it being also understood that taxes and charges imposed by the Republic of Panama upon vessels using or passing through the Canal which touch at ports under Panamanian jurisdiction, or upon their cargo, officers, crew or passengers, shall not be higher than those imposed upon vessels which touch only at ports under Panamanian jurisdiction and do not transit the Canal, or upon their cargo, officers, crew or passengers.

The Republic of Panama also has the right to determine what persons or classes of persons arriving at ports of the Canal Zone shall be admitted to the Republic of Panama and to determine likewise what persons or classes of persons arriving at such ports shall be excluded from admission to the Republic of Panama.

The United States of America will furnish to the Republic of Panama free of charge the necessary sites for the establishment of customhouses in the ports of the Canal Zone for the collection of duties on importations destined to the Republic and for the examination of merchandise, baggage and passengers consigned to or bound for the Republic of Panama, and for the prevention of contraband trade, it being understood that the collection of duties and the examination of merchandise and passengers by the agents of the Government of the Republic of Panama, in accordance with this provision, shall take place only in the customhouses to be established by the Government of the Republic of Panama as herein provided, and that the Republic of Panama will exercise jurisdiction within the sites on which the customhouses are located so far as concerns the enforcement of immigration or customs laws of the Republic of Panama, and over all property therein contained and the personnel therein employed.

To further the effective enforcement of the rights hereinbefore recognized, the Government of the United States of America agrees that, for the purpose of obtaining information useful in determining whether persons arriving at ports of the Canal Zone and destined to points within the jurisdiction of the Republic of Panama should be admitted or excluded from admission into the Republic, the immigration officers of the Republic of Panama shall have the right of free access to vessels upon their arrival at the Balboa or Cristobal piers or wharves with passengers destined for the Republic; and that the appropriate authorities of the Panama Canal will adopt such administrative regulations regarding persons entering ports of the Canal Zone and destined to points within the jurisdiction of the Republic of Panama as will facilitate the exercise by the authorities of Panama of their jurisdiction in the manner provided in Paragraph 4 of this article for the purposes stated in Paragraph 3 thereof.

ARTICLE VI

The first sentence of Article VII of the Convention of November 18, 1903, is hereby amended so as to omit the following phrase: "or by the exercise of the right of eminent domain."

The third paragraph of Article VII of the Convention of November 18, 1903, is hereby abrogated.

ARTICLE VII

Beginning with the annuity payable in 1934 the payments under Article XIV of the Convention of November 18, 1903, between the United States of America and the Republic of Panama, shall be four hundred and thirty thousand balboas (B/430,000.00) as defined by the agreement embodied in an exchange of notes of this date. The United States of America may discharge its obligation with respect to any such payment, upon payment in any coin or currency, provided the amount so paid is the equivalent of four hundred and thirty thousand balboas (B/430,000.00) as so defined.

ARTICLE VIII

In order that the city of Colón may enjoy direct means of land communication under Panamanian jurisdiction with other territory under jurisdiction of the Republic of Panama, the United States of America hereby transfers to the Republic of Panama jurisdiction over a corridor, the exact limits of which shall be agreed upon and demarcated by the two Governments pursuant to the following description:

(a) the end at Colón connects with the southern end of the east half of the Paseo del Centenario at Sixteenth Street, Colón; thence the corridor proceeds in a general southerly direction, parallel to and east of Bolivar Highway to the vicinity of the northern edge of Silver City; thence eastward near the shore line of Folks River, around the northeast corner of Silver City; thence in a general southeasterly direction and generally parallel to the Randolph Road to a crossing of said Randolph Road, about 1,200 feet east of the East Diversion; thence in a general northeasterly direction to the eastern boundary line of the Canal Zone near the southeastern corner of the Fort Randolph Reservation, southwest of Cativá. The approximate route of the corridor is shown on the map which accompanies this treaty, signed by the plenipotentiaries of the two countries and marked "Exhibit A."

(b) The width of the corridor shall be as follows: 25 feet in width from the Colón end to a point east of the southern line of Silver City; thence 100 feet in width to Randolph Road, except that, at any elevated crossing which may be built over Randolph Road and the railroad, the corridor will be no wider than is necessary to include the viaduct and will not include any part of Randolph Road proper, or of the railroad right of way, and except that, in case of a grade crossing over Randolph Road and the railroad, the corridor will be interrupted by that highway and railroad; thence 200 feet in width to the boundary line of the Canal Zone.

The Government of the United States of America will extinguish any private titles existing or which may exist in and to the land included in the above-described corridor.

The stream and drainage crossings of any highway built in the corridor shall not restrict the water passage to less than the capacity of the existing streams and drainage.

No other construction will take place within the corridor than that relating to the construction of a highway and to the installation of electric power, telephone and telegraph lines; and the only activities which will be conducted within the said corridor will be those pertaining to the construction, maintenance and common uses of a highway and of power and communication lines.

The United States of America shall enjoy at all times the right of unimpeded transit across the said corridor at any point, and of travel along the corridor, subject to such traffic regulations as may be established by the government of the Republic of Panama; and the Government of the United States of America shall have the right to such use of the corridor as would be involved in the construction of connecting or intersecting highways or railroads, overhead and underground power, telephone, telegraph and pipe lines, and additional drainage channels, on condition that these structures and their use shall not interfere with the purpose of the corridor as provided hereinabove.

ARTICLE IX (In Part)

In order that direct means of land communication, together with accommodation for the high tension power transmission lines, may be provided under jurisdiction of the United States of America from the Madden Dam to the Canal Zone, the Republic of Panama hereby transfers to the United States of America jurisdiction over a corridor, the limits of which shall be demarcated by the two Governments.

The Republic of Panama shall enjoy at all times the right of unimpeded transit across the said corridor at any point, and of travel along the corridor, subject to such traffic regulations as may be established by the authorities of the Panama Canal; and the Government of the Republic of Panama shall have the right to such use of the corridor as would be involved in the construction of connecting or intersecting highways or railroads, overhead and underground power, telephone, telegraph and pipe lines, and additional drainage channels, on condition that these structures and their use shall not interfere with the purpose of the corridor as provided hereinabove.

ARTICLE X

In case of an international conflagration or the existence of any threat of aggression which would endanger the security of the Republic of Panama or the neutrality or security of the Panama Canal, the Governments of the United States of America and the Republic of Panama will take such measures of prevention and defense as they may consider necessary for the protection of their common interests. Any measures, in safeguarding such interests, which it shall appear essential to one Government to take, and which may affect the territory under the jurisdiction of the other Government, will be the subject of consultation between the two Governments.

ARTICLE XI

The provisions of this treaty shall not affect the rights and obligations of either of the two high contracting parties under the treaties now in force between the two countries, nor be considered as a limitation, definition, restriction or restrictive interpretation of such rights and obligations, but without prejudice to the full force and effect of any provisions of this treaty which constitute addition to, modification or abrogation of, or substitution for the provisions of previous treaties.

ARTICLE XII

The present treaty shall be ratified in accordance with the constitutional methods of the high contracting parties and shall take effect immediately on the exchange of ratifications which shall take place at Washington.

In witness whereof, the plenipotentiaries have signed this treaty in duplicate, in the English and Spanish languages, both texts being authentic, and have hereunto affixed their seals.

Done at the city of Washington the second day of March, 1936.

CORDELL HULL SEAL

SUMNER WELLES SEAL

R. J. ALFARO SEAL

NARCISO GARAY SEAL

TREATY OF MUTUAL UNDERSTANDING AND COOPERATION

Between the United States of America
and the Republic of Panama

The President of the United States of America and the President of the Republic of Panama, desirous of concluding a treaty to further demonstrate the mutual understanding and cooperation of the two countries and to strengthen the bonds of understanding and friendship between their respective peoples, have appointed for that purpose as their respective Plenipotentiaries:

The President of the United States of America:

Selden Chapin, Ambassador Extraordinary and Plenipotentiary of the United States of America to the Republic of Panama,

The President of the Republic of Panama:

Octavio Fábrega, Minister of Foreign Relations of the Republic of Panama,

who, having communicated to one another their respective full powers, found in good and due form, and recognizing that neither the provisions of the Convention signed November 18, 1903, nor the General Treaty signed March 2, 1936, nor the present Treaty, may be modified except by mutual consent, agree upon the following Articles:

ARTICLE I

Beginning with the first annuity payable after the exchange of ratifications of the present Treaty, the payments under Article XIV of the Convention for the Construction of a ship Canal between the United States of America and the Republic of Panama, signed November 18, 1903, as amended by Article VII of the General Treaty of Friendship and Cooperation, signed March 2, 1936, shall be One Million Nine Hundred Thirty Thousand and no/100 Balboas (B/1,930,000) as defined by the agreement embodied in the exchange of notes of March 2, 1936, between the Secretary of State of the United States of America and the members of the Panamanian Treaty Commission. The United States of America may discharge its obligation with respect to any such payment in any coin or currency, provided the amount so paid is the equivalent of One Million Nine Hundred Thirty Thousand and no/100 Balboas (B/1,930,000) as so defined.

On the date of the first payment under the present Treaty, the provisions of this Article shall supersede the provisions of Article VII of the General Treaty signed March 2, 1936.

Notwithstanding the provisions of this Article, the High Contracting Parties recognize the absence of any obligation on the part of either Party to alter the amount of the annuity.

ARTICLE II

(1) Notwithstanding the provisions of Article X of the Convention signed November 18, 1903, between the United States of America and the Republic of Panama, the United States of America agrees that the Republic of Panama may, subject to the provisions of paragraphs (2) and (3) of this Article, impose taxes upon the income (including income from sources within the Canal Zone) of all persons who are employed in the service of the Canal, the railroad, or auxiliary works, whether resident within or outside the Canal Zone, except:

(a) members of the Armed Forces of the United States of America,

(b) citizens of the United States of America, including those who have dual nationality, and

(c) other individuals who are not citizens of the Republic of Panama and who reside within the Canal Zone.

(2) It is understood that any tax levied pursuant to paragraph (1) of this Article shall be imposed on a non-discriminatory basis and shall in no case be imposed at a rate higher or more burdensome than that applicable to income of citizens of the Republic of Panama generally.

(3) The Republic of Panama agrees not to impose taxes on pensions, annuities, relief payments, or other similar payments, or payments by way of compensation for injuries or death occurring in connection with, or incident to, service on the Canal, the railroad, or auxiliary works paid to or for the benefit of members of the Armed Forces or citizens of the United States of America or the lawful beneficiaries of such members or citizens who reside in territory under the jurisdiction of the Republic of Panama.

The provisions of this Article shall be operative for the taxable years beginning on or after the first day of January following the year in which the present Treaty enters into force.

ARTICLE III

Subject to the provisions of the succeeding paragraphs of this Article, the United States of America agrees that the monopoly granted in perpetuity by the Republic of Panama to the United States for the construction, maintenance and operation of any system of communication by means of canal or railroad across its territory between the Caribbean Sea and the Pacific Ocean, by Article V of the Convention signed November 18, 1903, shall be abrogated as of the effective date of this Treaty in so far as it pertains to the construction, maintenance and operation of any system of trans-Isthmian communication by railroad within the territory under the jurisdiction of the Republic of Panama.

Subject to the provisions of the succeeding paragraphs of this Article, the United States further agrees that the exclusive right to establish roads across the Isthmus of Panama acquired by the United States as a result of a concessionary contract granted to the Panama Railroad Company shall be abrogated as of the date of the entry into force of this Treaty, in so far as the right pertains to the establishment of roads within the territory under the jurisdiction of the Republic of Panama.

In view of the vital interest of both countries in the effective protection of the Canal, the High Contracting Parties further agree that such abrogation is subject to the understanding that no system of inter-oceanic communication within the territory under the jurisdiction of the Republic of Panama by means of railroad or highway may be financed, constructed, maintained, or operated directly or indirectly by a third country or nationals thereof, unless in the opinion of both High Contracting Parties such financing, construction, maintenance, or operation would not affect the security of the Canal.

The High Contracting Parties also agree that such abrogation as is contemplated by this Article shall in no wise affect the maintenance and operation of the present Panama Railroad in the Canal Zone and in territory subject to the jurisdiction of the Republic of Panama.

ARTICLE IV

The second paragraph of Article VII of the Convention signed November 18, 1903, having to do with the issuance of, compliance with, and enforcement of, sanitary ordinances in the Cities of Panamá and Colón, shall be abrogated in its entirety as of the date of entry into force of this Treaty.

ARTICLE V

The United States of America agrees that, subject to the enactment of legislation by the Congress, there shall be conveyed to the Republic of Panama free of cost all the right, title and interest held by the United States of America or its agencies in and to certain lands and improvements in territory under the jurisdiction of the Republic of Panama when and as determined by the United States to be no longer needed for the operation, maintenance, sanitation or protection of the Panama Canal or of its auxiliary works, or for other authorized purposes of the United States in the Republic of Panama. The lands and improvements referred to in the preceding sentence and the determinations by the United States of America respecting the same, subject to the enactment of legislation by the Congress, are designated and set forth in Item 2 of the Memorandum of Understandings Reached which bears the same date as this Treaty. The United States of America also agrees that, subject to the enactment of legislation by the Congress, there shall be conveyed to the Republic of Panama free of cost all its right, title and interest to the land and improvements in the area known as PAITILLA POINT and that effective with such conveyance the United States of America shall relinquish all the rights, power and authority granted to it in such area under the Convention signed November 18, 1903. The Republic of Panama agrees to save the Government of the United States harmless from any and all claims which may arise incident to the conveyance of the area known as PAITILLA POINT to the Republic of Panama.

ARTICLE VI (In part)

Article V of the Boundary Convention, signed September 2, 1914, between the United States of America and the Republic of Panama, shall be replaced.

Article VIII of the General Treaty signed March 2, 1936, as amended by Article III of the Convention between the United States of America and the Republic of Panama regarding the Colón Corridor and certain other corridors through the Canal Zone, signed May 24, 1950, is hereby modified by removing from the Colón, or westerly, end of the Colón Corridor the portion thereof lying north of North latitude 9°21′ and incorporating such portion within the boundary of the City of Colón as described above.

This Article shall become effective upon completion of the withdrawal by the United States of America from the sections of the city of Colón known as New Cristobal, Colón Beach and the de Lesseps Area, with the exception of the lots retained for consulate purposes, except that it shall in no case become effective prior to the exchange of the instruments of ratification of this Treaty and the exchange of instruments of ratification of the Convention signed May 24, 1950, referred to in the preceding paragraph.

ARTICLE VII

The second paragraph of Article VII of the Boundary Convention signed September 2, 1914, between the United States of America and the Republic of Panama, shall be abrogated in its entirety as of the date of entry into force of the present Treaty.

The landing pier situated in the small cove of the southerly side of Manzanillo Island, constructed pursuant to provisions contained in the second paragraph of Article VII of the Boundary Convention of 1914 between the two countries, shall become the property of the Government of the Republic of Panama as of the date of entry into force of the present Treaty.

ARTICLE VIII

(a) The Republic of Panama will reserve exclusively for the purpose of maneuvers and military training the area described in the maps (Nos. SGN-7-54 and SGN-8-54, each dated November 17, 1954) and accompanying descriptions prepared by the Comisión Catastral of the Republic of Panama, attached as the Annex hereto, and will permit the United States of America, without cost and free of all encumbrances, exclusively to utilize said area for the indicated purpose for a period of fifteen (15) years, subject to extension thereafter as agreed by the two Governments. This authorization includes the free access to, egress from, and movements within and over, said area. This utilization will not affect the sovereignty of the Republic of Panama, or the operation of the Constitution and the laws of the Republic over the mentioned area.

(b) The United States Armed Forces, the members thereof and their families actually residing with them, and United States nationals who, in an official capacity, are serving with or accompanying the Armed Forces of the United States and members of their families actually residing with them will be exempted within the said area from all taxation by the Republic of Panama or any of its political subdivisions.

(c) Prior to the expiration of the period envisaged in this Article and within a reasonable time thereafter the United States shall have the right to remove from this training and maneuver area, or otherwise to dispose of, without limitation or restriction all structures, installations, facilities, equipment and supplies brought into, or constructed or erected within this training and maneuver area by or on behalf of the United States. The Republic of Panama will not be required to reimburse the United States for any structures, installations, facilities, equipment and supplies not removed or otherwise disposed of as provided herein.

(d) The United States shall be under no obligation to restore this training and maneuver area or the facilities and installations thereon to their original condition upon the termination of this Article, except for the landing strip which will be returned in at least as good condition as that obtaining at the time of coming into effect of this Article.

(e) The provisions of this Article shall in no manner terminate or modify the provisions concerning the holding of military maneuvers in the Republic of Panama established by the Notes ancillary to the General Treaty signed March 2, 1936, other than as provided herein for this training and maneuver area.

ARTICLE IX

The Republic of Panama hereby waives the right under Article XIX of the Convention signed November 18, 1903, to transportation by railway within the Zone, without paying charges of any kind, of persons in the service of the Republic of Panama, or of the police force charged with the preservation of public order outside of the Canal Zone, as well as of their baggage, munitions of war and supplies.

ARTICLE X

The High Contracting Parties agree that, in the event of the discontinuance of the Panama Railroad, and of the construction or completion by the United States of a strategic highway across the Isthmus lying wholly within the Canal Zone intended primarily for serving the operation, maintenance, civil government, sanitation and protection of the Panama Canal and Canal Zone, and notwithstanding anything to the contrary in Article VI of the Convention signed November 18, 1903, the United States of America may in its discretion either prohibit or restrict the use, by busses or trucks not at the time engaged exclusively in the servicing of, or the transportation of supplies to, installations, facilities or residents of the Canal Zone, of that portion of such highway which lies between Mount Hope, Canal Zone and the intersection of such highway with the Canal Zone section of the Trans-Isthmian Highway referred to in the Trans-Isthmian Highway Convention between the United States of America and the Republic of Panama, signed March 2, 1936.

ARTICLE XI

The Republic of Panama agrees, notwithstanding the provisions of Article III of the General Treaty signed March 2, 1936, that the United States of America may extend the privilege of purchasing at post exchanges small items of personal convenience and items necessary for professional use, to military personnel of friendly third countries present in the Zone under the auspices of the United States.

ARTICLE XII

The United States of America agrees that, effective December 31, 1956, there will be excluded from the privilege of making purchases in the commissaries and other sales stores in the Canal Zone as well as the privilege of making importations into the Canal Zone all those persons who are not citizens of the United States of America, except members of the Armed Forces of the United States, and who do not actually reside in the Canal Zone but who are included in the categories of persons authorized to reside in said Zone; it being understood nevertheless that all personnel of the agencies of the United States of America will be permitted under adequate controls to purchase small articles such as meals, sweets, chewing gum, tobacco and similar articles near the sites of their jobs.

The United States of America further agrees that, effective December 31, 1956, and notwithstanding the provisions of the first paragraph of Article IV of the General Treaty signed March 2, 1936, the Government of the Republic of Panama may impose import duties and other charges upon goods destined or consigned to persons, other than citizens of the United States of America, included in class (a) in Section 2 of Article III of said Article III of said Treaty, who reside or sojourn in territory under the jurisdiction of the Republic of Panama during the performance of their service with the United States of America or its agencies, even though such goods are intended for their own use and benefit.

ARTICLE XIII

The present Treaty shall be subject to ratification and the instruments of ratification shall be exchanged at Washington. It shall enter into force on the date of the exchange of the instruments of ratification.

IN WITNESS WHEREOF, the Plenipotentiaries have signed this Treaty in duplicate, in the English and Spanish languages, both texts being authentic, and have hereunto affixed their seals.

DONE at the City of Panamá the 25th of January 1955.

For the United States of America:
SELDEN CHAPIN

For the Republic of Panama:
OCTAVIO FÁBREGA

MEMORANDUM OF UNDERSTANDINGS REACHED

In connection with the 1953–1954 negotiations between representatives of the United States of America and the Republic of Panama, which have resulted in the signature of a Treaty between the two countries, the following understandings have been reached:

On the part of the United States of America:

1. Legislation will be sought which will authorize each agency of the United States Government in the Canal Zone to conform its existing wage practices in the Zone to the following principles:

(a) The basic wage for any given grade level will be the same for any employee eligible for appointment to the position without regard to whether he is a citizen of the United States or of the Republic of Panama.

(b) In the case of an employee who is a citizen of the United States, there may be added to the base pay an increment representing an overseas differential plus an allowance for those elements, such as taxes, which operate to reduce the disposable income of such an employee as compared with an employee who is a resident of the area.

(c) The employee who is a citizen of the United States will also be eligible for greater annual leave benefits and travel allowances because of the necessity for periodic vacations in the United States for recuperation purposes and to maintain contact with the employee's home environment.

Legislation will be sought to make the Civil Service Retirement Act uniformly applicable to citizens of the United States and of the Republic of Panama employed by the Government of the United States in the Canal Zone.

The Unites States will afford equality of opportunity to citizens of Panama for employment in all United States Government positions in the Canal Zone for which they are qualified and in which the employment of United States citizens is not required, in the judgment of the United States, for security reasons.

The agencies of the United States Government will evaluate, classify and title all positions in the Canal Zone without regard to the nationality of the incumbent or proposed incumbent.

Citizens of Panama will be afforded opportunity to participate in such training programs as may be conducted for employees by United States agencies in the Canal Zone.

2. With reference to that part of Article V of the Treaty signed today which deals with the conveyance to the Republic of Panama free of cost of all the right, title and interest held by the United States of America or its agencies in and to certain lands and improvements situated in territory under the jurisdiction of the Republic of Panama, steps will be taken as provided in this Item.

(a) Legislation will be sought to authorize and direct the transfer to the Republic of Panama of all the right, title and interest held by the United States or its agencies in or to the following real property:

1. The J. N. Vialette and Huerta de San Doval tracts in the city of Panamá and the Aspinwall tract on the Island of Taboga.
2. Las Isletas and Santa Catalina Military Reservations on the Island of Taboga. This transfer will include the cable rights-of-way which have a width of 20 feet (6.10 meters) and extend between the Ancon Cove Military Reservation and the Santa Catalina Military Reservation, and between the El Vigia Military Reservation and the Las Isletas Military Reservation.
3. The lot in Colón now reserved for consulate purposes.
4. Certain lands on the westerly shores of the city of Colón described roughly as extending from the southerly boundary of the de Lesseps area (4th Street extended) to the Colón-Canal Zone boundary and bounded on the east by the east wall of the old freight house and, below that structure, by a line 25 feet (7.622 meters) west of the center line of the most westerly railroad track. This transfer will include the certain improvements consisting of the old freight house and Colón Pier Number 3.

(b) Legislation will be sought to authorize and direct the Panama Canal Company to remove its railway terminal operations from the city of Panamá and to transfer to the Republic of Panama free of cost all of the right, title and interest of the Panama Canal Company in and to the lands known as the Panama Railroad Yard, including the improvements thereon and specifically including the railway passenger stations. This action will also relieve the Government of the Republic of Panama of its obligation under Point 10 of the General Relations Agreement between the United States of America and the Republic of Panama signed May 18, 1942 to make available without cost to the Government of the United States of America a suitable new site for such terminal facilities.

(c) With respect to those areas in the City of Colón known as de Lesseps, Colón Beach and New Cristobal (with the exception of two lots in the de Lesseps area which the United States intends to use for consulate purposes), legislation will be sought to authorize and direct the gradual withdrawal from these areas and the conveyance or transfer to the Republic of Panama free of cost of all the right, title and interest of the United States and of its agency, the Panama Canal Company, in and to the lands and improvements thereon. Under this process of gradual withdrawal the United States Government, and/or its agencies, will not be obligated to install any new structure in such areas and, as severable parts of the areas cease to be needed, the lands and improvements would be conveyed or transferred. The severability of parts of the areas depends upon a number of practical considerations including those having to do with the present obligations of the United States, with respect to the subject areas, concerning water and sewerage facilities, street cleaning and paving, water supply, et cetera, as stipulated in the Instrument of Transfer of Water and Sewerage Systems, executed between the Governor of the Panama Canal and the Foreign Minister of Panama on December 28, 1945.

(d) With respect to the railroad passenger station and site in the City of Colón, legislation will be sought to authorize and direct the withdrawal from such site and structure at such time as the withdrawal from the areas known as de Lesseps, Colón Beach and New Cristobal, contemplated by the next preceding subparagraph, shall have been fully completed, and the conveyance to the Republic of Panama free of cost of all the right, title and interest of the United States and of its agency, the Panama Canal Company, in and to such site and structure. However, the railroad tracks and trackage area in Colón, being required for switching purposes serving the Cristobal piers, will be retained for such purposes.

(e) All transfers or conveyances of lands and improvements contemplated by this Item, subject to legislative authorization and direction, will necessarily be made subject to any leases which may be outstanding in the respective areas, and will also contain provisions fully protecting the Government of the United

States of America against any claims by lessees for damages or losses which may arise as a result of such transfers or conveyances

(f) The transfers or conveyances contemplated by this Item, subject to legislative authorization, are in addition to the conveyance of Paitilla Point as specifically covered by Article V of the Treaty signed today, and to the transfer of real property effected by Article VI of said Treaty.

3. Articles, materials, and supplies that are mined, produced or manufactured in the Republic of Panama, when purchased for use in the Canal Zone, will be exempted from the provisions of the Buy American Act.

4. Referring to the exchange of notes dated March 2, 1936, accessory to the General Treaty between the United States of America and the Republic of Panama signed on that date, relative to the sale to ships of goods imported into the Canal Zone by the Government of the United States of America, the United States of America agrees, effective December 31, 1956, and in benefit of Panamanian commerce, to withdraw wholly from, and thereafter to refrain from, any such sales to ships, provided that nothing in this Item shall apply.

(a) to sales to ships operated by or for the account of the Government of the United States of America,

(b) to the sale of fuel or lubricants, or

(c) to any sale or furnishing of ships stores which is incidental to the performance of ship repair operations by any agency of the Government of the United States of America.

5. Legislative authorization and the necessary appropriations will be sought for the construction of a bridge at Balboa referred to in Point 4 of the General Relations Agreement of 1942.

6. The United States of America agrees, effective December 31, 1956, to withdraw from persons employed by agencies of the Government of the United States of America in the Canal Zone who are not citizens of the United States of America and who do not actually reside in said Zone the privilege of availing themselves of services which are offered within said Zone except those which are essential to health or necessary to permit them to perform their duties.

7. It is and will continue to be the policy of the Panama Canal agencies and of the Armed Forces in the Canal Zone in making purchases of supplies, materials and equipment, so far as permitted under United States legislation, to afford to the

economy of the Republic of Panama full opportunity to compete for such business.

8. In general connection with the matter of the importation of items of merchandise for resale in the sales stores in the Canal Zone, it will be the practice of the agencies concerned to acquire such items either from United States sources or Panamanian sources unless, in certain instances, it is not feasible to do so.

9. With respect to the manufacture and processing of goods for sale to or consumption by individuals, now carried on by the Panama Canal Company, it will be the policy of the United States of America to terminate such activities whenever and for so long as such goods, or particular classes thereof, are determined by the United States of America to be available in the Republic of Panama on a continuing basis, in satisfactory qualities and quantities, and at reasonable prices. The United States of America will give prompt consideration to a request in writing on the part of the Government of Panama concerning the termination of the manufacture or processing of any goods covered in this Item as to which the Government of Panama may consider the criteria specified in this Item to have been met.

10. Prompt consideration will be given to withdrawing from the handling of commercial cargo for transshipment on Canal Zone piers so soon as Panamanian port facilities are in satisfactory operation in Colón.

11. The United States agrees that the term "auxiliary works" as used in the Treaty includes the Armed Forces of the United States of America.

On the part of the Republic of Panama:

1. The Republic of Panama will lease to the United States of America, free of all cost save for the recited consideration of one Balboa, for a period of 99 years, two parcels of land contiguous to the present United States Embassy residence site, as designated on the sketch (No. SGN-9-54, dated November 9, 1954) and accompanying descriptions prepared by the Comisión Catastral of the Republic of Panama, attached hereto.

2. The Republic of Panama assures the United States of America that the property, shown and described on the attached map (No. SGN-6-54, dated October 1954) and accompanying description prepared by the Comisión Catastral of the Republic of Panama, in front of the United States Embassy office building site and between the Bay of Panama and Avenida Balboa as it may be extended between 37th and 39th Streets, will be pre-

served permanently as a park and not developed for commercial or residential purposes.

3. So long as the United States of America maintains in effect those provisions of Executive Order No. 6997 of March 25, 1935 governing the importation of alcoholic beverages into the Canal Zone, the Republic of Panama will grant a reduction of 75 percent in the import duty on alcoholic beverages which are sold in Panama for importation into the Canal Zone pursuant to such Executive Order.

4. In connection with the authorization granted to the United States of America in Article VIII of the Treaty, the United States shall have free access to the beach areas contiguous to the maneuver area described in said Article VIII for purposes connected with training and maneuvers, subject to the public use of said beach as provided under the Constitution of Panama.

The provisions of this Memorandum of Understandings Reached shall enter into force upon the exchange of instruments of ratification of the Treaty signed this day by the United States of America and the Republic of Panama.

DONE in duplicate in the City of Panamá, in the English and Spanish languages, this 25th day of January 1955.

For the United States of America:

SELDEN CHAPIN
Ambassador Extraordinary and Plenipotentiary of the United States of America to the Republic of Panama

For the Republic of Panama:

OCTAVIO FÁBREGA
Minister of Foreign Affairs of the Republic of Panama

Index

V

W

Z